High-Tech Campaigns

HIGH-TECH CAMPAIGNS

Computer Technology
in Political Communication

Gary W. Selnow

Praeger Series in Political Communication

Westport, Connecticut
London

Library of Congress Cataloging-in-Publication Data

Selnow, Gary W.
    High-tech campaigns : computer technology in political
communication / Gary W. Selnow.
        p.   cm.—(Praeger series in political communication, ISSN
1062–5623)
    Includes bibliographical references and index.
    ISBN 0–275–94150–7 (alk. paper)
    1. Electioneering—United States—Data processing.
2. Communication in politics—United States.   3. United States
—Politics and government—1989-   —Data processing.   I. Title.
II. Series.
JK1973.S44   1994
324.7'0285—dc20   93–4258

British Library Cataloguing in Publication Data is available.

Library of Congress Catalog Card Number: 93–4258
ISBN: 0–275–94150–7
ISSN: 1062–5623

First published in 1994

Praeger Publishers, 88 Post Road West, Westport, CT 06881
An imprint of Greenwood Publishing Group, Inc.

Printed in the United States of America

The paper used in this book complies with the
Permanent Paper Standard issued by the National
Information Standards Organization (Z39.48–1984).

10 9 8 7 6 5 4 3 2 1

This book is dedicated to Cecil Edmonds,
a pioneer in computer communications.

Contents

Series Foreword

Those of us from the discipline of communication studies have long believed that communication is prior to all other fields of inquiry. In several other forums I have argued that the essence of politics is "talk" or human interaction.[1] Such interaction may be formal or informal, verbal or nonverbal, public or private but it is always persuasive, forcing us consciously or subconsciously to interpret, to evaluate, and to act. Communication is the vehicle for human action.

From this perspective, it is not surprising that Aristotle recognized the natural kinship of politics and communication in his writings *Politics* and *Rhetoric*. In the former, he establishes that humans are "political beings [who] alone of the animals [are] furnished with the faculty of language."[2] And in the latter, he begins his systematic analysis of discourse by proclaiming that "rhetorical study, in its strict sense, is concerned with the modes of persuasion."[3] Thus, it was recognized over 2,300 years ago that politics and communication go hand in hand because they are essential parts of human nature.

Back in 1981, Dan Nimmo and Keith Sanders proclaimed that political communication was an emerging field.[4] Although its origin, as noted, dates back centuries, a "self-consciously cross-disciplinary" focus began in the late 1950s. Thousands of books and articles later, colleges and universities offer a variety of graduate and undergraduate coursework in such diverse departments as communication, mass communication, journalism, political science, and sociology.[5] In Nimmo and Sanders' early assessment, the "key areas of inquiry" included rhetorical analysis, propaganda analysis, attitude change studies, voting studies, government and the news media, functional and systems analyses, technological changes, media technologies, campaign techniques, and research techniques.[6] In a survey of the state of the field in 1983, the same authors and Lynda Kaid found additional, more specific areas of concerns such as the presidency, political polls, public opinion, debates, and advertising to name a few.[7] Since the first study, they also noted a shift away from the rather strict behavioral approach.

A decade later, Dan Nimmo and David Swanson argued that "political communication has developed some identity as a more or less distinct domain of scholarly work."[8] The scope and concerns of the area have further expanded to include critical theories and cultural studies. While there is no precise definition, method, or disciplinary home of the area of inquiry, its primary domain is the role, processes, and effects of communication within the context of politics broadly defined.

In 1985, the editors of *Political Communication Yearbook: 1984* noted that "more things are happening in the study, teaching, and practice of political communication than can be captured within the space limitations of the relatively few publications available."[9] In addition, they argued that the backgrounds of "those involved in the field [are] so varied and pluralist in outlook and approach, . . . it [is] a mistake to adhere slavisly to any set format in shaping the content."[10] And more recently, Nimmo and Swanson called for "ways of overcoming the unhappy consequences of fragmentation within a framework that respects, encourages, and benefits from diverse scholarly commitments, agendas, and approaches."[11]

In agreement with these assessments of the area and with gentle encouragement, Praeger established in 1988 the series entitled "Praeger Studies in Political Communication." The series is open to all qualitative and quantitative methodologies as well as contemporary and historical studies. The key to characterizing the studies in the series is the focus on communication variables or activities within a political context or dimension. As of this writing, nearly forty volumes have been published and there are numerous impressive works forthcoming. Scholars from the disciplines of communication, history, journalism, political science, and sociology have participated in the series.

I am, without shame or modesty, a fan of the series. The joy of serving as its editor is in participating in the dialogue of the field of political communication and in reading the contributors' works. I invite you to join me.

Robert E. Denton, Jr.

NOTES

1. See Robert E. Denton, Jr., *The Symbolic Dimensions of the American Presidency* (Prospect Heights, Ill.: Waveland Press, 1982); Robert E. Denton, Jr., and Gary Woodward, *Political Communication in America* (New York: Praeger, 1985; 2nd ed., 1990); Robert E. Denton, Jr., and Dan Hahn, *Presidential Communication*

(New York: Praeger, 1986); and Robert E. Denton, Jr., *The Primetime Presidency of Ronald Reagan* (New York: Praeger, 1988).

2. Aristotle, *The Politics of Aristotle*, trans. Ernest Barker (New York: Oxford University Press, 1970), p. 5.

3. Aristotle, *Rhetoric*, trans. Rhys Roberts (New York: The Modern Library, 1954), p. 22.

4. Dan Nimmo and Keith Sanders, "Introduction: The Emergence of Political Communication as a Field," in *Handbook of Political Communication*, ed. Dan Nimmo and Keith Sanders (Beverly Hills, Calif.: Sage, 1981), pp. 11–36.

5. Ibid., p. 15.

6. Ibid., pp. 17–27.

7. Keith Sanders, Lynda Kaid, and Dan Nimmo, eds., *Political Communication Yearbook: 1984* (Carbondale: Southern Illinois University, 1985), pp. 283–308.

8. Dan Nimmo and David Swanson, "The Field of Political Communication: Beyond the Voter Persuasion Paradigm," in *New Directions in Political Communication*, ed. David Swanson and Dan Nimmo (Beverly Hills, Calif.: Sage, 1990), p. 8.

9. Sanders, Kaid, and Nimmo, *Political Communication Yearbook: 1984*, p. xiv.

10. Ibid.

11. Nimmo and Swanson, "The Field of Political Communication," p. 11.

Preface

A hand-signed letter and a personal call from a political campaign, a close-to-home radio spot and an on-target television commercial all inspire in voters a sense that at least some American politicians really are in touch with the people. These devoted few care to send the very best: the personal, insightful and responsive messages that assure voters that their concerns are deeply known to a sympathetic candidate. What constituent could resist the charm of communications so deftly precise and warmly personal? Who could not feel gratitude toward the busy sender who took the time to know the voters, one by one, and cared so much to touch them individually?

They say nobody really wants to know how sausages and laws are made, and by the same logic, voters may not really want to know how high-tech political communications are made. Anne Willette (1992), writing for the Gannett News Service, tells about Cali Communications, a Washington, D.C., outfit, one in a growing industry that puts "personal" touches in mass mailings. Willette explains how lawmakers bundle up constituents' mail and send it off to Cali for analysis. The company studies each letter, scours information-rich computer databases and finally shapes a detailed description of the writer. Cali computer-searches other constituents with similar characteristics then computer-generates a few thousand "Knowing of your concern about . . . " personalized letters with all the special bells and whistles that make each look like a handcrafted original. It's a twenty-first-century irony that these warm, compassionate letters are shaped by cold, compassionless computers.

Legislators don't just farm out their work; they also stockpile supplies to do the job themselves. Willette found that in 1991, lawmakers in Washington spent $14.5 million on computer equipment that composes letters and stores mailing lists, and another $127,000 on the rental and purchase of mailing lists. And this was just the taxpayers' contribution—in an off election year to boot! The largest investments in high-tech equipment come from the campaigns of incumbents and challengers, where the real sophisticated communication takes place.

Today, thousands of campaign workers operate computer equipment that analyzes minute details of individual voters. They study poll data that lay out a population the way blueprints lay out a new building. They use databases to size up audiences and break them down into separate clusters of like-minded voters. When campaigns reach out and touch these voters, they do so directly, often bypassing traditional media and dodging interpretative machinery of the press. Their communication programs are direct and efficient, aiming their laserlike messages at voters one by one or in small groups.

Bob Cali, owner of Cali Communication, says that "personalization is the key," and that's the philosophy and the practice in a nutshell. Since computers first made inroads into political campaigns during the mideighties, communications have become increasingly targeted and personalized. Knowing who you are demographically and how you think ideologically, campaigns aim their arrows at your emotional bull's-eye. Never before have there been more "Knowing of your concern . . . " letters and telephone pitches and more messages aimed at voters gathered around narrow-casting media such as cable television and specialized radio.

While it's true that mail and phone, television and radio have been tools of political communication for many years, today's bombardment is poll-driven, database-wired and computer-powered. Communicators once struggled to reach the greatest number of people with the biggest, broadest message. Big is beautiful no longer. The wisdom today: Smaller is smarter. Computers, polls, databases and small-audience media make such audience targeting possible, and they do so with a new standard of precision.

This book describes the tools and techniques of high-tech targeting. It examines the effects of these practices on individuals, the press and politics. But, readers beware: You need a stout heart for the making of sausages and laws—and for the crafting of new political communications.

Acknowledgments

Thanks to dozens of people in political campaigns, the media, the commercial information industry and academia. Special thanks to my friend and mentor, Dr. Richard Gilbert, a scholar and once heavy at NBC Television. For someone so evidently a natural enemy of computer technology, Dick was a remarkable resource for so many details in this book; his review and comments were priceless gifts. His love of the written word has been an inspiration and his unyielding faith in humankind an assurance that computers, at the end, will not prevail.

Thanks to Jo Laverde, who, for the past decade, has fed me the latest Nielsen numbers. I don't know what Nielsen pays her, but it's not enough.

K. C. Hullings, who directs the management information systems division of the Democratic National Committee, was a tireless source for computer information and a lead to others who work with it. Many of them may not forgive her. My appreciation to Katherine Folkes of Real Good Software in Washington, D.C., who answered a hundred questions throughout this project.

I'd like to thank David Broder, E. J. Dionne and Howard Kurtz of the *Washington Post*; Larry Grossman of NBC News and Harvard; Marvin Kalb, director of Harvard's Shorenstein Barone Center; Ed Miller, associate at the Poynter Institute; and Wes Pippert, director of the Washington Reporting Program of the University of Missouri. These journalists and media superstars helped put in focus the real impact of the new technologies on political campaigns. They made the point very clear that every action has an equal and opposite reaction, and that computers in campaigns not only do things for the voters and the system, but to them as well.

Finally, thanks to Ralph Daniels, former senior vice president of standards at NBC. One gray winter morning in 1991, Ralph and I were pounding the cold pavement of Pennsylvania Avenue in Washington, D.C., making official calls. We were promoting a new computer-based project that sought to reverse a growing trend—our plan would use technology to bring voters back into politics. It wasn't going very well. Sensing my frustration, Ralph offered comfort by explaining that the outstanding ideas often are missed by the best and the brightest in that town. These things take time, he said, and sometimes the leaders must be dragged by the followers to do what they should have been doing all along. That inspired this book. To lead the leaders, the people need to know what technology is doing to them and to their political system. This book lifts the page on that subject.

High-Tech Campaigns

Chapter One

Introduction

Gadgets do just about everything else for us these days, so we see no reason why they won't end up electing—or defeating—our presidents.
—Eric Sevareid,
CBS Radio news commentary
August 26, 1952

You are invited to look at something new in the oldest game since the Greeks invented democracy—the political campaign. From Athenian scrolls to modern newspapers, candidates for democratic office have played the game much the same: tell the voters one by one or work the crowds as far as the voice can carry, then depend on the press for the rest. A candidate's "intelligence" about voters' opinions and desires came out of that personal contact, pressing the flesh of the people. Then came the computer. Suddenly, software and hardware, databases and research techniques, targeted mailings and media have become the stuff of campaigns. Politics went high-tech, and the game changed forever. Today, the political sport is faster and more visible, and the candidates use techniques that put them one up on their opponents. It's something like the change in pole-vaulting from the old wooden poles to the new fiberglass models which whip the vaulter six feet higher. The game is the same, but the tools and the techniques have magnified the performances.

For all the talk about new electronic systems, though, we really are dealing with something very old. We are confirming the ancient wisdom, known well in Plato's Academy, that information is power: power to preempt what other people are likely to do, power to manipulate how they behave. That really is what this book is about: the acquisition of information and the wielding of power—now magnified beyond anyone's predictions of twenty years ago.

People have long known about the chemistry between information and power. The Book of Proverbs says that knowledge increases strength. Sir Francis Bacon wrote in *Meditationes Sacrae* that "knowledge is power." For thousands of years, armies have understood that information about the enemy can turn looming defeat into clever victory. Merchants and makers of goods have converted knowledge about the marketplace into personal profits. Political fortunes have been made and lost over the exchange of strategic information.

Our immediate concern with power is the capacity it grants one person to manipulate the behavior of another. This gets to the heart of the relationship between information and power in politics.

Suppose I want you to vote for me. If I were big enough, driven enough and if it weren't against my morals (not to mention the law), I could overpower you physically and make you pull the lever next to my name. You wouldn't like it, but I'd get your vote. That's a crude but workable scenario.

A second scenario is more likely. Suppose I could determine how you felt about a variety of public issues; suppose I understood your deeper feelings about the salient things in your life. If I knew your fears and passions, your preferences and prejudices, I could draw upon this information and pitch my arguments in a more convincing manner than an opponent without this information. In scenario two, you would walk into the voting booth and pull the lever with a smile, because I had overpowered you mentally, not physically. I brought about the same end, but by a more acceptable means. I traded the power of coercion for the power of persuasion. But power is power; I got your vote.

In the second case, my power derived not from the size of my fist, but from the effectiveness of my pitch, stemming from the depth and breadth of my knowledge about you. The more information I have, the better able I am to tug at the strings that lead you to behave as I wish.

Forms of information from many sources translate into the power to manipulate voters, other candidates, the press, funding sources and other players at the political table. Several examples show how.

During the 1980 presidential election, in a caper dubbed "Debate Gate," Ronald Reagan's campaign workers secretly obtained Jimmy Carter's briefing books for an upcoming round of debates. This proprietary information, rich with rhetorical strategy to coach Carter for his role in the televised contests, became a significant source of power to Reagan. Reagan knew in advance how and when Carter would thrust and parry, and so "the great communicator" was able to choreograph his own moves accordingly. This advance information enabled Reagan to control portions of the debate and so wield power over his opposition.

The tables turned with a high-tech twist in 1992. This time, the Democrats—intercepting television satellite feeds from the Bush campaign—got advance copies of the Republican's commercials, sometimes days before they went on the air.[1] This information gave Bill Clinton's "rapid-response" team an early look at Republican attacks. In response to one ad showing Clinton's Arkansas as a barren landscape, the Democrats conducted focus groups and prepared "instant" rejoinders, ready as soon as the spot ran. Advance information gave Clinton power over his opponent.

In 1992, the information-is-power game worked both ways. George Bush used information about Bill Clinton to manipulate and exercise power through the press. In one play, the Republican team said it found 128 instances of tax hikes during Clinton's gubernatorial reign in Arkansas. Clinton objected, but Bush and other Republicans used the figure at every opportunity. Many economists, including those on call to the conservative *Wall Street Journal*, challenged this claim, yet most major media continued to report the statistic as though it were fact. So cynical have reporters become about campaign statistics that ABC's Cokie Roberts dismissed the Democrats' protests by saying that all stats are challenged in the throes of a campaign, and that the challenge to this figure was more or less the same as challenges to any other figure hurled by candidates.[2] At any rate, the "128" statistic stuck like flypaper to Clinton throughout the campaign. The information—right or wrong—gave Bush power over his opponent, and this power was conveniently amplified by the press.[3]

Clinton learned many lessons from the failed Michael Dukakis White House bid of 1988. Dukakis—always a day late and a dollar short with responses to Republican attacks—was pummelled badly by GOP ads, speeches and mailings which assaulted his policies and accosted him personally.[4] This was not to be Clinton's fate. For instance, the candidate from Arkansas dug his claws deeply into Bush's flesh on the Iran "arms for hostages" story. It was a rare day during the 1992 campaign that Clinton did not pound home the claim that Bush was eyeball-deep in the mire of Irangate. Clinton's persistent reminders and releases of information scraps about the scandal kept the story alive with voters and the press. In the final hours of the campaign, it turns out, indictments against former Defense Secretary Caspar Weinberger gave the press additional incentive to pursue the story. Prior to this, however, Clinton and third-party candidate Ross Perot kept the issue in the press and on the public agenda. The information held power over Bush.

The information-is-power game in the 1992 race had other interesting twists as well. One came early in the race, when Bush accused then pre-candidate Perot of gathering personal information on Bush himself and his family. The president's campaign aides cautioned that the secret surveillance of the First Family told volumes about the shifty nature of the tycoon from Texas. Surprise-a-minute Perot employed a clever defense. He said, in fact, that he had received background information on Bush's sons in the mid-eighties and that he immediately turned everything over to Bush himself. Hardly a hollow claim, the billionaire then produced a handwritten note from Bush thanking Perot for his thoughtfulness and for passing along the details. Perot's information had enough power to derail the GOP locomotive. The 1992 campaign was a deck filled with wild cards and jokers.

In this book, we look with suspicion upon the power that information grants candidates to manipulate voting behavior. We gaze with uneasy wonder on the increasing amount of personal information about private citizens currently falling into the hands of political campaigns. Like a tidal wave beginning to crest, the widespread use of sophisticated equipment to obtain, store, tabulate, track and analyze voter information is threatening the coastline of democratic polity in America. Equipment with higher efficiency and lower costs and software now intellectually accessible to nonspecialists have granted access to computer-assisted communication for every mom-and-pop campaign in America.

What began as computer efficiency in campaign bookkeeping and administration now serves a host of functions well beyond these simple tasks. Now, computers process and manipulate data about voters in ways imagined only in sci-fi novels. Computers churn out remarkably complex and insightful polling analyses, personal consumer statistics, census data assessments and other intelligence evaluations that, once assembled, yield revealing and often proprietary information about individual voters. All that surveillance data becomes a campaign gold mine. The power to manipulate the behavior of others, the power to persuade someone to loosen the purse strings, the power to pull the right lever—no politician today can live without them.

Today, more than ever, political campaigns are, at heart, communication campaigns. Bagging the vote is the bottom line of politics, and in our political system this is achieved only through effective communications. Polling, the tools and techniques of audience analysis and all the computer technologies that streamline, focus and make communications more efficient have become the lifeblood of campaigns. More targeted, more responsive to audience information needs and better able to deal immediately with spontaneous events, running for office is no longer low art but high tech.

By nature and heritage, Americans are suspicious of power and resentful of authority. Indeed, our Constitution stands as a monument to the repudiation of state power. It is a well-developed mistrust that started early in our history among a group of the most ardent opponents of state power, who sailed here to escape the imposition of government control over personal will.

Columnist George Will found this basic impulse celebrated in the film *The Last of the Mohicans*. A British officer admonishes the colonial scout, Hawkeye, who is reluctant to fight for the king. Contemptuously, the elitist redcoat asks, "You call yourself a patriot and loyal subject to the Crown?" Laconically, Hawkeye replies, "Don't call myself subject to much at all." This idea of the self-created individual, says Will, with no social bonds or debts to society, lives in tension with the communal citizen, who is obligated to the society that shapes him (Will 1992).

We Americans come to the subject of central power with our eyebrows raised. This is appropriate in a discussion about the power to influence voting behavior. As we shall see, many campaign uses of information yield power with a potential for the abuse of citizens' rights and an intrusion into personal lives.

We need not stack the deck, however, and suggest unfairly that political power is derived from unholy sources—negative campaign data, personal files brimming with secrets, information gathered surreptitiously or at least unbeknownst to the subject. Occasionally, this is so, but most data gathering is aboveboard and honest. The problem is scope: As usage and data accumulation widens, so too do the boundaries of what we accept and what we do not. Presently, there is nothing illegal about most data collection, but whether or not it's ethical is a separate question we will save for later.

In the chapters that follow, political information—the grist for the mills of communication technology—is said to come from two general sources. The first is polling data, whereby a sample of voters provides the numbers for generalizable information about a larger population. Pollsters may not interview you personally, but they interview samples of people enough like you to have a pretty good idea of what you think and how you would react to various appeals, proposals and pitches.

The second source is "individual-level" data—that's tech talk for information specific to you. These databases range widely in detail. They can include your age, occupation and size of your paycheck. They can take in your marital status, a count of your children, the amount of your rent or mortgage, maybe something about the model car you drive, the magazines you read, the college to which you send an alumni contribution and the stocks in your portfolio.

The usefulness of such information grows in proportion to its mass. With more information, there is more of a chance to pinpoint the message, push the right buttons and boost effectiveness when pitching voters one by one. The power to persuade expands with the massing pile of information.

But it is not just the size of the pile that matters; the power is in the ordering of the pile. Here, technology works magic. Conceptually simple, the computer can match up databases (the process of concatenation) and arrange and assemble the many pieces of data into neat file folders—one per person, if you wish; clusters and groups, if you prefer. Computers unshuffle and sort the deck and add order and structure to the information.

And so, the mass of data that otherwise would be nothing more than an unwieldy traffic pileup of facts becomes as orderly and controlled as a Nintendo game. The resulting information translates into a usable foundation for communication specialists and professional managers. Targeted, persuasive strategies start by amassing voter information and continue with computer analysis and structuring of it all. That's the way political surveillance and planning is played today.

Before looking at the targeting process in the next chapter, let's step back a minute. This book considers only the last half-hour on the twenty-four-hour political clock. In the first half-hour, all they had were paper, pen and sufficient genius to write the Constitution. Later, the whistle-stop train tours of the mid–1800s gave candidates time to see and be seen by more voters, shake more hands and visit more districts than they previously could by riding on dusty buckboards. Then, the telegraph compressed time and space, connecting campaigns to faraway districts once accessible only by pony express. Soon after, telephones gave voice to the dots and dashes. In the 1920s, radio brought candidates—or at least their voices—into American living rooms. Finally, television provided voters with everything but the candidate's flesh and blood, Over the years, technology has shrunk the distances, reduced the delays, focused the energies and streamlined the efficiency of political campaigns.

Technology, therefore, is nothing new to American politics, but with each step in its evolution, changes take place in the candidate-voter relationship. In its simplest and oldest form, political communication involved one-to-one, press-the-flesh interactions. Politicians sold their ideas and their candidacies like shoes. They, and their precinct workers, measured up each voter in face-to-face discussions, then brought out the message that appealed best and fit most comfortably. Door-to-door politicking has always had a popular (and populist) appeal. Today, politicking is more like a mail-order operation.

The use of technology has brought about some interesting conditions. It has imposed a medium between the candidate and the voter. There are fewer and fewer occasions for direct contact, and when these do occur, they often are staged to serve media needs for camera footage, rather than to meet voters face-to-face. Today, we have mostly rubber-glove campaigning. Candidates don't touch voters directly; they send their messages through broadcasts, print and direct mail. These technologies separate and isolate the voters from the candidates.

But the rubber gloves block contact in two directions. Even for candidates who pound the pavement, the realities of contemporary elections make it impossible to know firsthand the needs of individual voters. There is not enough time. There are not enough occasions. There are too many people, and so, technology steps in with an answer. As we will examine, political campaigns gather detailed information about individual voters—often not from voters themselves, but from indirect sources that reveal something about them. It really is a very good solution from one viewpoint and a very bad one from another.

First, the good. Contemporary political campaigns have access to mountains of personal data. Linked with polling information, these yield a remarkably accurate profile. Campaign teams know voters' demographic statistics and what they like and dislike about news events, government leaders and political issues. They assemble other facts that illuminate revealing dimensions of voters' personalities.

Much of this is the kind of information one would expect to provide an affable candidate or campaign worker who dropped by for a pleasant chat. Information gathering today is an electronic surrogate for ward and precinct data gathering, which once provided a fairly accurate gauge of public concerns. Likewise, polls can clue candidates on real voter needs to supplement the information thrust upon them by powerful interests.

As for the bad side, it is dangerous to let the sweet smell of populist honeysuckle go to our heads. The truth is, facts today are seldom gathered from eager subjects. The level of information to the candidate rarely is rich with detail and the personal touch once well known to office seekers. Most people do not seek out a candidate to discuss what is on their minds, in their paychecks or near to their hearts. So, database building occurs impersonally, out of the voters' view.

People would be surprised, perhaps dismayed, to discover what is known about them. It's a safe bet that many wouldn't like it, because they value privacy and suspect those who intrude in their space. Driven, perhaps by the intuition that information is, indeed, power, most of us are uncomfortable at the thought of baring our souls to anonymous questioners. "Why do these electronic Peeping Toms want to know that? What will they *do* with it?" We don't like filling out financial statements or personal health forms or revealing to strangers the details of our personal history. Some people refuse to put their Social Security numbers on checks. They keep their phone numbers unlisted and generally guard details of their personal affairs. The growing efficiency of data collection and distribution increases the validity of concerns for lost privacy. Yet, even as these concerns rise, the capacity to remain anonymous diminishes. Data collection to a political campaign may be viewed as an efficient way of understanding voters, but from the voters' viewpoint, there is an annoying, intrusive quality about it.

Data collection procedures are only the means to an end. What about the application of these data? Essentially, the data provide a basis on which to establish and maintain a dialogue between the candidate and the voters. The information allows campaigns to determine the topics and appeals with which to confront each voter. Campaigns learn who is interested in Social Security, who is concerned about day care, who has a regard for environmental matters. They also learn whom to avoid: those totally disinterested in the issues, politics and voting, and those who are diehard fans of the opposition.

We noted that campaigns use data not only to select the topic but to position the pitch. How should these messages best portray the candidate's views on Social Security, day care and the environment? Advance information is indispensable. Some issues should be soft-peddled with some voters and pounded home to others. This is true of any conversation—one over coffee on the back porch or in a direct-mail letter. Audience data— or feedback from an audience—makes this determination possible and thereby increases communication efficiency and effectiveness.

So technology—polls, databases, computers and the rest—facilitate good communication in any political environment. Feedback is essential. If the goal of our political system is for elected officials to represent the will of the people, how better to determine the public will than by polls? How better to assure the public its will shall be done than through an efficient communication strategy? The argument is neat and clean. Candidates hear the voters; voters hear the candidates. There is feedback and information exchange. Political campaigns are communication campaigns. Effective communication translates into effective politics.

That's a soothing essay, but as Joe DiMaggio was begged to say, it just ain't so. Behind all the positive features of emerging high-tech political campaigning, a bell tolls a menacing warning. What happens to human communication when computers assume a major role? Sure, humans write the messages and make the decisions, so we don't have to worry about Hal of *2001* taking over, yet. But the process of political communication is still based on a sorting of icy statistics. That these statistics emerge from real people, 1,200 at a time, does not alter the impersonal truth. The richer the data, the more lifelike is the facade of intimacy. More receiver information means more hooks and references on which to shape the perfect "interpersonal" communication. The increasing application of cold technology enables strategists to project the appearance of greater warmth in one-on-one communications.

Without disparaging the efficiency of technology in political campaigns, we can be aware that a bomb is wired to this wonderful and sophisticated hardware and software. The ticking should alert us. How can you measure the merits of campaign technology solely by the newfound speed and precision of the equipment, the size of the databases and the capacity of machinery to map, sort, isolate and match voters with correct appeals?

There are enough bells and whistles in these technologies to please the wide-eyed kid in us all.

As students of the political campaigning process, however, we must step back and examine the implications both from a system-wide perspective and from the ethical tests of right and wrong, good and bad. We must ask not only what the equipment can do *for* us, but what it can do *to* us.

And so, with a healthy dose of skepticism about all things good and wonderful in political communication, we look hard at the information technologies. As Yogi Berra said, "You can observe a lot by just watching." Our goals are to describe the equipment and the software, to exhibit their uses and to explain their limitations. The views of experts in campaigning, computers, polling and database building will be aired, even though they don't agree among themselves.

The first half of this book presents the technology and the uses of that technology. It starts with a description of the targeting concept—the structural support for technology-driven communication. In mass communication, bigger is better; in targeted communication, smaller is smarter. We will pursue that logic.

A tech-driven philosophy of communication leads naturally to the key components of public opinion polling. The eyes and ears of a campaign—survey research—senses not only a candidate's stock within the general population, but also within small constituent subgroups. Polling has become an integrated and indispensable tool of the new technologies, and its innovations in recent years have written new agendas for candidates.

Ever since the Athenians numbered those who could vote in the purest of democracies, campaigns have used databases in one form or another. Today, databases are maintained on computers, and these provide an enormous advantage over the old three-by-five card files. They are bought and sold like baseball cards. Small ones can be joined to big ones, and big databases can be sorted, analyzed and synthesized to reveal a great deal of information about individual voters. As said before, this information gives campaigns power to know their audience, and this knowledge enables candidates to craft messages that offer the appropriate appeal to voters and contributors. A description of campaign databases and their anatomy, along with four primary sources, completes part I—the information technology.

Part II flips the coin to the other side. It looks at the effects of the new technologies on three levels.

First, the effects on individual voters. Data are collected about individuals, stored individually and used to affect individuals. The process raises questions of values: What does it mean to voters when information about them is used to persuade them? What about their privacy; what about their susceptibility to persuasive gambits?

Level two: the effects on the press. Targeting means ever more narrow and specific messages sent to each voter group—even to each voter individually. Targeting expands the number of channels through which these messages are delivered. As a result, the press today finds it almost impossible to keep tabs on all that the candidates say to the voters. Reporters cannot gain access to the many mailings and phone solicitations or even to the flurries of messages disseminated through cable television and targeted radio (we refer to all of these narrow communication outlets as the back channels). Direct mail, telephone solicitations and narrow-channel radio and television communications are difficult to inventory and analyze. Much of what is said to voters today goes by without press scrutiny.

Level three describes the effects of technology-driven campaign communications on government itself. Direct access to individual voters and small groups of voters allows candidates to shed the restraints of party discipline, and this has reconfigured the whole political process.

Such effects do not stop at the water's edge of the campaign, but are carried into government offices along with the successful candidates. In concert with other forces, the new technologies are having a significant effect on governance and particularly on the ways presidents and Congress run the day-to-day affairs of state.

Unarguably, the new technologies are efficient. They effectively pitch voters with personalized, targeted messages. The simple fact that candidates know more about their audiences than ever before means that they can deliver direct, one-on-one communications more accurately. The information they control grants them power they have never known. But the consequences, like so many blips on a radar screen, are ominous. This book is about the information and the power and the effects of technology-driven campaign communications.

NOTES

1. The Clinton campaign actually had two possible sources for this advance information. One was the satellite feed, as I indicated. This was the more likely source. The other source may have been Democrat-friendly employees at one or more television stations, who surreptitiously fed the Clinton people advance copies of the Bush spots. Clinton campaign adviser and spokesman Frank Greer would not reveal the source, although he said their methods were "very aboveboard" (Kurtz, November 6, 1992, p. A7).

2. Vice presidential candidate Albert Gore contested Roberts's use of the statistic during an interview on "This Week with David Brinkley" (ABC News, August 30, 1992). Roberts dodged the challenge to examine the underlying logic of compiling the number of tax hikes.

3. Claims about this tax statistic, along with statements on school voucher proposals and Middle East arms sales, earned George Bush the 1992 Doublespeak

Award, conferred by the Committee on Public Doublespeak of the National Council of Teachers of English.

4. The Democrats were not nearly as successful in getting the press to pick up their agenda. The Bush team seemed to stay one step ahead of the opposition and dictated Dukakis's agenda. Dukakis spent much of his time fending off the darts hurled at him by the opponent. Other information that wielded power with the press included the Willie Horton, Boston Harbor and Massachusetts school prayer legislation issues.

Part I

Description of the Technologies

Political communication during this century has run in cycles, moving from personal contacts in the hurly-burly of the ward and precinct system, to mass communication and the bullyboys of network television, then back to personal contacts again—only this time, the "personal touch" is computer-driven. There are both similarities and differences between the personal discourse of the past and exchanges today, not just in approach but in effect.

The next five chapters examine the high-tech tools of today's political communication. They look at the information that grants campaigns the power to influence voters as never before. They look at feedback theory and demonstrate how so much information can be gathered so quickly, analyzed so skillfully and applied so precisely to voters, who are often unwitting of the entire process.

Twin engines drive the political information machine. The first is public opinion polls, which sound out a population and reveal pockets of like-minded voters. They disclose how voters feel and why they feel that way, and they illuminate the scores of tiny voter bull's-eyes at which targeted communications are aimed.

Two chapters describe public opinion polling. Chapter 3 offers a thumbnail sketch of the process—the sampling, the data collection and the questionnaire design. Building on these three elements is the craft of data analysis.

Chapter 4 discusses the contributions of new technologies to political polling. Since the mid-eighties, when desktop computers stole into campaign headquarters, the polling approach has changed dramatically. Access to this technology also has changed. Polling, now a fixture in most campaigns, is open to the smallest candidate on the block.

The other engine of political information machines is the database. Guided by polls, databases single out individual voters by age, race, income, education, gender and party affiliation. If that isn't enough, they can combine dozens of other traits. They hold the names, addresses and phone numbers. They know other points of individual contact. They amass huge quantities of information. They store it, order it, sort it and apply it to communication programs so sensitive to audience feedback that campaigns can reach out and touch each voter, one at a time. Thanks again to the accessibility of computers, even the smallest campaigns can manipulate the most sophisticated databases. Chapter 5 describes how.

Chapter 6 puts the twin engines of polling and databases in tandem through data analyses. What can you do with polling data, and how do you feed this information into database operations? Chapter 6 looks at several approaches, and it also looks at something new—high-tech display functions that enable campaigns to gain instant insight into their audience targets.

Most of these functions, like polls and voter files, have been around in one form or another for a long time. But what hasn't been around until a dozen years ago is the dramatically increased power of inexpensive personal computers that open up a technical universe to shoestring operations. Technology has put within the reach of all the same powerful tools once restricted to high-budget operations. With computers, the Davids can out-communicate the Goliaths, and the mouse can out-remember the elephant.

Because of the growing popularity of and expanding market for information and analytic tools, technology does magic that no campaign could have managed just a few years ago. Take the new mapping programs. These twenty-first-century innovations offer a visual and intuitive inspection of a database. They reveal in an instant what could not have been known after countless days of laborious analyses. Furthermore, the ability to map data has encouraged the development of related products. Even the U.S. Census Bureau got into the act by providing its 1990 data in a form suitable for geographic mapping.

The following chapters describe these dynamic innovations that have renovated political campaigns while raising new questions about the use and misuse of political information born of the new technologies. Recall from Greek mythology that Prometheus stole fire from heaven for earthly use. Giving this mighty tool to man angered the gods, who sent Pandora to earth with her box of evils. For politicians—indeed, for all of us—the computer is the mightiest tool since fire. The question is: Are computers accompanied by a Pandora's box of manipulations and exploitations, evils that deprive us of our privacy and infringe on our democracy?

Chapter Two

The Targeting Concept

A whole bushel of wheat is made up of single grains.
—Thomas Fuller[1]

OVERVIEW

Voters were grazing peacefully in the pastures of network television and daily papers, when, in the early eighties, an elephant herd of new electronic media trampled onto the scene. Information rushed in from every direction. Cable television barreled in first, then a new genre of talk radio, then the stampede of computers, faxes, EMail, computer-driven direct mail, electronic bulletin boards, fancy phones and a daily drumming of innovations that blink and buzz and appeal for a few minutes of the voter's precious time.

Political communications—just a few years after the first cable was spliced on-line and the first desktop computer fired up—are now faster, more efficient and better able to reach the right audience with the right message. There are more messages, more media, more audiences—especially diverse and fragmented audiences—clustered by common traits.

Voters face packed warehouses full of electronic media, even as they continue to suffer print by the racks full. In the closing hours of this century, political and commercial communicators alike offer Americans information options once divined only in science-fiction novels. Remember stodgy, old Ma Bell? Her firstborn son, AT&T, will soon enter home news and entertainment markets, thanks to an FCC ruling that promises customers an assortment of interactive video media. Just think: Very soon, through compressed digital technology, you will have access to more than seven-hundred channels and video-on-demand. Select any of ten thousand titles, and your choice will be sent immediately, via telephone lines, to your television. IBM and NBC are preparing "News on Demand" for instant videotape retrieval. Bill Clinton has promised to criss-cross the nation with "data highways" that will traffic a rich, new assortment of communication services.[2]

Most of these new communications are targeted, aimed at tiny slices of the audience pie. None of the new media embraces network-size multitudes or seeks the throngs once drawn broadly to *Look* and *Life* magazines or to national, network radio. The new media are focused, directed and custom built to reach users one by one and in small groups.

Communicators rejoice because they know audiences respond best to personal pitches—that's an old truth known to hucksters of brushes and mules and to politicians. It's easier to sell tonic to one person than it is to a mob, and now computers and technology are making that intimacy possible, paradoxically on a large scale. The "personal" pitch to multitudes of individuals is the logic of audience targeting.

The techniques of targeting depend wholly on computers. These mighty brutes crush granite mountains of data into tiny gravel piles, sorting entire populations into useful clusters of like-minded voters. Computers store the data, order it and give campaigns the power to analyze and understand the voters in ways never before possible. In short, computer specialists analyze data with a singular goal: to divide up an audience for personal communications.

Sometimes called personalization or commoditization, targeting occurs in two steps. First, it takes the public's pulse by means of a representative voter sample. The polls record the vital signs and examine typical cases. By inference, the polls reveal the condition of the whole population.

Second, lessons learned from the sample are projected onto the population. This occurs through the manipulation of personal databases that contain the DNA of each voter. Thus, you draw general lessons from the polls and apply them to specific voters. It is like studying a sample of patients to learn who is most susceptible to the flu, then inoculating everyone in the population who meets the criteria.

Targeting, guided by the samples, enacted on the population, identifies, defines and isolates the subgroups most susceptible to political pitches. Then it's a matter of matching the right message with the right audience, each group getting the right prescription. It's simple in theory, but with real voters and real issues, it is complex in practice. This chapter lays out the concept and highlights the practical challenges.

TARGETING FOUNDATIONS

The paradigm for targeting is the one-on-one conversation, what ABC-TV sports immortalized for Olympic interviews with the phrase "upfront and personal." Two people talking over coffee enjoy rich interplay. Each processes information from the other and produces information designed to affect the other—like moves in a chess game, each based on previous moves, each anticipating those to come. In one-on-one conversations, the participants are linked, both analyzing and anticipating, processing and projecting information. Try having a dialogue without any feedback from your partner—it soon becomes a meaningless monologue and a testament to the claim that information drives interpersonal communications.

How eagerly people seek information about anticipated encounters! They scramble to learn everything possible about a job interviewer, a blind date, future in-laws, a yet unknown office mate. Many would trade a winning lottery ticket to learn what makes the IRS auditor tick and what sways the traffic judge to go easy. Such curiosities spring from the belief that effective communications grow from a knowledge of the audience. The information offers something to go on, something with which to craft an effective appeal—in other words, a better way to target the message. Information is the key to successful targeting.

In order to project from one person to many, it is necessary to examine the elements common to both interpersonal and mass communication. Essentially, how are interpersonal and targeted communications related? How is communicating with one person similar to communicating with a group of like-minded people?

AUDIENCE COMPOSITION

Let's start with an examination of mass and targeted communications, concepts best distinguished by the kinds of audiences each addresses. There are clear differences, but the main distinction is not audience size. Big audiences are not necessarily mass audiences, and small audiences are not necessarily target audiences, even though it often works out that way.

To crystallize the point, assume one audience (the mass audience) has one hundred members, each with traits and perspectives unlike anyone else in the group. Everyone is different in every way. Reactions, views, needs and abilities are distinct. These innate differences make it difficult to create informative or persuasive messages, since everyone wants and needs to know something different and will respond uniquely to any message. Call that the heterogeneous audience.

Now, think about another audience of one hundred—a narrow, targeted audience—where every member is identical to every other member. Each holds the same views and knows the same things, each has the same disposition and the same skills. There is no variance here. Learn about one, know about the others. A message fashioned for one would interest the remaining ninety-nine. Call that the homogeneous audience.

Neither of these extremes really exists, but each helps define the issue. Whether heterogeneous or homogeneous, the audience size is immaterial. Each has one hundred members, and yet one audience has mass characteristics, the other narrow. The real distinction, then, is the nature of the members in a given group and, consequently, the kinds of messages that can be pitched toward it. Ordinarily, the roughest-hewn messages drive at common denominators of the heterogeneous audience; a precise, responsive message strikes at the homogeneous audience. In the second case, it is as though we were interacting with a single person. Such a level of precision is the goal of targeted communication.

What are the defining traits of an audience? Uniformity and focus. For example, the television networks—although now tired, aging giants, slugging their way through the information marketplace—still draw mass audiences counted in the millions. Not only do network prime-time audiences remain large by any standard, but they are heterogeneous, a fusion of people with every conceivable view and characteristic. They are blended audiences, near ideal national samples whose features cut a broad swath through the American population.

Thus, along with demographic heterogeneity comes interest heterogeneity. To network programmers, the large audiences are sweeping statistical collectives. Each viewer is different, but some things are bound to appeal to most. This is the common denominator—usually called the lowest common denominator—the thread that weaves through the fabric of every audience. Network assessments are blunt but functional. What makes most audience members laugh, what makes most of them weep, which subjects draw in the largest group? The raison d'être of a network programmer is learning the answers and responding correctly with shows that grab a respectable share of this wide viewership.[3] It is a broad brush with which the networks sweep, and while millions may rebuff their shows, other millions tune right in. The goal is to impact the largest audiences with subject matter sufficiently general to please everyone and offend no one. This broad, open-arm philosophy results in large numbers. Like sausage stuffers, networks measure audiences by the pound.

In contrast, targeted communication is precise and focused. Interpersonal communication, the most obvious targeting case, occurs whenever two people talk. Communication scholars are quick to point out that not all one-on-one interactions are responsive and interlocking.[4] People often talk past each other, ignore feedback from each other and follow their own agendas. Remember the televised 1992 vice presidential debates? During the five-minute discussions, Vice President Dan Quayle and Senator Albert Gore shared the same stage and occasionally the same topics, but each locked into a preset agenda that ignored the opponent—and for that matter, the reporters' questions. The two candidates never fully recognized each other or each other's arguments. Instead, they spewed the lines packed into their briefcases long before the debate began. That happens in a lot of discussions when feedback fails.

Nevertheless, many one-on-one encounters achieve the prized goal of interlocking exchanges and operate in direct response to each other. Unlike mass-mediated messages aimed at a statistical average—or a lowest common denominator—these messages are uniquely crafted for one person whose individual traits are well known. Successful interpersonal conversations are interactive, each comment contingent on the one preceding it, anticipating the one to follow. Good talkers are good listeners, sensitive to subtleties—the transient smile or the flitting glance, brittle tension in a voice or the clipped ending to a sentence. Each message is responsive and tailored for an intended effect, one time, to one person. This is pinpoint, targeted communication at its best.

Leave it to communication specialists to exploit a good thing. Political communicators yearn to emulate the patterns of successful interpersonal exchanges. It is a reach that exceeds their grasp, but it is, nonetheless, the model that drives an emerging genre of political communication. Targeting begins with the assembly of audience information—through polls and databases—and continues with data analyses that determine targetable clusters—those groups of people sufficiently like-minded that they will respond similarly to the same message. Databases can inventory the details with which communicators assemble targeted audience clusters. By fixing on small like-minded groups, they attempt the precision of interpersonal communication. Its success improves in proportion to the amount of information that can be stockpiled, then manipulated.

How does the stockpiling work? The answer is found in audience stratification, a notion intuitively simple, a practice inherently complicated. First, the easy notion. Think about a traditional grammar school. Children are divided into grades that correspond to their ages, experiences and abilities. A school-wide cross-section reveals layers of students with these easily identifiable traits.

Similarly, mass audiences can be layered by measurable traits, these traits revealed by polling data. In politics, most campaigns have an idea of their candidate's strengths and weaknesses and some of the strengths and weaknesses of the opposition. They also have a list of the hot issues, and they know which of these work for them and which work against them. They know the population's voting history, and they have access to polling data that reveals current voter thinking about the issues and the candidates. These data and other audience feedback are critical when stratifying an audience.

But the challenge lies ahead. On what variables should the campaign stratify? Age, party affiliation, education level? How about occupation, income and gender? Maybe it is best to start with voter predispositions to certain issues—for instance, thumbs up or down on gun control, for or against abortion, save the ancient forests or saw them down. Look then at the demographic traits of like-minded people, and allow strata to form accordingly. Such decisions are made even more complicated in the face of several realities.

Successful audience stratification is rarely based on a single characteristic, but on several. For instance, audiences are seldom divided just into men or women, young or old, educated or uneducated, but into combinations of these traits, each audience defined by some level of these and many other characteristics. Three age categories (young, middle age, senior) may be combined with four income categories (under $10,000, $10,000 to $20,000, $20,000 to $50,000, $50,000 plus) and with three education levels (less than high school, high school graduate, some college plus). The deck is cut many times. In deciding such groupings, the analyst looks for traits that discriminate audience thinking on an issue.

That matching of demographic groups to issues, however, has its problems. People don't always stay with their group mates on all the issues that come along. Upper-income, professional males may think as a group about tax policy but share little on abortion. That being true, communicators can accurately develop strategies to deal with tax proposals by selecting media and messages that reach this upper-income, male group. At the same time, they must avoid discussing abortion with this audience, because there is so little consensus. For abortion, planners must turn to other audience formulas.

Because the voting public never stands still, other complications make planners miserable. People change their views, shift their allegiances among candidates and issues, some even revel in their ability to shuffle aimlessly around an issue. Communicators learn quickly that, for many voters, consistency and logic are not proud virtues. Neat audience clusters dissolve and reform through the course of a race as persuasion tactics work their spell and thinking evolves. That species of upper-income professional males, in such harmony at the outset, may, over time, become discordant and no longer serve as an ideal target—for taxes or any issue.

How can audience stratification be made to work in such chaos? The process may never be neat and clean, but computers and other technological aides have been recruited for the heavy pick-and-shovel work that mines the information essential to targeted communication. Computers store and sort the data and assist in the analysis of patterns that lead to target group selection. Then, they assist campaigns in preparing messages that distribute information to target clusters and to individual voters.

Audience stratification then—with or without computers—relies on the ability to sort an audience into meaningful clusters that represent the confluence of audience and issue. They are formed of the largest audience group that holds reasonably consistent views on a given issue. Look for homogeneity within groups and diversity across them.

Let's take an example: an orbiting space station, a perennial favorite of Congress. Suppose a public opinion poll found three distinct views: (1) proponents—"spend money for it," (2) opponents—"don't spend money for it" and (3) fence-sitters—"haven't decided yet." What kinds of people most likely hold each view?

The analyses may turn up something like this. The proponents of the space station are young and middle-aged, college-educated professionals. Opponents are older, high school–educated, blue-collar workers. Fence-sitters come from both groups and are concentrated in the southeastern United States. These are broad categories, and not everyone within each group agrees completely, but there is enough unity within groups to focus targeted messages. And that is what a campaign will do. It will discover ways of reaching these individual groups—through targeted media such as radio and cable television, direct-mail and telephone solicitations—with messages designed just for them. The informative and persuasive content will appeal to their predispositions, interests and understanding of the issue.

The voter template is constructed from bits and pieces of information gathered in public opinion surveys. This feedback is essential. Stop the feedback, stop the communication.

FEEDBACK

Feedback can be an electrical impulse, a sound, an odor or a flash of light. Feedback can be a slap in the face, a kiss, an arm around the shoulder or public opinion data gathered from likely voters. The one feature common to all feedback signals is information. Feedback IS information.[5]

The notion of feedback was first used to describe the regulatory processes in guided missiles and other automatic-control systems.[6] Mathematicians Norbert Wiener and Claude Shannon are among the first to build the bridge from feedback in the physical sciences to feedback in communication and the social sciences.

Feedback is involved in the operation of a simple thermostat in your home heating system. The temperature maintenance of your body is based on feedback. Feedback information allows control in robotic technology, rocket operations, in hundreds of systems aboard commercial airliners and in today's computer-controlled automobiles.

Electrical engineer and writer Arnold Tustin (1952) argued many years ago that feedback may function as a controlling mechanism as long as at least three conditions are met: (1) The required changes must be physically attainable, (2) the controlled quantity must be measurable and (3) modification must be rapid enough to allow the system to function properly.

Before applying these three points to political communication, go back to our model.

A model campaign identifies the audience strata based on accurate polling data. It develops appropriate messages and coordinates them with media strategies involving television and radio, billboards, direct mail and telephone. As sure as Adam bit the apple, audience responses, recorded in polling data, flow back to the campaign and provide the information necessary to develop subsequent strategies and messages. Obviously, some appeals work, some do not, but updated, responsive information flows smoothly and quickly to the voters, and follow-up information flows smoothly and quickly from the voters, and this is used to construct new messages. All the elements are accurate, speedy, and contingent. That's the ideal model.

Now, test the model using Tustin's three points. First, the required changes must be physically possible. That means a political campaign must have the technical skill and the financial resources necessary to enact a program responsive to audience feedback. If the campaign cannot read the signals—understand what the polls convey—develop a fitting strategy or put the plan into place, then the required changes cannot occur. The system breaks down as would any feedback-controlled system that cannot respond appropriately to information. It is like a shot in the dark with a rusty Howitzer, the gunner unable to move the barrel according to the spotter's range and azimuth information.

Second, the controlled quantity must be measurable. Not just any thruster burst will keep the missile on course; it must be directed and calibrated, and it must be calculated to have a desired effect on the missile's trajectory. Similarly, campaigns must react to audience information with a response calibrated for an intended effect. Implications of the message must match indications of the data. Discover audience concerns, understand their viewpoints and shape messages sensitive to these positions. Messages must be audience-responsive; one persuasive message or strategy is not the same as another. With one group, you promote a candidate's stand on abortion; with another, environmental policies; with a third, the candidate's ability to form a consensus. Feedback-based targeted messages are custom-made, one to an audience. That is the magic of targeting. It is a process of disseminating focused messages to small groups whose needs are well measured and understood. We shape messages with specific goals and expectations for each audience and thus assemble each component to achieve an intended effect. That is the objective of targeting. Tustin reminds us it is the same for all feedback-controlled systems.

Finally, the modification must be rapid enough to allow the system to function properly. Imagine a rocket that fired its thrusters a casual few seconds after it received an "off-course" signal. Delayed reactions would zigzag the lazy rocket into the void. In this, the age of instant communication, there is increasing pressure on communicators to respond rapidly to changing conditions. Audience movement must be recognized, analyzed and answered quickly, sometimes within hours or minutes. Voters are volatile, particularly the uncommitted souls in the middle who shift and shimmy throughout a campaign. They are driven by the political ebb and flow. Candidates must track these voters and quickly adjust messages to meet their emerging concerns and evolving agendas.

In the 1988 presidential campaign, Michael Dukakis was riding high in the polls just after the Democratic convention. Within weeks, the gap closed, and opponent George Bush left a bewildered Dukakis in a cloud of dust. Most analysts believe Dukakis whistled in the dark too long and failed to act at the first signs of danger. He allowed public thinking to veer too far off course, and his campaign soon lost control, drifting off into the political void.

This was a lesson not lost on Bill Clinton who, in 1992, hit the ground running after the Democratic convention. He never let the sun set on a Republican charge without confronting it head-on, and he never allowed public sentiment to gel around an allegation. At the first sign of a charge, Clinton would issue a press release or make a public statement, and then, within hours, he would release radio and television ads to sustain the initial response. Appropriately enough, Clinton's staff called this "operation war room" to connote instant responsiveness.

Political communicators these days must fire rapidly and return fire immediately. The norms for quick responses have inched ever upward, and the voters have come to expect immediate responses and rejoinders.

SUMMARY

Tustin's thinking is helpful for political communication systems. Goals must be achievable, measurable and rapid. Campaigns take maximum advantage of feedback information when they mint spontaneous messages, responsive to audience feedback. It is pointless to lay out a complete, ready-to-run communication program months in advance, because campaigns encounter unavoidable eddies and currents throughout a race, and these demand spontaneous heading corrections. Successful campaigns chart a general direction, but they pilot the specific course every day of the race.

Knowing your capacities, measuring your feedback and meeting your deadlines are prescriptions for success in any campaign. Targeted messages today must be precise and well crafted, they must yield a desired effect with specific audiences and they must be instantly fed into the candidate's responses.

Why is speed so important? Electronic communications have conditioned audiences to expect instant responses. Within seconds, we know about major events around the world. Instantly, we learn about crises and major government decisions. CNN gave us the Gulf War live and in living color. Exit surveys give us results moments after the polls close. In the 1992 presidential debates, networks reported accurate, representative poll results minutes after the gavel closed each session.[7] Voters have been treated to the sensation of instant communications, and now they expect flash facts from everyone. Campaigns must be perched for instant replies and immediate reaction to unfolding events. Audiences demand quick answers, and the opposition will not relent on a candidate who is slow on the draw. As the westerns used to say, there are only two kinds of gunfighters: the quick and the dead.

CONCLUSION

Targeting is the password that opens doors for political communicators today. The methods and media single out, size up and shake down small audience groups, then craft messages to meet the needs of each. Some observers believe that these techniques don't serve audiences' interests as much as they sense audience weaknesses and strike at audience vulnerabilities. These are judgments saved for later.

Contemporary techniques of targeting involve two components born of and wedded by computers. The first is political polling, by which campaigns take the pulse of a population. The second is political databases, by which campaigns read the genetic code of each voter. Together, the two form a powerful instrument of persuasion. We turn next to these components and their uses.

NOTES

1. Thomas Fuller, *Gnomologia* (London: B. Barker, 1732), p. 456.

2. Business reporter Don Clark writes: "Information utilities will deliver computerized text, graphics, video images and stereo sound into the home. Consumers will be able to call up movies, hear the latest record, play new video games and tap into libraries and schools. They may also browse through so-called video malls, examining images of goods and paying for them electronically" ("New Vision of Communications," *San Francisco Chronicle*, November 23, 1992, p. B1).

3. For a thorough account of how the television industry seeks to produce popular shows, see Gary W. Selnow and Richard R. Gilbert, *Society's Impact on Television* (Westport, Conn.: Praeger, 1993).

4. For an excellent treatment of interpersonal communication exchanges, see Gerald Miller and Mark Steinberg, *Between People: A New Analysis of Interpersonal Communication* (Chicago: Science Research Associates, 1975).

5. In the strict application of the concept, control of a system is maintained by negative feedback, or the amount of deviation from a desired condition. For instance, your furnace will fire up only if the room temperature drops below the target 68 degrees. A rocket will ignite corrective directional thrusters only if it deviates from its desired course.

6. The role of feedback is articulated in cybernetic theories that examine control systems and look at the flow of information within self-adjusting mechanisms. Alfred Smith describes the process in a missile: " 'Do X until Y happens and then do Z.' If the missile swerves from its course by doing X + 1 instead of X, its deviation is fed back to change the original instructions automatically from Z to Z - 1" (Smith 1966, p. 2).

7. The networks and Public Broadcasting reported telephone poll results a half-hour after the debates ended. These polls were based on more than seven hundred randomly selected respondents.

Chapter Three

The Anatomy of a Public Opinion Poll

> Even though counting heads is not an ideal way to govern, at least it is better than breaking them.
>
> —Judge Learned Hand,
> Speech before the Federal Bar Association (1932)

The historical roots of political polling run deep. The first poll may have taken place when the senate divided the people of Athens—excepting women and slaves—into two sides of the city, the yea votes on the east and the nays on the west. This "sample of the whole," by the way, voted for war, two to one. More scientific opinion surveying has served campaigns since the mid–1930s—and a lot earlier than that, if you consider the informal techniques used to gather voter information scraps during the nineteenth century (Bradburn and Sudman 1988).

But polling found its modern voice in the thirties and forties. Paul Lazarsfeld used polling technology in his celebrated studies of the 1940 presidential race, and his work contributed much to the academic respectability of the technique. George Gallup improved sampling procedures through the late thirties and early forties. Ever since—despite a few obvious disruptions, such as the infamous Dewey-Truman blunder—polls have been trusted fixtures in political campaigns.

Polls deliver more for the money today than they ever have. Statistical programs pry loose more usable information, questioning techniques test concepts never before examined in large-scale surveys and ingenious display software transforms dreary tables of numbers into colorful charts and maps for instant interpretation—even by the untutored. Integrated programs, often called "campaigns-in-a-box," allow campaigns to run their own polls on a shoestring—perhaps a tad imprecise, but dependable enough to obtain usable data. The result is that more races are using more polls for ever-more guidance in a widening range of campaign decisions.

Computers now deftly join the population discoveries of opinion polls to the individual details of personal databases. Together, opinion poll data and voter databases provide a one-two punch for political communication. Polls shake down voter thinking by subgroup and issue, and databases tell campaigns where to land the best shot with each voter.

In this chapter, we will review the basic components of public opinion polling. The discussion is designed as a refresher for readers away from the subject a while and as an overview for readers new to polling.

Here is the polling process in a nutshell. First comes the sample. Researchers select a group of people (i.e., the respondents) to answer their questions. Whom they select, how they select them and what they do about those who decline the honor—these questions dominate the sampling effort, and they are the detail devils that pester the pollsters.

Second is questionnaire development. This step is concerned with what to ask and how to ask it. Questionnaires reflect a list of issues the candidate favors, but the answers they elicit can change that agenda as well. The heart of any survey, the questionnaire, often called the "instrument," is constructed by the pollster in coordination with the campaign.

Third, there is data gathering. In this phase, interviewers pose questions and record respondents' answers. This is accomplished through the mail, in face-to-face (in-person) interviews or over the telephone. But not all techniques are equally sound. Mail surveys seldom deliver data representative of the population and have no place in legitimate survey research. In-person surveys, once the darling of the industry, are rarely used anymore because of their expense, logistical hassles and other complications. That leaves the telephone, the prevailing method in most political and commercial research.

Fourth, and finally, is data analysis. Here, researchers process the data to understand what respondents mean, how they feel and how they may vote on issues and candidates.

These four components of survey research are conducted sequentially, and they are very much interrelated: Whom you interview depends on the kinds of information you want, the questions you ask and the forum for data gathering you select. Your intended analysis dictates the design of questions and responses. I have isolated the survey components for discussion in this chapter, but you might think of this as a juggling act, with each of the four components as a plate. When any one is in hand, the other three are in the air, each dependent on the others.

SAMPLING

Recall a scene in the Peter Sellers movie *Revenge of the Pink Panther*, when Inspector Clouseau faces an old man and overly attentive dog. Clouseau asks the man, "Does your dog bite?" The man assures Clouseau his dog does not bite. Clouseau then pets the dog and, of course, is bitten. He challenges the man: "I thought you said your dog didn't bite!" The man replies, "That is not my dog." Clouseau asked the right question; he just didn't ask it of the right person.

And so, your questions are useful only if you ask them of the right people; you must draw a correct sample. In surveying, the fruits of poor sampling may look sweet, but beneath the skin lies a poison. The data appear sound, since there are statistics and tables and other trappings that seduce us into believing one sample is as good as the next. The truth is, poor samples yield poor data.

What then is a good sample? Let's look at two techniques—one misleading and the other sound.

Nonrepresentative sampling is a body of techniques with no skeleton. Respondents are chosen because they are willing and accessible. Even worse, some are chosen in order to avoid unwelcome opinions. You can gather them at shopping malls, cocktail parties, churches or anywhere you wish. You can select them from phone books, voter lists or neighborhood sign-up sheets. One of the most ludicrous "samples" is the showpiece of TV's "Family Feud." To establish a "national sounding," the show sounds out people in the studio audience. Contestants are then asked to answer questions like, "What should you do on your first date?" They are to answer not what they think, but what they think the "average Americans" from the studio audience think. The use of code words and phrases like "polls" and "average Americans" implies that the results are representative. Of course, this is not so. People with the means to visit Hollywood, then with luck or connections to obtain seats in the audience just don't represent the nation. From the expressions on the faces of contestants who are told they are "wrong," it is obvious that they are genuinely surprised at the silly "average American" answers. This is an example of bad sampling.

The problem is not so much where you choose respondents but how. There is nothing wrong with studio audience or "person-on-the-street" samples when you need interesting and entertaining anecdotal material. The techniques employed may help you refine items on a questionnaire and thereby support development of a full-scale poll. These findings, however, never ought to be used for campaign decisions, because they are not representative of the voter population.

Representative sampling is another matter. The techniques are precise; they are based on the scientific principle of random selection. Underwriting all representative methods is the notion that every member of the population has an equal chance of being chosen. Friendships and proximity to campaign headquarters hold no advantage. Party membership, ideological compatibility and the ability to articulate one's views mean nothing in a random population sample. Everyone is equal in the eyes of the random sampler, and everyone has the same chance for selection into the group. Compare this with the "Family Feud" studio sample.

Sampling specialists stop at nothing to ensure that Lady Luck deals an honest hand. In the past, respondents were selected with help from a table of random numbers, under the reasonable assumption that few things are less biased than an arbitrary assignment of numerical codes. Random samples are also drawn from telephone books and other published directories using stratified random-selection techniques. Random-digit dial (RDD) procedures are most popular for telephone interviews today. They are computer-generated, and so they minimize staff time and effort. They eliminate the nagging problems inherent to phone book samples: unlisted and out-of-date numbers.

It is inconceivable that legitimate polling organizations would consider anything but a true random sample. Research with recognized companies, then, is usually safe from the dangers of nonrepresentative samples. Still, it isn't a bad idea to have the sampling procedure spelled out.

RDD sampling programs are built into most campaign software packages. They require only the entry of preliminary information specific to the local area. After a few minutes of staff time, the programs generate numbers and print them in lists, on call sheets, or store them electronically for integration with other survey software. Pollsters can also purchase random samples for the desired population from companies such as Survey Sampling, Inc.[1] These companies specialize in sample designs and preparations, and they will consult with clients about recommended approaches. Their sophisticated databases ensure accurate sampling and maximize the success of reaching eligible respondents.

A pollster's use of the term "population" deserves a note of explanation. When samplers refer to a population, they mean the universe from which a sample is drawn. It has a floating definition based on the characteristics of the target audience. For instance, a population may be defined as everyone in the United States, everyone in California or everyone in Texas who is Methodist, over 18 years old, has graduated high school and who owns a Chevy. Geographic, demographic, behavioral or other distinguishing characteristics alone or in combination may be used to define a population. You can't talk about a sample without talking first about a population.

Survey research discussions usually work around to the question of sample size: How many people need to be in a sample to provide an accurate reflection of the population? That question is more easily asked than answered, due to a number of factors. The most obvious concern the degree of confidence (confidence level) and the level of accuracy (confidence interval) one wishes to place in the results—and the cost.

The confidence level reveals how many times out of one hundred replications (repeated identical surveys) you would expect your results to occur. The confidence level most experts have settled on in survey research, 95 percent, means that you can expect reported results to occur ninety-five times in one hundred replications.

The confidence interval describes the margin of error associated with the percentage of respondents selecting an answer. For instance, an error of +/– 4 percent means that if half the sample selected candidate Johnson, you can be confident that the true support level for Johnson lies between 46 percent and 54 percent. Putting the confidence level and the confidence interval in the same picture, you can be confident your results would show that 95 percent of the time, between 46 percent and 54 percent of the people would vote for Johnson.

There is a natural give-and-take between the confidence level and the confidence interval. Without changing the number of respondents, you can increase your confidence in the results if you are willing to accept greater error. You can be more certain that the real value is between 40 percent and 60 percent than you are that it is between 48 percent and 52 percent. There is just more room to be right. Conversely, if you wish to report greater accuracy, you must become less confident.

Think about this example. How confident are you that ABC newsman Peter Jennings weighs between 170 and 180 pounds (that's your confidence interval). Not too sure? Good reason. That's a pretty tight interval. Lets say you are only 60 percent certain (that's your confidence level). Now, how sure are you that Jennings weighs between 135 and 215 pounds? There's a safer bet. The level of your confidence shoots up to, say, 95 percent. That is why you can be more confident if you are willing to accept a greater interval.

Most researchers use the 95 percent confidence level. This is not a magic number; it just happens to be a convention reflecting a reasonable level of risk comfortable to most.

If you increase the sample size, you can improve both the confidence level and the confidence interval. As long as you employ identical sampling techniques, larger samples will yield improvements in both features. Here, too, is a trade-off: larger samples cost more. You may remember the story about JFK's father, millionaire Joseph Kennedy. According to talk, he told the ward captains getting out the vote in New York to buy every one as long as the election looked close, but, said Joe, "Be careful, because I'm damned if I'll pay for a landslide." The same thing is true in polling. Why pay for four thousand respondents when twelve hundred will give dependable, accurate data?

There are perennial debates about how much accuracy campaign managers should buy. If the race is a cakewalk for one of the candidates, both probably can tolerate a little less accuracy, since the gap is undeniably wide. You don't need a micrometer to measure the Grand Canyon.[2] Photo-finish races, though, demand more accuracy just to know whose nose is ahead, and so they necessitate larger samples that unfortunately (for candidates, not pollsters) incur higher costs.

We need to consider one more element before leaving this discussion of sample size. So far we have been preoccupied only with overall results of the entire sample: What is the candidate's overall rating? If the race were held today, would he or she win or lose? In fact, targeting strategies, so critical to contemporary campaigns, demand an examination of responses from audience subgroups. However, such categorical analyses rapidly reduce the numbers, as the sample breaks down into ever smaller component parts, and as we have seen, smaller numbers reduce confidence in the results. Principles of sampling error govern the sample overall and each subgroup as well. As it is with entire samples, the smaller the subgroup, the greater the potential for error. So, to improve the accuracy within subgroups, you need larger overall samples, or you need to over-sample among the subgroups in which you have particular interest.

Say you want to know how American viewers feel about the level of sex on tabloid TV. If that's all, a sample of four hundred is probably dependable, because the $+/-5$ percent margin of error (at the 95 percent confidence level) would probably be accurate enough for your needs. But suppose you wanted to discover what percentage of high school–educated homemakers under 40 felt about TV sex? To measure that subgroup with any accuracy, you would need a larger total sample, since only a small portion of all respondents would fit the subgroup characteristics. You could also screen for and over-sample people in this group to increase their numbers to improve the accuracy. Either way, increasing the overall sample or over-sampling a subgroup, runs into money. This returns us to the top of our discussion about sampling: How much accuracy do you need, and how much can you afford?

In summary, the determination of sample size must account for these factors: How much confidence do you wish to have in the results, how accurate do you want them to be, what subgroups do you plan to examine and what sample size can you afford? Answers depend on the phase of the race, the strength of the competition and the size of your checking account. As a point of reference, polls typically sample between four hundred and twelve hundred respondents, but it is not uncommon to see much larger samples.

P.S. What about the relationship between the size of the population you draw from and the size of the sample itself? It is natural to suspect that larger populations require larger samples. Surprisingly, this is not so. With equal subgroup requirements, district-wide campaigns require samples of about the same size needed for state and national races. This curious fact is described below.

• Why the population size is not very important to the sample size.
• Why the sample size is important to the accuracy of the sample.

Imagine a two-gallon fishbowl filled with an equal number of red, white and blue marbles (about 33 percent of each color), all mixed and churned and scattered evenly (randomized) throughout. If you didn't know the proportion of colors and you didn't have the time to count them all, you might consider counting just a sample. You could do so by dipping in a measuring cup and filling it with marbles. You could count the marbles in this sample and find that you came up with a third red, a third white and a third blue. You could do this several times, if you wished, and each time you would come up with roughly a third of each color (on a bet, several of my students did this and demonstrated it works!).

Now, consider a larger population, represented this time by a swimming pool full of red, white and blue marbles in equal proportions—a third of each—and all mixed together (randomized). Again, take a measuring cup sample and count the contents; once again, you would find a third of each color.

In both cases, from the small population (the fishbowl) and the large population (the swimming pool), you took the same-sized sample (the measuring cup). Yet, in both cases, your sample accurately revealed the proportion of marble colors to be the same.

The same principle holds for human samples from small and large populations. A predetermined number of respondents extracted from both populations (using random selection methods) is necessary to describe each, despite its size.

Consider one more point. Suppose you used not a measuring cup but a shot glass to draw your marble sample from the fishbowl and then the swimming pool. Suppose an average shot glass can scoop up four marbles. With such a small number, there is a much greater chance you will obtain marble colors disproportionate to their representation in the population. By the luck of the draw, you may scoop two reds and two blues, or two whites, a blue and a red. That would be easy to do. Because the number is so small, you increase the risk of developing a sample that does not accurately represent the total population.

If you increase the size of the container and thus increase the number of marbles in your sample, you also increase the chances of obtaining a sample that represents the total population.

In summary, the size of the population (fishbowl/swimming pool) is not as important as the size of the sample (measuring cup/shot glass) in determining accuracy.

QUESTIONNAIRE DEVELOPMENT

Oliver Goldsmith didn't have political pollsters on his mind when he said, "Ask me no questions, and I'll tell you no fibs," but his remark touches a critical issue: How can you draft questions that elicit the truth—not just the truth in terms of a respondent's honesty, but the truth in terms of the genuine beliefs and perceptions of that respondent?

If I could answer that question, I would be a Nobel laureate. The best I can do is outline the pitfalls in question writing and suggest ways to assemble survey instruments that have a reasonable chance of yielding accurate and usable information. Question writing is a science and an art. Learning the science is easy enough, but the art comes slowly and by practice—by chiseling a few blocks then chipping away at the questions, the phrasing and the placement of items in questionnaires.

Let's start with a short inventory of question types. There are two broad categories: closed-ended and open-ended. Closed-ended questions involve selecting one answer from the alternatives—for example, the multiple choice test. Open-ended questions ask people to fill in the blanks and so permit infinite response possibilities. Closed-ended questions are fast to administer, quick to code for computer manipulation, easier to tabulate, lend themselves to more sophisticated statistical analysis, get results in minutes and, because they save time, they save money. On the other hand, they force respondents to chose from an array that may not include their preferred answers, and they allow reporting of no personal views.

Ironically, the greatest drawback of closed-ended questions results from the ease with which they can be answered. Even respondents who are without a clue about the meaning of a question can pick an answer—any answer—and it is recorded alongside the thoughtful choices of others. Researchers sometimes demonstrate this eagerness to respond by asking people to rate their views (excellent, good, fair, poor) on some fictitious subject, say a country called the Grand Duchy of Pourchnick. Lots of people are bound to say they think it's a pretty good place. They may not want to appear stupid or to disappoint the interviewer, so they select an easy answer. Some may actually believe that they have heard of Pourchnick—a few may swear they've visited there! Easy selection gives body to specious answers.

Open-ended questions, by contrast, present almost a mirror image of advantages and drawbacks. They take time to administer and hours to code, and there is little a computer can do to manipulate them. They are the last thing anyone needs in a hurry. The human effort required to process them pumps up their costs. There are wide-open spaces for subjective interpretations, and so ambiguity over the meaning of answers can loom like a storm cloud.

Still, open-ended questions offer information that can endear them to analysts interested in understanding why people feel as they do about an issue. Well-phrased, open-ended questions can often pry loose valuable audience thinking about critical issues not easily budged by less demanding, closed-ended items. In political campaigns, the hectic pace, budget constraints and reluctance of some survey researchers may discourage the use of open-ended questions. This is too bad, because these slow, awkward devises often can cut keys that open a treasure chest of voter thinking. Many researchers have discovered the rewards of open-ended questions, and they not only are continuing to use them, but they are coming up with new designs and applications.

Back to closed-ended questions. Writers select from several conventional types. Dichotomous questions allow two responses: yes or no, for or against, good or bad. Resulting information can be useful, because it reveals the direction of respondent thinking. With a little adjustment, though, and no additional cost in time or money, the campaign can get a sense for the intensity of thinking as well. This is no small matter when trying to assemble a voter mosaic.

It is accomplished by moving from a dichotomous (yes/no) to a scalar format, which also captures intensity of feeling. For instance, rather than asking, "Are you in favor of or opposed to a fifty-cent per gallon gasoline tax," as Ross Perot proposed during his bid for the presidency, you would ask, "Are you strongly in favor of, somewhat in favor of, somewhat opposed to or strongly opposed to a fifty-cent per gallon gasoline tax." From the second version, you would learn not only if respondents favor or oppose the tax, but whether they are strongly or mildly committed to their stated position. The strength of respondent views factors prominently into audience analyses and would be sorely missed if questionnaires were reduced to dichotomous items. Scalar questions also open up additional possibilities for data analysis. The variance revealed by such responses allows statisticians to perform more detailed investigations of the data and so to construct better portraits of the audience.

The closed-ended category also includes other kinds of scalar questions (e.g., Likert scales, Osgood semantic differential scales) and multiple choice questions, which have nominal categories (e.g., "Who is your favorite past president: Ford, Carter, Reagan or Bush?").

Open-ended questions can stand alone but are often used to clarify and elaborate issues raised in a closed-ended question. For example, after asking a scalar question to gauge the intensity of pro and con feelings on the gasoline tax hike, ask respondents why they favor or oppose the increase. Open-ended questions may be as simple as a single word: "Why." When you get back responses like, "I oppose a gas tax because it will hit the poor hardest," or "I favor a hike because it will force Detroit to make more efficient, less polluting engines," you learn a lot about people's true feelings.

As survey research books will tell you, questions should be simple. Let's say very simple. Respondents become confused by complex phrases or difficult concepts. They are as likely to volunteer spurious answers as to balk at the survey and provide no answers at all. Use everyday words, then keep the sentences short. Stay away from esoteric references. In other words, aim at the prime-time television audience. Enough said.

Consider some broad guidelines:

- Beware of compound questions; they make lots of trouble. ("Do you support gas tax hikes and road improvements?")
- Stay neutral, even if it hurts. ("How do you feel about the sad state of this nation's highways?")
- Watch out for questions with fatal loops. ("Did you finally decide to become a good citizen and vote?")
- Don't put the respondent on the spot. ("Did you vote last year?" What good citizen didn't. How about, "Did you get a chance to vote last year?" Even model citizens sometimes find themselves unable to get the chance to vote.)

Sometimes it's fun to catch prestigious pollsters using questions that yield more heat than light. Can phraseology sway a respondent? You bet. A *New York Times*/CBS News poll demonstrated this by phrasing questions on abortion in two ways. First, it asked, "Should there be a constitutional amendment prohibiting abortions?" The majority said, "No." It then asked, "Should there be an amendment protecting the life of the unborn child?" Twenty percent of the "nos" switched position and said, "Yes" (Brower 1988, p. 146).

What can you make of this? Anything you want. That's the problem. Abortion foes read one set of numbers; choice advocates read the other. Volatile issues such as abortion can be seen in many ways. We may not be able to find the simple truth, because there is no simple truth. The public is torn by the complexity of such issues, and the polls reflect this— even if negatively by discrepancies in their results.

Campaigns cannot afford the philosopher's luxury of debating audience riddles. They need to gather data and analyze it on the fly as they prepare positions and persuasions. In these most difficult matters, when closed-ended questions cannot sort the wheat from the chaff, it may be helpful to use an open-ended question to identify the assortment of population views. People don't always know what they think, and sometimes they don't know why they think as they do. It is helpful, however, to understand even such uncertainty. Learning the depth of indecision and the range of confusion often can be uncovered best through open-ended questions. Do not be afraid of the interpretive work they demand. Well-phrased open-ended questions can clarify and help a campaign recognize underlying beliefs and contribute to a communication agenda.

The nuances of phrasing a question lead to a related issue: Where in a survey do you ask a given question? The same question, perfect in every way, can yield different responses depending on where you position it— early, middle or late—in the questionnaire. For instance, respondents may react to a question about military spending differently if it follows a series of items about conflicts in the Middle East rather than items about funding infant inoculations and food subsidies. Lead-in questions predispose respondents' views.

Generally, it's a good idea to place more sensitive questions (e.g., about income and other personal data) late in the survey, after the interviewer and respondent have had a chance to bond. After a few minutes, respondents tend to talk more freely about personal matters than they would if you popped the tough questions early on.

When rating someone or something on several dimensions, ask the more general questions first. Asking about details first may plant thoughts in the respondent's mind and change his overall views. For example, if you want a respondent to rate an office holder's overall performance and also his performance on four specific items (e.g., agricultural policy, economic issues, environmental concerns and education), ask the overall question first, then the others.

Here's why: Suppose the respondent forms his overall impression on the office holder's policies toward child care, abortion rights and foreign policy. If you started with your lineup—a different lineup—of items, you would induce him to consider yet another agenda. In other words, while you haven't told the respondent what to think, you have told him what to think about when rating the candidate. By doing so, you render that individual no longer a true representative of his population subgroup. The results would be misleading.

A good questionnaire captures information about the issues of greatest importance to the candidate, but it also allows respondents to reflect on issues important to them personally. It makes room for the respondent to introduce his own agenda. After all, this is a feedback tool and should be sensitive to matters that arise within the target population.

The integrity of the pollster rides on the ability to create an instrument that avoids distortions and captures responses that are accurate and totally representative. Anyone can draft questions that elicit confirming responses; it takes work to make a question truly neutral. Candidates rejoice in cheery survey statistics, but they need the truth.

DATA COLLECTION METHODS

You have selected the representative sample, crafted a penetrating questionnaire and now you are ready to meet the respondents. You can choose several approaches for the interviews. Let's examine a few of them briefly.

Before the telephone became a universal household appliance, in-person surveys were the stock and trade of survey research. We don't use them much anymore in political communication research—not legitimate research. We know some local campaigns send workers out to "gather data," but this really is a pretext to get a foot in the door for some heavy campaigning and database building. This is not real research. It yields poor quality data that, if treated seriously, can ruin a campaign. It also distresses legitimate pollsters, because it uses the good name of research as a wedge into voters' homes. After a few "campaign researchers" come calling, even legitimate researchers get the cold shoulder.

Today, there are many reasons to avoid in-person data collection. Cost is one. It takes much longer to gather data door-to-door than it does on the phone, and time is money. Then, sampling is generally not as clean. Because of logistics hassles, researchers often resort to cluster sampling techniques, and to achieve the same accuracy as a simple random sample, these require a larger number of interviews.

Even if there were money and time to burn, in-person data gathering would not be the expert's first choice. In the old days, people let strangers into their homes, but today they are less likely to do so. The society has changed. There are too many sad stories, too many shocking television accounts of innocent victims. Chances for trouble may be one in a million, but people are reluctant to run the risk, and many will decline an interview. This increases the time it takes to complete the requisite number of interviews, but more importantly, it imposes a troubling sampling problem. People who let interviewers in may not be representative of the population, so the sample becomes biased. It is a good bet that, in many neighborhoods, only the daring and the trusting will consent. One could argue persuasively that they hold atypical views, and so the survey will not be a true sounding of the voters.

There are other problems with in-person interviews, but in fairness, there are positive elements as well. The technique builds a better rapport than does faceless phoning, and respondents may be more forthcoming. Compared to the phone survey, door calling makes for longer and more thorough interviews. It also allows respondents to look at pictures, examine charts and study logos and artwork. This accommodates data collection when visual inspection is required.

On balance, though, in-person interviews are ill-suited for most campaign research needs. They just take too much time and money. Except for rare occasions when respondents must inspect something visually, there is little information that cannot be collected faster, cheaper and more efficiently by telephone.

What about mail surveys, clip-and-return newspaper and magazine surveys and dial–900 surveys? These techniques do not allow a representative sample, so therefore, they are of little use in gathering comprehensive population data. They are cotton candy. They give the illusion of substance but offer little of value other than public relations hype. Such approaches rarely figure into campaign polling schemes.

The mail-in and 900-number surveys would hardly be worth noting except that some campaigns have been known to use them in place of authentic research. Why should they be avoided? One flaw is fatal: These techniques fail to deliver a random sample of voters. Without random selection, you might as well gather information on a street corner. Take the mail survey. Only a handful of people in the general population ever choose to respond, and those who do often represent not the mainstream voter, but people on the political fringe—those deeply committed or opposed to a single issue.

The 900-number techniques suffer from the same distortion. They allow respondents to select themselves into a sample, often many times. Voters with rolls of quarters can ring in early and often, destroying any semblance of representativeness of the results. Meanwhile, people who may be likely to vote but who are not particularly motivated enough to call will fail to register their views, leaving a gap in the sample. Unless anecdotal information is all you need, forget these methods. They may help generate copy for campaign spots, but they can only mislead the policy and planning activities of a campaign.

A similar indictment can be made of the town meetings proposed in 1992 by presidential candidate Ross Perot. Only voters deeply committed, particularly angry or especially curious will bother to tune in after the first few sessions. Public town meetings will become fringe-public town meetings, and decisions will be based on samples fundamentally flawed, because the deck will be heavily stacked with all but the mainstream, the "silent majority."

Some candidates drop off campaign literature and include a survey in the packet. Returns from this approach, too, are useless for reasons now obvious. Still, there are different and exciting reasons to avoid the survey handout. Consider this true story.

A friend who brought up his kids in Princeton, N.J., says that during the fifties, the Gallup organization enlisted high schoolers to take its questionnaires into selected homes and neighborhoods. The surveys were to be mailed to Gallup (postage free) after completion. The response rate was disappointingly low. Years later, it was discovered that most of the kids, hired for a pittance, simply waited for the leaders to leave, then unceremoniously dumped the questionnaires into sewers. No wonder the returns were sparse.

Focus groups play a part in many campaigns. Some representation can be built into small groups—selecting people by age, sex, profession and so forth—but it falls far short of a scientific sample. What focus groups can deliver is color and idiosyncratic information, which trigger public relations decisions. For instance, it was a focus group in Cook County, Illinois, that convinced Lee Atwater, President Bush's first campaign director, that the antitax theme was a winner (Woodward 1992). At a fraction of polling costs, focus groups provide a first-blush response to new ideas, themes, slogans and audience reaction to untried campaign programs. They also serve as a precursor to general telephone surveys and sometimes provide visible and convincing evidence that the big polls really are right, or that the gut instincts of a candidate are sound. Focus groups supplement representative polling techniques.

Despite a squall line of trouble moving in on telephone surveys, they remain the best current approach to gathering large amounts of data from a representative voter sample. Researchers can ask questions about all but the most intimate topics. There is a respondent fatigue factor to consider, but in the time of an average survey, ten to twenty minutes, you can cover a lot of topics in some depth.

Phone surveys are as fast as they are efficient. Interviewers complete calls one after the other and never need to leave their office chairs. Thanks to Computer Assisted Telephone Interviewing (CATI) equipment, responses can be encoded directly into a computer. (See chapter 4 for a discussion of CATI equipment.) This allows instant analysis.

Viewers of the presidential debates in 1992 were treated to poll results no more than twenty minutes after Bush, Clinton and Perot were finished. Some eight hundred Americans were called, questioned, charted, analyzed and copied to the anchor desks while the experts were still analyzing the debates. Suddenly, before they could change the channel, viewers learned who won. America had spoken—or at least eight hundred randomly selected voters had rendered a national verdict.

That's only one example. Critical, time-sensitive feedback requirements of today's electronic media campaigns demand instant information. *Washington Post* reporter Howard Kurtz noted that campaigns these days expect a twenty-four-hour turnaround for their broadcast spots—that's twenty-four hours from inception to airing and includes the completion of an entire survey, its analysis, the development of scripts, shooting a spot and its distribution to broadcast stations nationally. Such fast production pays off only when fed by fast audience assessments. Pollsters, therefore, must be spring-loaded to deliver processed information an eye blink after it is collected. Today, such wizardry is commonplace. One totally computerized system now undergoing refinement will be able to gather data from as many as 650 respondents in the time it takes to cook a few soft-boiled eggs.[3]

A word about the squall line. There are two sources of potential trouble for telephone surveys, although it is difficult to predict if either will impose serious problems for the future of this technique.

First, there is an expanding line of electronic hardware designed to separate the caller from the respondent. Tape machines with screening features allow people to monitor incoming calls and to make determinations about whether or not to answer. While most people will agree to an interview if they actually pick up the phone, there is a running debate about their willingness to do so when they know the yet unanswered phone has an interviewer at the other end. Linda Piekarski, research manager at Survey Sampling, Inc., completed a study in 1990 that demonstrated little interference from answering machines (Piekarski 1990). She found that screening, or "cacooning," as she called it, did not interfere.

Caller ID is a phone company innovation that gives people advance information about incoming calls. It provides an LED printout of the caller's phone number. Few people will recognize the number of a survey research phone bank, and since it is not in their repertoire of "friendlies," they may let it ring on. Curiosity may not be stimulus enough for many people to answer the call. This is especially so in the evening, when they suspect that survey researchers and telemarketers are lurking about—to say nothing of charity appeal callers. Caller ID is now available in only relatively few locations, so even if it did interfere with telephone research, it is not pervasive enough to be a serious problem yet. Expansion of the service will not work in favor of survey research.

The second threat to telephone research are the pesky telemarketing wolves who like to dress in researchers' clothes. They often begin their pitch fraudulently by pretending to be surveyors; although this works with many people, targets soon realize that they are being pitched and forever after tar all "research callers" with the same dirty brush. Like Caller ID, telemarketers are not yet a big problem, but the matter is stirring a lot of concern in the industry. Some have proposed legislation that prohibits such tactics, but these efforts run head-on into the First Amendment. The problem is not unlike the occasional garment in your laundry that runs all over the other clothes, discoloring everything it touches.

Phone surveys remain the method of choice. They are fast and versatile, they cost less and deliver the most reliable sample possible and, best of all, they can explore all but the most intimate of issues.

Occasionally, a poll misses the mark and calls a race that refuses to follow the script. This doesn't happen often, and usually there are logical reasons when it does. Presidential candidates who dismiss their low scores in the polls often refer sarcastically to "president" Dewey, but they really are reaching. Feeding the skepticism of the lay person is the commonsense suspicion—even resentment—toward a process whereby twelve hundred individuals can be projected as "What America Thinks?" It's hard to swallow. Of course, the overwhelming evidence supports the success of this method. Just remember the red, white and blue marbles.

ANALYSES

The analysis shapes a pile of numbers into an audience profile—plus a vision of the subgroups. Computers allow more insight into the meaning of the data, and since computers and software are usually available, nearly all campaigns have the capacity to dig more aggressively into their numbers. New analytic tools are helping campaigns understand their audiences better.

Data analysis is a special subject, best saved for a separate chapter. We take up the discussion in chapter 6.

WHEN ARE SURVEYS USUALLY USED IN A CAMPAIGN?

Finally, it would be helpful to review the kinds of surveys typically used in a political campaign. We draw from a discussion by Berkman and Kitch (1985), who outline four categories of polls.

A benchmark poll assesses voters before a campaign is launched. It takes a broad sweep of the issues and of the potential candidates. These omnibus surveys often are lengthy as they paint a broad picture of the pre-campaign political landscape.

Follow-up surveys pick up on dominant themes—many of which may have evolved from the benchmark survey—and track them through a campaign. These surveys are shorter and more focused than the benchmark poll, but like the larger study, they seek to develop a database that feeds information necessary for targeted communications. These are the workhorse surveys that keep campaigns tracking the critical issues in the population and in the subgroup targets.

Panel surveys, viewed with skepticism by some researchers, monitor voters' movement through a campaign by returning periodically to the same respondents. Advocates say panel surveys show how thinking evolves over time. Critics say there is limited projection of the findings, because the participants become tainted by their involvement. Participation renders panel members unlike the population they are chosen to represent. Data from such studies may help identify looming problems, but there is a strong case against panels as reliable sources of detailed information.

Tracking polls are conducted daily among small samples to sense emerging problems or helpful trends that may evolve into significant factors. A "moving average" system collapses new data in with data from the previous few days. Trend comparisons reveal population shifts and help a campaign staff become aware of patterns before they reach unmanageable dimensions.

CONCLUSION

The French say, the more things change, the more they stay the same. Today, as fifty years ago, pollsters contact a sample of voters, ask them questions, and try to figure out what their answers mean. They seek to learn how voters think and to understand how voters align on issues and form allegiances around candidates. They strive to engineer the best strategies to keep the faithful in the fold and rustle a few sheep from the opposition. Some things never change.

But some things do change. At every step of the polling process, from sampling to analysis, technology has significantly transformed what pollsters do and how they go about doing it. Sampling is more sophisticated. Questionnaires look different. Data gathering, while still a human activity, is computer-guided, and analyses are taking on the look of a George Lukas production. These changes—or threats—become our next subject.

NOTES

1. Survey Sampling, Inc., One Post Road, Fairfield, CT 06430, (203) 255–4200.

2. As the candidates become farther apart in the polls, the accuracy actually increases, and fewer respondents are required to achieve the same level of precision necessary for a closer race. Of course, high accuracy at this point is rarely necessary.

3. Hypotenuse, 15 Bloomfield Avenue, Verona, NJ 07044, (201) 857–8500.

Chapter Four

Technical Advances in Polling

Save Time, Stress & Money. Get the Best. It's a paradox—a survey program that does it all, is easy to use yet powerful. Create unlimited question and scale types, questionnaire forms. Branching. Does interviewing & self-administrated. Reports & graphics with export options. Source code available. Call Now For Special Introduction Offer. Save $$$.

—Ad for Programming Technology Software,
PC World, December 1992

Sixty years ago, researchers armed with clipboards and stacks of survey forms pounded the pavement, asking their questions, penciling in answers. Some early researchers used telephones, but this approach was considered too expensive, too limiting and too likely to miss major portions of the population (Lumley 1934). Of course, in the thirties, this was true; telephone surveys made no sense.

But then, all survey procedures had problems. Sampling was not yet a science. In-person interviewers were told to "call at one in every fifty homes." Phone interviewers were instructed to pass "completely through the telephone book at frequent intervals to obtain numbers" (Lumley 1934, p. 227). These are not the fastidious random procedures with which we sample today.

Questionnaires consisted of a few simple true/false questions and a scattered assortment of open-ended items. They often were more like free-flowing newspaper interviews than the formal survey research formats we use now.

Analyses produced tabulations and descriptive summaries. They weren't fancy, and they were painstakingly compiled by hand, but they reported the information simply and in a way people could understand.

So, early polling was like early aviation. People flew by the seat of their pants, the equipment was basic, and it took a while to get from here to there. But still, the early pros delivered the goods. With such austere beginnings, who of that generation envisioned the technology that later would advance their trade? For commercial aviation and survey research, as well as a thousand other budding enterprises sprouting from the virgin soil of the 1930s, there was a future that would be transformed by a tiny silicon chip.

Economies of scale introduced aviation and other heavy industries to the computer early in the 1960s. Mainframe computers, although big and bulky by today's standards, make possible John Glenn's inaugural space flight in 1962 and seven years later the landing of two astronauts on the surface of the moon. A decade would pass, then miniaturization, mass production, affordability and the visceral appeal of technology conspired to place personal computers in the hands of politicians hungry for such innovations. Quickly, it became obvious that computers offered enormous advantages to a campaign, and sometime in the early 1980s, politics took its leap to the moon.

POLITICAL SURVEY RESEARCH

Even without the chip, survey research already had changed in many ways over the years. Sampling became more sophisticated than "hit every fiftieth house." In-person surveys used complex cluster sampling strategies, which concentrate on randomly selected blocks rather than randomly selected households. These saved interviewers time and effort and provided higher precision at lower costs than did earlier techniques. Telephone sampling still involved the phone book, but the procedures for selecting names were more precise, and they delivered a sample with known accuracy.

Questionnaires changed in several ways. They became more formal instruments, using precise wording and prescribing for each item an exact order and sequence. Over the years, there developed an entrenched belief in uniform questionnaire administration that encourages objectivity and contributes to accuracy. These days, you wouldn't expect to hear a professional interviewer paraphrasing questions, discussing peripheral issues and chatting about the weather. In the early days, they thought small talk greased the skids. In all fairness, that was due, in part, to the in-person format, which benefits from a little table talk.

The content of questions changed as well. Researchers learned a lot about the importance of neutral phraseology and recognized the need for precise language. A variety of scaling techniques was introduced which reported a respondent's leanings and intensity toward issues. These methods became increasingly more valuable as sophisticated analytic tools were forged to squeeze out ever more information and insights from survey data. Questions became more compact and specific. In part, this was due to the growing dominance of the telephone survey. It is easier to hang up a phone than it is to throw an interviewer out of your kitchen. So, to save the survey, researchers wrote questions that maximized the use of time and minimized the burden on a respondent. Punchy, easily understood, quick-answer questions best served the needs of the telephone format. This thinking is currently being challenged by some pollsters, who are introducing ever longer and more complex questions. We will examine that later.

By the early 1980s, nearly all political surveys were conducted by phone. It made perfect sense to abandon the in-person approach. Ninety-five percent of American homes had telephones by the late 1970s. The 5 percent that did not were most likely disenfranchised nonvoters whose absence mattered little to a campaign. Phone samples were better than in-person samples; data collection was cheaper, faster, more efficient and more successful in getting honest and accurate data. Besides, during the past fifty years, Americans had grown suspicious of strangers at their door, and it was increasingly more difficult to gain access for in-person interviews. The fact is, it just isn't necessary to stare people in the face when asking them questions. There is almost nothing you can do in-person that you cannot do by phone. Nearly every survey researcher understood this by the late 1970s.

By this time, the analysis, which makes data ore into information ingots, changed in two ways. First, early analyses were aided by mainframe computers which, like industrial blast furnaces, melt down raw data almost instantly. Number crunching that once took days now took minutes.

Second, computer-smelted information was richer and more refined than manually processed information. Multivariate analysis, which seeks to understand a population by examining several traits at the same time, and other procedures too involved for hand calculations disclosed unsuspected relationships in the data. Compared to previous simple frequency counts, these analyses told more about the population overall and about the subgroups within. They gave campaigns a new vantage point from which to view the voters.

Each of the survey components contributed to and benefited from advances in the other components. Improvements in analytic techniques required question formats that yielded more elegant data; the movement to telephone surveys demanded better sampling techniques. The improvements ratcheted up the overall quality of survey research and thus improved the contributions of technology to the political communication process.

Surveys delivered more information that was faster, less expensive, more accurate and more revealing about voter populations. By the late 1970s, survey information was a staple of political campaigns and an indispensable source of knowledge about constituents. Political candidates were quick to discover the power that flowed from this knowledge.

POLLING IN THE 1990s

Political polling has changed more during the past decade than during all of its first fifty years. Speedier data processing, easier and better sampling and faster and sharper reporting of information have made polling more efficient. I will discuss these advances later in this section, but the real changes are found not in the way polls are run, but in the way they are used and how they provide advantages to smaller campaigns once locked out of polling technology. Clearly, computers have changed the operation of state and local campaigns, where polling has been greatly popularized as a result.

Let's begin with the technology of polling in the new political campaign. What a difference a decade makes!

Mark Blumenthal, vice president at Donilon and Petts Research in Washington, D.C., describes a major overhaul in campaign structures. Before 1980, he says, campaigns tended to rely on a few principals who called the shots. There was the candidate, of course, backed up by a campaign manager, maybe a consultant and a covey of volunteers. Any polling, media strategy and fund-raising were contracted out. Often, consultants were hired guns brought in during the heat of a campaign, when the regular troops found themselves in the middle of a turkey shoot.

Today, in congressional and gubernatorial campaigns—even in state senate and legislative races—a new team concept has taken hold, according to Blumenthal. Early in the campaign, before the fusillade begins, candidates are likely to assemble a group of paid advisers to run the campaign. It is not unusual to find a media adviser, a mail consultant, a fund-raiser, a pollster and a general strategy adviser assisting the campaign manager. They form a spectrum of talent integrated to deal with the hassle of contemporary political campaigns. Each function has evolved rapidly into a highly specialized activity requiring the efforts of experts who make a living immersed in the waters of their profession.

Ross Perot provided comic relief during the 1992 race by hiring two of America's top guns—Ed Rollins and Hamilton Jordan—and then firing them along with every other specialist before they had had time to load up, much less squeeze off a few shots at Bush and Clinton. Capitalizing on his east Texas range-hand act, Perot told the nation during the debates that he was the only candidate without spin doctors and pollsters to feed him lines. "Why, I even made them charts myself," he boasted, referring to the pie graphs displayed in his thirty-minute infomercials.

Perot may not have needed political pollsters, but everybody else seems to. Why is that? The answer is blowing in the winds of technology.

One clue is found in the behavior of people who buy a new car because the neighbors have one. But keeping up with the Joneses is pretty thin. Pollsters are expensive, and if they weren't worth it, they would go the way of tail fins on a 1956 Cadillac. The fact is, competitive forces have become fierce, and the complexity of communications has grown since the late 1970s. This is as true for political campaigns as it is for commercial marketing and advertising.

Consider changes in the most popular medium ever to assault mankind: television. In the cozy, pre–1970s, it was easy to reach an audience. If you wanted to blanket the U.S. population, you ran ads on the networks or network-affiliated stations. Ninety-five percent of Americans watching prime-time television were watching the networks. The strategy also worked for local campaigns. Buy time on the network affiliates, and you blanketed the market.

Then, in 1975, RCA launched SATCOM I, and the world changed. A few entrepreneurs at Home Box Office, a subsidiary of Time, Inc., realized they could bounce movie signals off this geostationary satellite. Uncut movies, the programming source for cable television, instantly became a hit. Since then, more than 60 percent of American homes (Nielsen 1993) have tied into cable, and the once simple task of choosing between the three big networks has become a nightly scramble to select from dozens of choices. Act III Communications, Inc.'s research confirms that many people (i.e., "the grazers") never settle happily on one show, but instead bounce fitfully between two and three (Frank M. Magid 1988).

Add to this the burgeoning VCR rental shops that stock thousands of program options, the scores of choices on the radio dial and the ticker-tape parade of print, and you have communication by total immersion.

Analysts of mass media yell themselves hoarse about the power of these technologies to change the way people receive information. These changing patterns continue to evolve, and, no doubt, the pattern of viewer influences will evolve as well. The question for political campaigns is how to hit that moving target?

The challenge facing anyone in a crowded market is how to get public attention. How do you reach your audience—not just with any message, but with an attention grabber that is also convincing? From Hill and Knolton to hometown consultants, the answer is to fight fire with fire. Technology wrought it; technology can address it.

Communicators on Madison Avenue, Pennsylvania Avenue and Main Street have turned to technological solutions. Survey research is now among the most powerful tools available to understand how audiences think and how and where they acquire information. Polls guide the lasers of political and commercial communications. Without polls, it's a shot in the dark.

From this arises a second answer to the question of why political campaigns need pollsters. It's a matter of competition. The ragtag band at the Alamo lost to Santa Anna because they were outgunned. In political battles, it is well accepted that underfinanced campaigns are disadvantaged despite the inherent value of their message. In the same way, campaigns without audience information are at a great disadvantage. Britain's *Independent* reported in a story about the 1992 U.S. elections that campaigns were forced to maintain technological parity or simply be overwhelmed by the high-tech muscle of the opposition (Simons 1992). And so it comes down to keeping up with the Joneses, especially the incumbent Jones, after all. Campaigns have notched up their need for power during the past fifteen years, and candidates must field competitive resources to match the opposition.

NEGATIVE POLLING

Around 1986, beginning perhaps with an article published by Irwin ("Tubby") Harrison of Harrison and Goldberg Research in New York, pollsters with time to burn found a new surveying twist that has moved like a brushfire through political campaigns. If nothing else, "negative research" demonstrates that idle hands are the devil's workshop.

Here is how the two-phase process works. In phase one—using a technique around for many years—a team of library and database researchers examines every scrap of information ever generated about their own candidate and about the opposition. They begin with the individual's college years, or even before, and work up month by month, searching newspaper stories, speeches, position papers, anything ever written by or about the person. They look at police blotters, bankruptcy proceedings, divorce court records, hospital admissions squibs, anything that may hold a nugget of negative information. During the 1992 campaign, an overzealous group of State Department officials took this to new highs by rummaging through the passport files of Bill Clinton and Ross Perot. They even visited the records of Clinton's poor, old mother!

The motivations are clear. For opponents, they are attempting to unearth any dirty detail that can provide a rich campaign issue. In the hands of these political alchemists, lead slag can be made into gold. A slip of the tongue, an unpopular vote, a domestic dispute, a pile of parking tickets can serve the purpose. But evil can be made of simple blunders, and the worst of it is that candidates can suffer not for what their pasts are, but for what their pasts are made out to be. One political cartoon showed a baby Clinton spitting out his pabulum from the crib, while nearby, George Bush says, "And he never came clean about this to the American people!"

Candidates sift through their own dustbins for the same information possessed by the opposition. So, everyone's past is carefully examined for sharp, jagged things that can hurt when thrown. This background search is nothing new, although the use of on-line databases gives the activity a "Star Trek" look.[1] Ten years ago, Republican campaign strategist Ken Khachigean said, "Campaigns are won and lost in the library." Negative research advocates, no doubt, would agree.

Getting the goods (or the bads) on the opposition sets the stage for phase two, the hatchet job. The question becomes: "Which of these items, if developed properly, has the greatest potential for damage?" Here is a particularly virulent form of survey research. Without mentioning a candidate's name, researchers assess the relative liabilities of behaviors and events dug from the past. "How would you feel if you heard that a candidate ... ?" "How serious would you say it is if a candidate ... ?" "Which would you say is more of an offense, this behavior or that behavior?"

Pollsters then spade the soil deeper to probe well beneath the surface of the issue. Campaign advisers in Washington, D.C., members of the Beltway fraternity, come to surveys fully armed. Interviewers read to respondents negative campaign spots and determine which evoke the strongest responses. Plowing through long scenarios recounting a candidate's past "indiscretions," they coach respondents to identify the most troubling or most intriguing portions. They may test negative phrases and slogans, hard-punching strategies and themes, all of which meld with the negative events dug out of the library and on-line computer files.

The use of information cuts both ways—against foe and for friends—for friends to anticipate retaliatory strikes, for foes to prepare bruising assaults.

While negative campaigning is not new, the recent polling adaptations fine-tune these strategies and increase their firepower. Computers, on-line databases, polling facilities and a wave of new pollsters magnify the impact of negative research. Anyone with a passing sense of fair play and ethics must find this distressing. Indeed, many voters were appalled by the 1992 presidential street fights. Bill Clinton hit George Bush hard on the economy and domestic issues. Bush slugged Clinton, even referring to the Democratic ticket as "bozos" and sardonically calling environmentalist Albert Gore "Mr. Ozone." Perhaps such strategies have an impact as they appeal to the dark side of voters. People claim they are sick of negative politics, and yet focus groups and the polls suggest the tactics work. Unless candidates call a truce, which is not in the cards, or voters harshly punish the perpetrators, it is unlikely the practice will cease anytime soon.

Washington-based pollsters willing to talk with me about negative research were unwilling to accept responsibility for the consequences of the activity. They see themselves as hired to do a job, to enhance the mission of a campaign, and if the message takes a negative tone, it is not their doing. The pollsters see themselves as small wheels in a big machine. Candidates will be candidates, and during the past twenty years, with or without polls, campaigns have become more negative.

Over a decade ago, Don Todd, executive director of the "Anybody but Church Committee," said, "A lot of mud gets thrown in a campaign. The trick is to throw more dirt at the other guy than he throws at you" (*Regardies* 1986, p. 130). This quotation is worthy of the Lee Atwater Award. Credited with raising negative campaigning to an art form, Atwater renounced the techniques after contracting an incurable illness. Even after his death, however, negative campaigning still dominated his party's strategies.

NEW TRENDS IN SURVEY RESEARCH

New technological developments will shorten the delivery time, increase the precision and reduce the requirements for manpower, money and expertise in political surveying. They neatly wrap a variety of elements into a single package. Happily, such advances lessen the logistics effort that once complicated polling.

THE SAMPLE

Sampling always has been the Achilles heel of a poll. It has been more difficult to develop a good sample than a bad one, yet both look the same. For instance, the once staple of pollsters, the phone book samples, were hassles and took time, and for all their trouble, they yielded lists plagued by outdated and incomplete information. Until the past few years, the difficulty of obtaining good samples was a significant impediment to survey research and a real barrier to entry for would-be pollsters.

Things today conspire to make the sampler's life a lot happier. First, swarms of companies (e.g., Survey Sampling, Inc.[2]) now sell low-cost, high-quality samples. A survey researcher can order a sample by phone in the morning and receive an electronic file of phone numbers that afternoon. She can order printed lists, call sheets or labels for overnight delivery.

How good are these samples? Very good. The vendors invest heavily in the refinement and maintenance of computerized databases. They assemble general population samples or highly targeted groups based on age, race, gender, geography, income, education and other characteristics. That's specialization for you. An economy of scale permits these outfits to deliver excellent samples for less than it would cost to generate them at home. The richness is there, too. The quality is difficult to match—good, representative samples that improve the hit rate (that is, the incidence of suitable respondents who answer the phone), thus increasing the probability of fewer calls. As a result, candidates get faster, cheaper and richer samples.

These firms charge by the size of a sample and the number of setups, or characteristics, on which they sort the data. For instance, you could pay for three additional setups if you wanted a sample of Hispanic, white-collar workers in Los Angeles. Prices have dropped considerably since the mid-eighties due mostly to lower equipment costs, economies of scale and competition.[3] In short, one of the neatest developments in the sampling field is to let specialized firms do the job.

Second, a campaign can draw a home-built sample with do-it-yourself software. Cost competition among pollsters and budget-conscious campaign managers have given rise to programs that allow small campaigns to draw their own random samples. They are not as efficient as purchased samples, but they are less expensive and can save quite a bit of money for a campaign that runs routine surveys. Many statistical and survey packages, such as StatPac and the Survey System, provide these programs. So, too, does nearly all "campaign-in-the-box" software.

Unfortunately, these low-cost, random-number generators do not always yield the best sample. Their shortcomings are governed by the GIGO (Garbage In Garbage Out) dictum. In order to configure the program, you must provide information about telephone number prefixes within the survey area. Easy-to-make mistakes or incomplete information will fail to yield samples that are random—the fatal flaw of polls. The problem is not so much that the sample is flawed, but that it does not look flawed. Bad samples look just like good ones. And yet, like the first domino to fall, they can be the cause of flawed analyses, conclusions and campaign decisions.

Still, for the campaign on a shoestring, do-it-yourself computer samples merit consideration. Follow the procedures closely, and spend time to feed in the best setup information you can. These samples may be lacking compared to vendor samples, but they are a sight better than phone book samples used in the dark ages of polling.

Finally, survey sampling from voter lists is becoming more popular. Several companies now maintain comprehensive voter files. Aristotle Industries, for instance, has a set of sixty CD–ROM disks that contain information about every voter in the United States. You don't need to buy (actually rent for one year) the whole collection; campaigns can purchase any geographic area they wish. These files have two strong advantages: (1) They contain just registered voters. Thus, from the campaign viewpoint, they separate the wheat from the chaff (even though roughly only half of eligible voters vote). (2) They have valuable, supplemental demographic information. They can be joined with other information sources to fortify databases. They can also be computer-sorted and so facilitate targeting.

Of course, there are drawbacks. Commercially fortified voter lists are costly. While it's true that such lists have many uses in a campaign, polling samples alone do not justify the sums most campaign managers would have to spend. Moreover, these lists often lack many phone numbers, even after developers go through extraordinary efforts to assemble complete files. As a result, the sample suffers from the anemia typical of telephone directory samples: unlisted numbers.

Random-digit dial methods used by software programs and sample vendors avert this problem. Until the missing-number problem with voter lists is solved by firms selling this information, these databases will not be ideal for drawing survey samples.

QUESTIONNAIRES

Technology has changed questionnaires directly and indirectly. Directly, Computer Assisted Telephone Interviewing (CATI) systems have made it easier to design more sophisticated branching questionnaires, in which the answer to one question determines which question is asked next. Indirectly, the increase in polls has meant that pollsters can experiment with different questioning techniques.

CATI systems bring computer technology directly into the data collection process in two ways: (1) questionnaire construction and (2) development of a database structure. In the first, typists input the questions and response options, usually according to an established format recognized by the computer. For simple questionnaires, this process is no more than a typing job. CATI systems are particularly facile at handling meandering "road map" questionnaires. For instance, they accommodate complex "if-then" routines that make the sequence of questions contingent on the sequence of previous answers.

Now, as Dan Quayle was fond of telling Al Gore, "Take a deep breath." It's time for compound contingent responses. In this procedure, if a respondent answers "yes" to three of four "indicator" questions, he will be introduced to a different follow-up series than someone who answered "yes" to only one or two of the four. Example: You want to identify people who hold strongly liberal positions. Maybe you anticipate a fund-raising pitch to liberals and need to test some "hot button" ideas in your survey, but only among the most committed liberals.

In order to distinguish the hard-core liberals, you give all the respondents in your sample questions on abortion, minority rights, aid to the poor and gun control. Now, you operationally define hard-core liberals as those who answer at least three questions with the most extreme liberal view: strongly in favor of abortion, strongly for civil rights legislation, strongly for funding of poverty programs, strongly in favor of gun control. The computer keeps a tally of responses, and if a respondent passes the "liberal test," you have your target audience. Just route them to a special question series (hoping to elicit your fund-raising ammo) before returning to the other questions asked of all respondents.

If you really want to be cute, you can come up with a formula that sends interviewers down one of the questioning paths leading to combinations of any number of questions. Now we're having fun, but contingencies built upon such complex formulas would, without CATI, drive interviewers crazy. There would be too many mistakes, too much paper, too many delays and too many miscues to long-suffering, disgruntled respondents.

Human interviewers may not be able to work with awkward contingency patterns, but the process is a natural for CATI. Programming CATI for the task is the only trick, and this, of course, is accomplished before surveying begins. Program complexity grows proportionately with the complexity of a questionnaire, and while most CATI systems allow some level of contingent routing, most require a reasonable level of expertise to tell CATI where to go. But formatting is getting easier all the time with new, friendlier software.

CATI also develops a structure for the configuration of data. Most of these systems recognize the flow of questions, and from the answer pattern, determine the space required to store data for each answer. Simple "yes-no" questions or four-point multiple choice questions need one space (sometimes called one column) in the database to record an answer—a single digit, 0 to 9. Others, such as home state, require two or more spaces, or columns (Alabama [AL], New Mexico [NM], California [CA]). In most cases, CATI assigns spaces and columns to each question, then tells you the sequence in a file for each of these elements. Operators can override CATI's assignments, and they may also be required to step in for open-ended and other tricky questions. Designing a database structure is not usually a difficult or time-consuming task; CATI just makes it easier.

Question formats and questionnaire design would have evolved with or without technology, but it was technology that fueled the rapid growth of political survey research, so it is partially responsible for the acceleration of changes. Technology allows more surveys, so there are more opportunities to push old limits and try new techniques. The Washington pollsters who contributed their thoughts to this book reported using a few new techniques worth noting. Each is based on the growing need for larger amounts of voter information.

Several researchers said they are using split-sample techniques more than they did ten years ago. This method essentially involves the administration of two (or more) questionnaires which are distributed randomly among respondents. Both share a set of core questions, but they also boast others dealing with separate topics. Split samples obtain information on a larger number of subjects, but there is a cost. They involve a smaller number of respondents for many questions, and so for these items, they have less statistical accuracy. Still, the technique offers a way of obtaining information on a wider range of subjects than if a single questionnaire were used.

Some Washington researchers said they are using long scenario-based questions to pretest campaign concepts and strategies. Scenario-based questions are used, for instance, on college boards, which ask test takers to answer questions about an essay or other long narrative they are first asked to read.

Let's say that your survey begins with a description of an unnamed candidate—voting record, public service background, views on public issues.[4] Based on this description, respondents are asked what they think of the candidate—what they like, what they find offensive. They may be asked to identify the most damaging, the most flattering and the most intriguing features. Clearly, campaigns need to anticipate the best and the worst traits of the candidate and the opposition alike.

The purpose of these long and often difficult questions is to help a campaign identify useful issues. Many survey researchers, though, are skeptical of the technique and believe it does not yield information reliable enough for important campaign decisions. They question the ability of average people to recall the many points raised in these often protracted descriptions. They also wonder if most people can stay with an interview that requires them to focus for long periods on endless descriptions. Respondents have not been known to have endless patience, and a series of lengthy monologues may weed out those with shorter attention spans. What then happens to the representativeness of the sample? At the end of such a survey, these critics argue, there will be data—there will always be data—will it be of value? Will the survey measure what pollsters think it measures, and will the numbers be reflective of the true feelings of the voting population?

Scenario-based questions are popular in negative research applications. Consequently, they draw fire from another direction. Critics argue persuasively that the growing use of negative research has contributed to the rise of negative campaigning. Survey research just dumps jet fuel on the blaze.

Doubtless, research contributes to negative campaigning, but it need not inspire it. More likely, the negative techniques betray a system that has placed a higher priority on destroying the opposition than on touting a candidate's virtues. It's hard to blame this on survey research. Author of best-sellers *Truman* and *Brave Companions*, David McCullough said, "Blaming our political problems on the polls is like blaming the ax for a murder."[5]

Nevertheless, pollsters have lent their skills to support these modern campaigns and the fashionable smears. The Washington pollsters I spoke with think of themselves as hired guns and nothing more: sergeants answering to the generals. All the same, it's hard to believe they enjoy a role that shields them from the ethical questions.

Finally, in the quest for ever more voter information, pollsters say they are using more open-ended questions, in which those phoned can free-associate instead of selecting from a dictated list of answers.[6] Early in a race, these narrative answers fill in the blanks for campaigns deciding on strategies and positions. Open-ended questions provide greater detail and often explain why people feel as they do about issues referenced in closed-ended questions. The proliferation of polls permits the inclusion of a few open-ended questions in each survey without incurring much additional cost or slowing the data analysis process. But, open-ended questions are nothing new; technology has just made them a bit more convenient to include in a questionnaire.

Of the survey components, questionnaire development is the least effected by new technologies. CATI has accommodated the use of more targeted questionnaires, and the general increase in polling activities has expanded the opportunities for experimentation with scenarios and open-ended items. But, all the power of computer hardware and software cannot do much to overcome the limitations inherent in human interactions required for the delivery of an instrument. We still need to ask questions and wait for answers. We need to probe for detail; people do not volunteer such information. We need to display the assortment of choices; people cannot anticipate them. We still must operate within a set of rules governing human interaction—telephone etiquette and the recognized obligations of someone who wants information from someone who has it.

No matter how impressive the growth of computers and software routines, it is unlikely that technology can do much to change the contact points of human interactions. Technological advances in spacecraft, library catalogue systems, stereo equipment, digital watches and VCRs face limitations when they confront humans. The weak link in survey research always has been the respondent, and it is unlikely technology can change that. This leads to the next topic.

DATA COLLECTION

Some adventurous, although annoying, telemarketers have discovered the technological limits to computer involvement in data collection. Driven to cut costs and exploit technology, several entrepreneurs during the mid–1980s programmed computers to dial numbers, ask questions and record responses. Maybe you were blessed with a phone call that sounded like an answering machine calling an answering machine. Fortunately for humanity, the results they obtain are spotty and threadbare. In the process, however, the public distaste for this technique has rubbed off on legitimate survey research. Computer voices are not yet able to fake a live human voice, so the interviewer's job is safe—for now. The time, no doubt, will come.

Still, data collection through computers will not go away. There is a growing use of touch-screen computers to gather from average consumers data about a variety of subjects. CareQuest, Inc., a computer information outfit in Roanoke, Virginia, has been using stand-alone computers to disseminate information and to collect data from people at shopping malls, work sites and other public places. Their tests among more than 100,000 users demonstrate great success in the use of computers for simple data collection, where users enter their own responses by touching appropriate places on a special screen. Although they can do no more than tape-record open-ended responses, these computers have been successful in obtaining personal information not easily gathered by human interviewers. CareQuest research demonstrates that people will tell a computer things they will not tell their bartender—or an interviewer with a clipboard.[7]

Computer-driven telephones successfully gather information from people who phone organizations. You may have called an employment agency for job information and ended up giving a machine all your vital statistics! This information is limited, of course, and because of some special need, the respondent is beholden to the computer. Remember, the respondent initiated the call.

In survey research, the tables are turned. People have no incentive to oblige a brassy computer voice. Also, the level of information sought by surveys is generally more complex than an impersonal system can handle. At this point, computer evolution is too primitive and human expectations too demanding. We still need a human at the respondent touch point for most survey research.

While technology cannot replace human interviewers, it can aid them. Computer Assisted Telephone Interviewing systems are a case in point. They automate much of the activity before and after the interview, and they facilitate the interviewer's activities during the discussion.

CATI equipment has been around since the early 1980s, although advances in hardware and software have greatly changed how it functions. Major computer cost reductions have expanded the use of CATI systems among pollsters, even those with small budgets. It is impossible to offer a comprehensive description fitting all of the CATI systems, but most packages assist polling in several important ways.

Although computers make terrible interviewers, they make terrific assistants. They manage the random telephone numbers by selecting callees from a list obtained from sampling companies, generated by campaign software or drawn from voter lists. These data simply are loaded into CATI software.

When you see these machines in action, you can't help but be amazed.

CATI dials the number. It notes completed interviews and ineligible numbers (e.g., businesses, refusals, nonworking numbers) and retires them from the file. It detects busy signals and no-answers and calls these back at programmed time intervals. It makes note of people who cannot start or finish an interview, then dials back later to complete the session. CATI flags the stopping place of discontinued interviews and stores notes that allow interviewers to pick up the pace very quickly: "We were talking last night about your view of the economy when you had to pick up the kids from drum lessons."

During the interview, CATI directs the flow of a questionnaire, popping up on the computer screen questions in sequence according to contingencies we discussed earlier. Researchers often ask respondents to rate lists of items. To avoid bias from the order of presentation, it is customary to rotate the items. Usually, interviewers reverse the order of the list for each interview, starting at the top one time, at the bottom the next. CATI, though, can mix and truly randomize the order each time. It's a better approach.

CATI checks for ineligible responses. For instance, if the only two possible answers are "1" or "2" and the interviewer mistakenly strikes a "3," CATI will call the error.

Programmers can direct CATI to insert previous responses into the context of questions. Suppose a respondent said in one question that she attended Rutgers University. Subsequent questions dealing with university attendance may reference the name of the school: "During what years did you attend Rutgers?" or "Did you join any political groups when you attended Rutgers?" Interviewers could fill in the blank on their own for nearby questions, but it's easy to forget such details much later in the interview. CATI remembers.

Most CATI systems allow interviewers to back up and review earlier questions. Programmers can decide whether or not to permit changes, although some researchers argue against the practice, saying it ruins the spontaneity of a question and the validity of an answer. CATI doesn't much care and will comply with instructions either way.

As an interviewing aid and coordinator, CATI is a wizard:

- Its dialing and number management keeps the calls moving along.
- Question sequencing focuses questionnaires and reduces mistakes and disruptions in the flow.
- It checks for ineligible responses and thus helps reduce errors.
- It notes times and dates for each interview and clocks completion times. This helps management identify and work with particularly slow or fast interviewers.

CATI facilitates interviewing without actually confronting the respondent.

All the while CATI is assisting interviewers, it is working away quietly at perhaps its most important function: the construction of a database. As interviewers enter respondents' answers through a computer keyboard, CATI adds that information—one keystroke at a time—to a data file. Alpha or numeric codes (data stored as letters or numbers) and open-ended responses are stored in the format determined during the planning phase.

Without CATI, this task is accomplished by keypunch operators or coders who transfer information from questionnaires to optical scan sheets. This approach can be reasonably fast, although not as fast as CATI. It also has the potential for error. Every step in the data handling process introduces the possibility that someone may misread a response, get answers out of sequence or just strike the wrong key or pencil in the wrong bubble. It's true that most researchers have rigid quality-control procedures to reduce these occurrences, but as an old chess master once said, the mistakes are all there waiting to be made. Chances for errors are minimized by taking the shortest route between the respondent's utterance and its entry into the database. CATI does this best by skipping the middlemen.

ANALYSES

The speed of data entry contributes directly to the speed of data analysis. In the rush of a fast-paced electronic campaign, this speedy turnaround is critical. Feedback information, such as survey data, is only as good as it is fresh, and in the heat of a political campaign, the shelf life of data can be very short. Consequently, a lot of energy has gone into the development of procedures that shorten the time from the start of a survey to the delivery of results. Computers and statistical packages have advanced immeasurably the tabulation and analysis of data. CATI's instant database compilation improves even on that.

At any time in a survey, researchers can analyze the growing database. They can monitor trends and obtain early indications of public views. At the end of an evening's interviewing, they can instruct CATI to provide response summaries. Data can be examined incrementally for the impact of powerful external events that may occur while data collection is underway. The revelation of a candidate's extramarital affair or the release of GNP figures may change the way people think. We would expect such shifts in public thinking to be revealed through a running examination of the data.

Wary researchers would issue a big caution here: Running interim analyses may be helpful in many cases, but they can also be misleading. Depending on sample layout, there may be a built-in bias. Unless the selection of phone numbers is randomized—the random numbers are called in random order—interviewers may be calling regional blocks of numbers. For instance, numbers may be grouped by state, and so Wednesday's sample may represent people only in Oregon, California and Arizona. It would be foolish to draw conclusions for the nation based on such a sectionalized sample. Consequently, for this and other reasons, it is better to randomize the list of random numbers when possible, even though time zone differences may require special handling.

Even when the numbers are so randomized, however, researchers must be aware of the relatively few respondents that often result from a single night's calling. Since margins of error grow inversely with the sample size, one day's slice of the sample likely will have considerable error. Following day-by-day trends is one thing; drawing conclusions and making strategic decisions is another. CATI assists researchers in the possibility of instant analyses, but it does nothing to ensure accuracy or to instill the wisdom to use the information wisely.

Finally, like an official NFL statistician, CATI provides a summary of events. How many surveys were completed, what was the average administration time and which interviewers had trouble? It tells the hit rate, the number of businesses, the number of disconnects and all the other facts that describe the success and efficiency of the sample.

This helps managers improve subsequent surveys. They may choose another sampling approach and maybe use a different sample company or software package. Some interviewers may need additional training, some questioning techniques better design.

AVAILABILITY OF LOW-COST COMPUTERS

The really big break for survey researchers came with the availability of high-power, low-cost personal computers and data analysis software. Before the early to mid-eighties, pollsters could conduct analyses on rented mainframes, or they could wrestle with awkward, homespun software on feeble, underpowered desktop computers. Mainframe users paid high rents and faced awkward logistics arrangements getting data in and out. Early desktop computer users were courageous pioneers who suffered endless torments along the trail. They deserve our respect.

IBM released its first personal computers in the early eighties and adopted a nonproprietary strategy that allowed any vendor to copy its hardware components and utilize its software protocols. This open policy was as important as the excellence of IBM's computers in exploding the worldwide computer industry. By 1985, clones began flooding the market, which drove down computer costs. IBM deserves our thanks. Meanwhile, computer capacity has expanded, and software options have grown at extraordinary rates.

As we noted, the evolution has changed political polling in many ways. For the analysis of data, it placed sophisticated tools in the hands of anyone with even a few dollars to spend. The barriers posed by the need for mainframes fell overnight.

Today, most pollsters conduct data analyses on desktop machines using any number of software programs. SPSS and SAS, the granddaddies of mainframe number-crunching software, have PC versions. StatPac, StatPlan, and NCSS are a few other packages currently in popular use.[8] Nearly all campaigns-in-the-box software have analysis routines among their inventories of tools.[9] So, too, do public opinion survey programs.

Each program has twists and turns that make it unique and give it something to be loved by one statistician and hated by another. At the hearts of most, however, are these features:

Development of data structure and labels. Programmers allocate the number of columns per variable and specify where each should be placed in the file. They also can give labels to the variables (e.g., "Rating of the President") and to the responses (e.g., "Excellent, Good, Fair, Poor").

Data Entry. Data can be keyed in directly or provided in the form of electronic files. These files can be entered through optical scanners, key punches or CATI systems.

Analysis. They will do just about any kind of statistical analysis—for example, frequency distributions, cross-tabulations and a host of multivariate statistics. There is almost nothing a mainframe can do that today's PCs cannot do as well.

Graphics. It didn't take long for software houses to pack into their releases all the statistical routines a survey researcher could want. Next, they began improving the means of displaying those statistics. Good thinking. Raw numbers are something only a statistician could love; charts, graphs and pictures breathe life into these numbers for everyone else. They make statisticians look good to the boss. Most analysis packages these days make it easy to transform gray numbers into Technicolor graphic depictions.

Of the survey activities, data analysis has enjoyed the greatest benefits from computer technology. A wide array of statistical routines are now available, and processing time has greatly improved. As the six-shooter of the Old West was the great equalizer among men, the computer has become the great equalizer among campaigns. Analytic power, once the luxury of well-endowed political organizations, is now accessible to all.

CONCLUSION

Survey research, and particularly political survey research, has been revolutionized by technology. As a profession and as a business, it has been changed from an elementary activity in the hands of a few to a complex operation available to an ever-expanding field of players.

Campaigns have been caught up in these changes. Few candidates for anything but the local school board would dip a toe in political waters without the guidance of a poll. Most congressional-level and larger races employ a resident pollster who works with other staffers to comprise a nineties campaign team. Pollsters gather more data than ever before, do more with it and affect more of the campaign strategy.

Of particular concern is the effect of survey research on campaign communications. The value of feedback in any communication event is critical, and with the sharpening voter image projected through campaign polling, political communication is developing a new sophistication. Candidates know more about the voters than ever before. They have better databases with which to begin a campaign and to track voters through the election. Polls measure the subtle changes and report evolving troubles. Themes, speeches, slogans, pitches, votes, strategies—all are processed through polls, where they are refined, reinforced or rejected.

These things are accomplished because they are possible and affordable, and because technology has made polling in the nineties easier than it was in the early eighties and before.

Some of my interviewing highlighted this change. In response to a question about why campaign pollsters use computers in nearly all of their activities, Todd Ballinger, an assistant administrator in the computer division of the Democratic Congressional Campaign Committee, said: "Because they are there. Like a telephone or a car, we use the technology at first because it's there, and we want to see what it can do. Then, over time, we develop a dependence, make psychological and financial commitments and seek to justify the investment through additional applications."

And so, computers were invited into survey research because they could crunch numbers and do analyses, but since they have been there, people have found other things for them to do. Now in place, like a "temporary" puppy that moves in to stay, computers have become fixtures in political campaigns.

Much of this smacks of science fiction. CATI selects the numbers and dials them, tossing viable calls to human interviewers. It then gives interviewers the questions and carts away the answers to an electronic depository. CATI keeps human assembly-line workers moving, reporting the best and the worst of them to authorities. It marks the time, keeps the pace, makes the data-gathering sessions operate orderly and correctly. Then it crunches the numbers and gives humans a report card on their successes and failures. Computers have worked their way into the front office.

It may be overplaying the scenario to call them coworkers. Human beings still drive the process and impose any pains or pleasures derived from the technology. Remarkably, a simple support device has quickly assumed new and important responsibilities. (The most dreaded phrase in the nineties: "Sorry, our computer is down.") The computer has changed survey research, and survey research, along with high-tech implementing functions such as database manipulations and direct communications, has changed political campaigns.

Without a doubt, campaigns will continue to evolve in the face of technological advances in feedback information. We have just begun to understand the capacity to gather, store and sort information on voters. As some sage once said, the future isn't what it used to be. It is dangerous to place any bets on what lies just over the hill. We suspect, though, that it isn't more of the landscape we see right now.

One of the areas of greatest change in information gathering likely will come from the interplay of survey data and sophisticated electronic databases that, like a strand of DNA, hold the political, psychological and economic makeup of voters. Computer technology is making possible the construction of remarkably detailed personal voter maps. These maps, drawn from databases, guide our trip in the next chapter.

NOTES

1. These searches typically begin with an examination of NEXIS files. NEXIS, an on-line database, allows instant review of newspaper, magazine, television news program and other public media reports. The complete text of every news story carried by the major U.S. and many foreign media is included on computer files. Researchers can search these by topic, date, media or key word. Anything ever reported about a person in these media becomes immediately available.

2. Survey Sampling, Inc., One Post Road, Fairfield, CT 06430, (203) 255–4200.

3. Currently, a typical completed sample of six hundred respondents (three thousand to five thousand numbers) costs around $550. Remember that you often need to call several numbers for each eligible respondent reached. You usually order (and pay for) between five and seven times the number of people you want in your final sample.

4. This is also a place for researchers to describe in detail the negative traits of a candidate, as described earlier in this chapter. Sometimes these descriptions run a page or more in length.

5. McCullough offered this comment in response to a question posed at the California Commonwealth Club on July 14, 1992.

6. The inappropriateness of some closed-ended questions is illustrated by a cartoon that once hung in the office of George Gallup, Sr. It showed a teenage girl asking a boy, "Do you love me very passionately, somewhat passionately, somewhat dispassionately, or very dispassionately, or none of the above!"

7. CareQuest, Inc., has experimented with computer dissemination of health care information. The company has loaded touch-screen computers with information about symptoms, descriptions and treatments for over two hundred common illnesses. Users select a topic, provide demographic information (to bring up the

information appropriate for their age group and gender), then answer basic questions that route them through the discussion of an illness.

CareQuest research found a regular group that accessed the computers (in twenty-four-hour pharmacies and grocery stores) at late-night hours for information on subjects such as AIDS, genital herpes and sexual dysfunctions. Thus, they found nonjudgmental answers in a computer. In the process, CareQuest confirmed that people freely provided to the computer personal data that they might not give to case workers or medical professionals.

8. Here is a sample of statistical software vendors. Dozens of others are commercially available.

NCSS
329 North 1000 East
Kaysville, VT 84037
(801) 546–0445

SPSS
444 North Michigan Avenue
Chicago, IL 60611
(800) 543–5837

StatPack Gold
StatPac, Inc.
3814 Lyndale Avenue
Minneapolis, MN 55409
(612) 822–8252

StatPlan V
The Futures Group
80 Glastonbury Boulevard
Glastonbury, CT 06033
(203) 633–3501

9. This is a small sample of campaign software. *Campaigns & Elections* (February 1992) offers the names, addresses and phone numbers of seventy-six popular vendors. All of the following are nonpartisan.

Apian Software
P.O. Box 1224
Menlo Park, CA 94026
(800) 237–4565

Aristotle Industries
205 Pennsylvania Avenue, S.E.
Washington, D.C. 20003–1164
(202) 543–8345

Brock Control System
2859 Paces Ferry Road, #1000
Atlanta, GA 30339
(800) 221–0775

Micro Research Industries
3027 Rosemary Lane
Falls Church, VA 22042
(703) 573–9538

Politech/SD Associates
1021 Asylum Avenue, #418
Hartford, CT 06105
(203) 278–3434

Chapter Five

Databases in Political Communication

The whole concept of building these files is to narrow-cast your message.

—Richard D. Schlackman[1]

Just beneath their aeronautical skin, a crop duster and a high-speed jet aren't much different. Both use petroleum to power their engines. Both are operated by pilots who control direction and speed. Both have wheels and wings, rely on the same principles of lift and are slaves to the same gravity that works unyieldingly against the unnatural state of flight. You might miss it at first, but the old biplane and the jet are distant relatives.

Similarly, dusty boxes of three-by-five cards with voters' names and phone numbers are related to the new electronic databases. Both have demographic information with which to sort voters into groups; both can be updated as information changes. Both scope out individual voters, but like the jet, electronic databases leave their distant cousins in the dust, performing so much better and faster.

Let's define a database as any systematic collection of information (called a file) about individuals in a defined population. For instance, each entry in a database (a record) may contain someone's name, address and phone number (variables, or data items). Expanded entries may list marital status, occupation, income and education. These are standard demographics. For politics, however, you need data items such as party affiliation, voting history and, if possible, information about political contributions. All of this information will be stored in the same location (field) in each record to allow computer processing.

Big used to be beautiful in political communication, but not anymore, now that targeting small, some would say exotic, audiences allows communicators to put exactly the right information into the right hands at the right time. The more communicators know about the audience, the better able they are to make correct decisions about the allocation and content of campaign messages. Database manipulation, guided by polling analyses, is the key to message targeting.

Like political polls, databases deliver information about voters, but unlike political polls, which accumulate information about the population, databases stockpile details about individual voters. Moreover, polls obtain data from willing participants; databases usually are compiled out of sight and out of mind of the subjects. Both elements—individual detail and unwitting participation—raise the hackles of critics who denounce databases as too intrusive and too secretive.

Consider these points about polling methods. First, respondents provide information voluntarily. They'll tell you what they wish you to know. They'll hang up or refuse to answer when they think the interviewer has crossed the trip line. Second, survey respondents enjoy anonymity. Most pollsters assure participants that their answers will never be linked directly to them. This guards their privacy and encourages their veracity. Such a contract between pollsters and their respondents is the bedrock of survey research ethics. Woe onto the researcher who breaks the promise!

By contrast, most databases bought and sold in political campaigns have been assembled without the consent or knowledge of their subjects. They are constructed of information that arises from a person's activities, possessions and life-style.

Bear in mind that there are many sources for a person's address, Social Security number and birth date. Drivers licenses, insurance records and voter registration lists are a few. On my last birthday, I received a half-dozen cards from merchants offering best wishes. I never shopped at any of these stores and never volunteered my birth date. How did they know? Easy! They bought a database that contained my birthday and God knows what else. Comparing my dossier with others, the merchants determined that I fit a promising demographic profile, including membership in a group with expendable income (were they ever wrong!). They made my day with these personalized, computer-generated, heartfelt greetings and a few coupons.

In addition to such core information, there are databases that reveal the kind of car you drive, the schools you attended, the value of your home and your membership in professional associations. Have you ever sent for a mail-order catalog? Request just one, and like rabbits, they multiply quickly, bringing on a dozen look-alikes. This multiplier effect is made possible through database sharing—or, more likely, selling and renting—

because the field of "commercial intelligence" is increasing as privacy is decreasing.

It is a safe bet that most people on whom such dossiers are compiled have no idea that they are on file or that their file can be bought and sold like a garage sale trinket. It's only a guess, but if they knew about it, they probably wouldn't like it. They might be even more offended to learn that a computer operator can sort, match and compile a lot of little databases into a larger, more comprehensive personal file. This is a common computer operation, called concatenation, which assembles the contents of several databases, the way a police artist assembles a sketch from the description of several eyewitnesses. The resulting picture often can be a remarkable likeness of the subject, and it can be produced with the speed of a Polaroid. Disturbingly, the pictures are made from hidden cameras, and the subjects rarely know it is happening (for the ethical treatment of this issue, see chapter 7).

OVERVIEW

As noted elsewhere, computers have been around political campaigns in one form or another for more than two decades, even though in the early days, they generally served national races, typically for fund-raising among wealthy donors. It was not until the mid–1980s, with the arrival of IBM 286 PCs and friendly campaign software, that computers became familiar appliances in smaller congressional and state-level races.

Even now, some campaigns are just warming to the technology, but the next few years likely will see even the die-hard holdouts holding out no longer. One seasoned, local office holder told me that he had decided to "computerize" his operation next time around. He admitted that he didn't know what that meant, although his staff said he should do it, and he didn't want to appear old-fashioned. That's a bold move for someone who doesn't know how to set his electronic watch or tune his car's digital radio, to say nothing of programming his VCR. When people like this spring for technology, we know the market has reached true saturation.

Given the eagerness to adopt computers, it is easy to project great change, as campaign workers get their hacker's licenses with these new technologies. Now is the period of experimentation and exploration, as amateurs gaze with wonder upon databases, new polling techniques and impressive analytic tools.

With all its scientific trappings, the use of computer technology in political campaigns remains very much an art. There just has not been time for resolving procedures, establishing standards and setting routines. Political and computer scientists are meeting at the campaign level with the pols (politicians) to explore how computers can best serve a modern campaign. For the time being, communication art and communication science equally share the same space. It is reasonable to assume that over time the science will dominate, as scholars and field crews discover what works and what does not so as to codify and set norms where none now exist.

In both national parties, consultants and campaign officials are standardizing databases. The Republicans have the lead on this effort, although even they are far from establishing a standard database archive. Former independent, Washington-based information systems consultant and now consultant to Vice President Albert Gore, William L. Krause said that not only are campaigns operating with totally different databases and formats, but within a single campaign, there often are several incompatible databases loaded on various computers in the same office.

Krause said fund-raisers may use one database, field contact workers another, volunteer coordinators yet a third. Furthermore, he said, "When consultants come in to straighten things out, they set up the files using their favorite program, and everyone has a different favorite." This means that not only are the databases different, but even the software used to manipulate the databases often are different—among campaigns and within a campaign. This does not mean that data couldn't be shared if people on the campaign staff had a mind to do so; it just would be easier if everyone were playing from the same score. Krause asks, why transpose when everyone could play in the same key?

This disarray should be a comfort and a challenge: a comfort to campaigns that think their database operations alone are disheveled; a challenge to everyone using computers in targeted communication programs to tighten database operations within a campaign and to work on some level of standardization among sibling campaigns.

Campaigns that share databases, analytic tools and expertise are more efficient and save money. Krause believes that if such standardization should occur, it likely would be at the national party level. He said the "break camp" mentality that follows in the aftermath of most statewide and smaller campaigns disrupts the continuity necessary to establish long-range direction. Only the permanent party structure is in a position to look beyond the next two-year political cycle. The Republicans got an early and aggressive start, and there is a consensus among the computer experts I interviewed that they are outpacing the Democrats. The Republican Party maintains sophisticated databases and, according to several Washington sources, often loans computers and expertise to local candidates. The Democrats, despite a large push during the 1992 campaign, admit their second-fiddle status. One Democratic consultant in Washington joked about his party's efforts to assist local campaigns. He said the Democrats are "at the bleeding edge—or just behind the Republican cutting edge." The fact is, both parties will find it necessary to pour money into computer facilities during the nineties.

As the parties and individual campaigns become more coordinated and grow more sophisticated, there will be a coincidental demand for more raw material—for the databases, on which the analysts work their magic. Unlike the increasingly sophisticated data analytic tools, the databases remain pretty much unchanged from years past, when they were used mainly by direct-marketing firms. Databases continue to warehouse the personal facts and figures they always have. True, they hold more data gathered from more sources on more people, but they have not changed much in form and layout. Like the standard gray business suit one wears for years, the essential database structure looks like a dowdy old friend.

ANATOMY OF A DATABASE

The characters in a database can be alphabetic or numeric, and variables can be comprised of elements that are all alphabetic, all numeric or mixed.[2] The data on voter Sandra L. Dillon might look like this:

Name:	Sandra L. Dillon
Address:	34 Penn Avenue
	Wilmington, DE 19456
Phone:	(302) 876-5432
Occup:	Newspaper editor
Income:	$43,500
Relig:	Methodist

To make it easier on people who key in the data and on those who later must study it, use a simple form that configures the information for quick inspection. Note these nine elements of personal information on a typical computer form:

Name:
Street:
City: State: Zip:
Phone:
Occup:
Income:
Relig:

Using such a form is not only easier and less error prone than typing in data as would a keypunch operator, but inappropriate entries can be spotted more quickly. Fail-safe mechanisms can be developed. Let's say you are entering zip codes in the phone number block or typing a city in the state slot. A wrong entry will sound an alarm. You always can review the data on screen by matching the data for each case next to its appropriate descriptor.

When stored in a computer, however, data take a different form, usually as one long string of information. Most database programs establish a long line of numbers and letters, separated by markers and notes that help the computer configure the data. ASCII files (data in a "universal language" format), which are readable by nearly all database programs, appear as one of two long strings or single lines of data. Since ASCII files are universally understood, let's use them to illustrate.

ASCII data can be stored in "fixed-field" or "free-field" formats. Consider first the fixed field. Think of one hundred spaces—numbered consecutively—into which we will put data. In order to keep things orderly, we earmark clusters of spaces for each variable. For instance, spaces 1–25 are for the voter's name, 26–45 for street address, 46–55 for city, 56–57 for state, 58–62 for zip code, 63–72 for phone and so forth. A data file in a fixed-field format so designated may look like this:

Sandra L. Dillon	34 Penn Ave.	Wilmington	DE 19456 3028765432
Howard D. Johnson	1029 Winston Place	Elk City	MO 98765 4029876543
John Worthington Jr.	16th St., Apt. 997	Bethesda	MD 30087 3012397392
Ednapearl Billings	RFD 2, Box 55	Dublin	VA 24987 7033949887

1||||5||||10||||15||||20|||||25||||30||||35||||40||||45||||50||||55||||60||||65||||70||||75||||80||||

Most databases will have more than one hundred spaces; within reason, programmers use the number they need. Computers process fixed-field data quickly, because they can skip to the exact location in each field to find the information they need. Rapid processing speed is a strong argument for fixed-field formats, but as Gilda Radner's character Roseanne Roseanna Danna used to say, "With everything, it's always something." Fixed fields take up more storage space, and they do so because they must account for even the longest entries. This adds a lot of blanks for shorter entries, and blanks take up space.

Free-field formats do not run into the space problem, since they use only the room they need for each entry and no more. With free fields, column designations are not relevant; instead, the computer looks for delimeters—commas or semicolons—to recognize where one variable ends and the next begins. Programmers tell the computer the order of variables (which always must be the same within a database) and let the delimiters separate them. Consider our last example, converted now to a free field.[3]

```
Sandra L. Dillon,34 Penn Ave.,Wilmington,DE,19456,30287665432
Howard D. Johnson,1029 Winston Place,Elk City,MO,98765,4029876543
John Worthington Jr.,16th St.","Apt. 997,Bethesda,MD,30087,3012397392
Ednapearl Billingsworth,RFD 2, Box 55,Dublin,VA,24987,7033949887
```

Note, without all the blanks, this format uses less space, although reading delimiters does consume more computer time. Depending on the software package, fixed or free formats may be used. Most database vendors can provide campaigns with either. They are also likely to prepare the data in a format designed specifically for some of the more popular database programs—for instance, dBase and Paradox.

A WORD ABOUT RELATIONAL DATABASES

The term "relational database" suggests a particular kind of database, and this can create some confusion. Actually, the term refers to a relationship between databases, rather than anything specific within a single database. Consider this example.

Suppose two separate databases had the following information:

Database A: Party Affiliation

City or County	Voter Registration	
	Democrat	Republican
Alameda County	391,304	157,307
Berkeley	49,287	8,511
Contra Costa County	224,086	162,567
Marin County	69,512	45,135
Oakland	137,287	23,226
San Francisco	260,995	78,482
San Jose	177,029	116,251
San Mateo County	157,428	104,110
Santa Clara County	353,421	264,696

Database B: Income

City or County	Average HH Income
Alameda County	$41,800
Contra Costa County	51,700
Marin County	65,400
San Francisco	43,000
San Mateo County	53,900
Santa Clara County	54,300

The party affiliation and income tables come from two separate data-bases, but each has information common with the other—the city or county data. This becomes a useful coincidence.

Suppose we wanted to know the party split (how many Republicans and how many Democrats) for the three cities/counties with the highest average incomes?

- First, we would identify the three highest incomes from the right column in Database B ($65,400, $54,300, $53,900). Looking to the left column, we match up the counties of Marin, Santa Clara and San Mateo.

- We then go to Database A, find these counties in the left column and trace across to the Democrat and Republican columns. We find Marin (D: 69,512; R: 45,135), Santa Clara (D: 353,412; R: 264,696), San Mateo (D: 157,428; R: 104,110).

These databases are related through the city/county column, and thus the two are called relational databases—they are said to fit the "relational model." As long as two or more databases share a column of information that can identify a record—contain the same identifying variable—they are related. This relationship becomes a valuable link in joining two or more smaller databases into larger, more thorough ones. Note the process. It is used with increasing frequency in political campaigns.

DATABASE SOURCES

Political campaigns use information from a variety of database sources, most of which can be categorized into one of four groups.

In-house Databases

Nearly all campaigns maintain databases generated entirely by staff, and these, unsurprisingly, are called in-house databases. With campaign software or one of several database programs such as dBase, Paradox, FoxPro and Q&A, staffers may build a database from the ground up. They construct a file using data collected by campaign workers and the candidate and generated from other local sources. Data originate from newspaper clippings, letters sent to the candidate, phone calls or attendance records at public forums. In-house databases are usually one-of-a-kind, campaign-specific, labor-intensive collections. They are the closest kin to the trusty three-by-five cards.

Such files often identify contributors from among those who attend talks, ask for help with special concerns or express an interest in a key issue. The data even may begin on an index card or on the back of an envelope. It may be collected from door-to-door canvassing or generated from pass-along information offered by friends. These data are typed into the computer, then used in special mailings, on campaign calls or as fact files for the candidate's personal visits. The files also can be joined to other files and used in a variety of analytic and word processing programs.

For this discussion, let's use a simple but versatile program called Q&A by Symantec. Although Q&A lacks some of the bells and whistles of more complicated database programs, it's a real workhorse and demonstrates nicely the software elements that build in-house databases for small to midsize campaigns.

Q&A allows users to enter, store and manipulate voter information. It also makes it easy to print summary reports of voter particulars and to integrate voter information into campaign letters. When the time comes to move a Q&A database file to another program (for mapping, graphics, statistical analysis or the integrated functions of campaign software), it will create export files in ASCII, dBase, Paradox and other formats.

To create a database, you first develop a form for the data. This form is like any you've ever filled out for a driver's license, college admission or credit card. It tells you what information is needed and where to put it on the page. A database form lets you indicate what information will be included and specify where on the computer screen (instead of a page) that information will be entered. Screen layout concerns more the human operator than the computer, since the layout has little to do with how the computer actually stores the information. As long as users follow a few simple rules, they can define whatever configuration is easiest for them to use.

Suppose a campaign wanted to build a voter database with this information: name, address, phone, income, education, occupation, religious affiliation and age. Assume also that the campaign wanted a "comments section" for general notes and observations. This information could be arranged in a dozen ways, but suppose staffers chose this one:

First Name:
Middle Initial:
Last Name:
Street:
City: State: Zip:
Phone: (   ) -   Income:
Education: Occupation:
Religion: Age:
Comments:

Variable labels—"First Name," "Middle Initial," "Last Name" and so forth—could have been called anything, for instance, "First," "Middle," "Last," or "FN," "MI," "LN." The operators lays out all the information, shifting around the variables like furniture until the arrangement is pleasing and functional. A keystroke stores the form in computer memory for use later to input and retrieve the data.

Now, whenever the campaign workers wish to enter new data, they call up the form and type in the corresponding voter information. When they have finished with each voter, the computer will store the information and place on the screen a new, empty form. A completed form may look something like this:

First Name: Sandra

Middle Initial: L.

Last Name: Dillon

Street: 34 Penn Ave.

City: Wilmington   State: DE   Zip: 19456

Phone: (302) 876–5432   Income: $43,500

Education: Coll deg   Occupation: Newspaper editor

Religion: Methodist   Age: 34

Comments: interested in freedom of information matters and has agreed to advise staff on such issues.

Typos, inaccurate information and data changes can be corrected and updated at any time. Campaigns always are adding new comments and new voters, and they even can add new data categories. It is best to determine all the needed information categories when a form is planned, but when circumstances require additional information, a new category should be added.

Suppose it became apparent several months into a campaign that date of birth—one's astrological sign—was actually a revealing variable. Credulity aside, let's say that a "star-driven" constituency was found to have belief patterns traceable to astrological signs. If true, think how valuable it would be to know who was a Virgo, Pisces, Leo and so forth. The campaign could update the form with this killer variable, then key in the birth date for the records already on file and for new names entered henceforth into the database. Happily for voters, astrological signs don't help campaigns much, or else it would mean, as the little old lady in the Solid Gold Cadillac said, defining astrology, "Once you're born, you're done for!" The point is, we can add the birth date variable—or any variable—whenever we wish.

Importing Database Files

Much of the information that begins in-house can be joined with other sources generated outside the campaign. Suppose, for example, a congressional candidate assembles a respectable list of voters with whom s/he has had some personal contact. These are good friends, people who have asked for help and voters who have expressed an interest in the candidate. Suppose also that local candidates in the same party also have developed computerized lists of friendlies and are willing to share them with the congressional candidate.

To merge sources, computer technicians will first join their in-house list with lists from the local campaigns. This expands the number of contacts and even may add data to the records already on file. The local candidates may provide religious affiliation or income—data not already included in the congressional candidate's records. When campaigns add such information, they are said to "append" their files.

Second, computer techs will purge files of redundant names. John P. Sledgehammer and J. Paul Sledgehammer may be the same person, and if they are, Sledgehammer would rightly be unhappy with two very personalized, heartfelt appeals from a candidate who did not care enough to learn that only one J. P. Sledgehammer lived at that address. Redundant mailings are counted among the deadly sins of campaign mail and particularly campaign fund-raising.

So, a campaign can merge an in-house file with an imported outside file, creating a new, improved, hybrid database. This organic, changeable quality of databases demonstrates their adaptability and flexibility and shows a creative element of database art.

The Elements of Importing Data. Most campaign and generic software will accommodate database files from other programs. Usually, it is a two-step process involving, first, a setup to receive the file and then the actual importation. Many database programs can even receive an assortment of programs directly, without the setup requirements.

A setup—when it is needed—is much like the form development process we described earlier. Choose and label the variables that will constitute the database, and configure them on the computer screen in an easy-to-use array. You may adopt all the variables from the imported file or just some of them; it is easy to pick and choose which you want to enter into your new database.

Database programs use various importing procedures, depending on the kind of file being imported (e.g., standard ASCII, fixed ASCII, dBase, Paradox). Generally, though, when a setup is required, you will indicate where the program can find each variable in the imported database.

For instance, to import a free-field ASCII (delimited) file into Q&A, you note next to each variable label a number representing the field in the file from which data will be imported. In this example, the first variable is the first name, the second variable is the middle initial and the third is the person's last name.

Imported items:	Jennifer, C, Higgens
	1 2 3
Instructions to Q&A:	First Name: 1
	Middle Initial: 2
	Last Name: 3

In a fixed-field ASCII, you indicate the starting column number of the imported variable, followed by the number of columns it occupies. For instance, in this example, the first name is in a field allowing a total of 15 columns (1–15), the middle initial has one column (16) and the last name, 20 columns (17–36):

Jennifer	C	Higgens	Data
1														15		16	17														Column Number
First Name: 1,15			
Middle Initial: 16			
Last Name: 17,36			

Specific data importing procedures vary by program, but the concept is universal. The main point here is to demonstrate that the process is simple and requires little expertise. Software documentation will provide the details needed to bring in databases from just about any source.

Cleaning up the Lists. List cleaning for in-house databases involves three operations. First, since much of the data may have been entered by hand, editing is needed to ensure correct spelling, letter transpositions, the proper use of upper- and lowercase letters and other standard editing features.

Second, to avoid the deadly sin of duplicate mailings, redundant entries must be purged. Most database programs allow the designation of variables (data items) on which to check for duplication. For instance, the computer can be cued to examine the entries for first, middle and last names and for street addresses. When the computer comes across an exact duplicate based on these variables, it usually will save the first and discard (or save to another file) all the remaining records that duplicate.

You can increase the probability of discarding only true duplicates by adding additional search variables. For example, have the computer add phone numbers or ages to names and addresses. Additional variables take longer, and sometimes because of error, some information contained in two records for the same individual may not match exactly. Records that probably should be discarded might be retained.

Database complications have caused more than a few headaches. Suppose the computer was instructed to match on income and a few other variables. Income data entered this year may differ from income data entered last year (on records from two databases), and accordingly, the computer would save both records as though they described two different people. On the other hand, you don't want the computer to toss out the records of dozens of different John Smiths and Mary Joneses just because you programmed it to zap duplications on the basis of too few variables.

The perfect matching variable would be one that was uniquely assigned to every person at birth and stayed with that person until death. The social security number comes closest in the United States, but it is not always available. Although database specialists yearn for the social security number, critics fear a total invasion of privacy when not only Big Brother, but thousands of little brothers have your number. The ancient Hebrews were on to something when they read mystic power into names. Tell outsiders your name, and they suddenly possess power over you. Beware, today, the release of your number.

Perhaps fear for your social security number has diminished now that computers have been able to accomplish almost the same level of data gathering without it, but the intrusion is no less. It may take a little longer and have a few more mismatches, but the absence of a universal nine-digit I.D. is no longer much of a deterrent to the construction of large personal databases.

When definitive designators (such as the social security number) are unavailable, computers cannot be left alone to run through your lists. After the computer goes through the database once to cull obvious duplicates (using just name and address matches), a person—or "human technology," as one computer consultant I interviewed insisted on calling people—is required to assist the computer in order to make subjective decisions. On this second pass through the list, the computer matches on just last name and address and forces the operator to determine if John and Jane White are husband and wife, if John P. Sledgehammer and J. Paul Sledgehammer are one and the same. An operator can scan the remaining information in the record—say, number of children, make of automobile or other stored information—and usually make a reasonable determination about record duplication. It isn't all that difficult to see that John and Jane are a couple, or that there really is only one J. P. Sledgehammer, a 35-year-old, $25,000-a-year tool-and-dye maker living at 123 Maple Street. Such judgments can be made quickly, and most good database programs facilitate the process by highlighting judgment cases and allowing the save or purge decision to be expressed in a single keystroke.

The third list-cleaning operation is checking for accuracy, and this is a lot more difficult. People change jobs, phone numbers and spouses. They get raises, convert to new religions, buy new cars, have additional kids and switch political parties. Short of checking with each individual, the latest available database information usually is considered most reliable. All else being equal, if an imported file was developed more recently than the in-house one generated during a previous campaign, it is logical to accept the more current data. Of course, as the list is used for canvassing, phone calls and direct mail, campaign workers will obtain information updates with which to freshen the lists. Additional contacts, newfound friends and the discovery of updated lists will call for the minting of new records and thus contribute to the continuing evolution of a database.

We began this brief discussion with a look at in-house database development and the concept of staff-developed format, data collection and entry. We saw how outside files can introduce new data items and add new records. In a process that is dynamic, names come and go; information expands, improves and transforms over time. Good databases, like the living organisms their information describes, are ever changing. Automation and standardization during the next ten years may eliminate some of the hands-on database dough-kneading. Staffers, instead, will become more involved in coordinating the care and feeding of these lists by outside handlers.

List Brokers

Perhaps it is a mercy that average consumers know little about the diversity and accuracy of commercially available databases—at least those with their names on them. They are innocent of the thousands of lists holding countless details about audiences of every conceivable stripe. Catalog companies use databases to zero in on high-probability customers, and once the target is identified, these companies market their tested lists, often earning millions every year by doing so. Fund-raisers generate lists of supporters with demonstrated political and ideological leanings. Associations compile lists, as do religious organizations, universities, magazine publishers and audience-sponsored broadcasters. Newspapers are even in the game. The *Atlanta Journal and Constitution* held a contest among sports fans, then turned over its participant data files to Pizza Hut, which targeted the unwitting contestants (Fisher 1992).

Supermarkets with scannable check-cashing cards gather personal data from customers' application forms, then track purchase patterns. Safeway, for instance, has developed a marketing scheme that grants sale prices only after customers surrender their bar-coded, computer-scannable identification cards. This enables the store to track buying patterns more closely and facilitates the development of enormous and detailed customer databases.

Other businesses are in a position to obtain an even wider range of data. Take, for instance, the American Express Company, which tracks all the purchases of its 20 million customers. What you have bought says a lot about what you are likely to buy. Purchase databases become a Rosetta stone for reading a consumer population. The *Washington Post* described the American Express activities as follows:

[American Express] can sift through its card holders' transactions, sorting them out by categories, such as frequent air travel, car rental or use of hotels. From that information, it can create a list that can be offered to airlines, hotels and others interested in marketing to travelers.

American Express segments its card holders into six tiers, ranging from the least affluent, "value-oriented" customers to the most affluent, which it calls "Rodeo Drive Chic" (Crenshaw 1992, p. D11).

The *Post* went on to describe how this database development may become even more common as computers facilitate data processing and expand markets for the sale of lists: "Even small companies may have this sort of ability before long. Lotus Development Corp. and the credit bureau Equifax, Inc., last year said they were developing a package that would put millions of people's names, credit histories and other information onto compact discs that could be used with a personal computer."[4]

Everyone is getting into the list development act. They are doing so because it is profitable and because, with today's technology, it's easier to do than ever before. Lists, an effortless spin-off of direct-marketing activities, can earn a great deal of money. The net effect is the proliferation of lists and a blizzard of choices for groups in the database market.

In steps the list brokers. Like real estate and stock brokers, they provide a link between buyer and seller and serve both research and liaison functions. As researchers, they join with the buyer to analyze specific database needs and then search the list market for the best prospects to deliver a high proportion of key respondents (customers, supporters or contributors). Thus, brokers become personally and actively involved in the transaction, even though their liaison role is purely administrative. They approach the list owner, place the order, follow it through processing, obtain all clearances, handle billing and ensure payment for the transaction. Their cut is usually 20 percent (Stone 1988).

List brokers also help with list testing. Very often, several lists will have the characteristics sought by a buyer, and some objective measure must establish which is best suited for the specific marketing task. Direct markets live or die by the right databases, and it is important to land the best possible list. The list broker's role in testing is to acquire a sample of several lists and, when the results are in, advise the client on the best strategies.

Consider an example in direct-product marketing. The Rugged Prairie Outdoor Apparel Company of Dismal Seepage, Wyoming, sells outdoor clothes to indoor people. It aims at the same direct-mail customers who buy from Eddie Bauer and L. L. Bean, office workers who, when not in the office, want to project that "just-off-the-range" look.

Rugged Prairie contacted a well-known list broker in New York to beef up its customer list. The broker worked with the company to understand better its current customer base and to examine the customer frontier it wished to explore in its upcoming marketing drive. After checking many list sources, the broker arrived at five candidates. She arranged for the rental of seven thousand test names selected randomly from each source.

Rugged Prairie sent its catalogs and promotional materials to each name on the five lists—culling duplicates and coding the list source for each name—and sat back to see which would bring in the largest number of purchases and generate the greatest income—two very different measures. Without getting into the details of such a test, we can report that Rugged Prairie found one list earned 15 percent more income than any of the others, and so it instructed the broker to arrange for a full-scale rental of 100,000 names from that list vendor.

Direct-marketing expert and author Bob Stone (1988) notes that lists are almost never purchased, but rented. Moreover, he says, they are rented for one-time use, and then only for a purpose arranged contractually with the owner. Owners can refuse to release lists for whatever reasons they choose, and the lists must be used within a specified time period. Clearly, the owner retains considerable control over a list and does so to protect both the list itself and the owner's direct-marketing operation from campaigns that might threaten its own best interests. There are cases where the renting company's marketing moves were just too close to a list vendor's plans, and the vendor denied the rental. It does not make good business sense to let the competition have first crack at the customers.

Given the typically high costs, most political campaigns restrict their use of list brokers to fund-raising and other specialized targeting applications. List costs start at around $65 per thousand names, with an additional charge of $5 to $30 to sort and select names by various characteristics such as zip code and state. Since an average return in the direct-mail business for a first effort is 2 percent, that means twenty people respond out of a modest $80 sample. Unless those twenty average spending better than $4 each, you can't even pay for the lists, much less the other mailing and processing costs. Most campaigns can find far less costly alternatives for their general mailings. List brokers, though, can be money well spent in search of exotic audiences, usually those that yield a financial payoff that justifies the expense.

One of the largest list brokers serving political clients is Atlantic List Marketing (a division of Atlantic List Company, Inc.). It works hand-in-hand with political campaigns, just as it does with commercial customers. From its viewpoint, it doesn't much matter whether the end use is to sell Prairie outfits or seats at a political banquet. Lists are lists. The common goal in all cases is to discover which list delivers the greatest concentration of people sought by the client. Selection, research and arrangements are practically the same.

Once brokers have narrowed the list search to a few vendors, clients can examine rate cards that explain the composition and history of the list, its common uses and successes, restrictions and other factors that help decide its suitability. (See Figure 5.1 for a sample rate card.)

List titles offer a quick fix on the nature of a list, and descriptive squibs on the rate cards provide a little more detail. Consider these examples provided by Atlantic List Marketing:

Agenda for Freedom Donors: Composed of donors to political campaigns across the country, this list features Christians and Conservatives dedicated to preserving family and moral values by building a strong America. They have tried to enforce—through their activism and campaign donations—a new commitment by the Republican Party along with Conservative Organizations to adhere to traditional principles, especially in regard to social and family issues.

Dynamic American Donors: Direct mail donors to Democratic candidates and organizations. A wide range of Democrats—liberal, moderate and conservative— are represented on this list of donors who have given to support candidates espousing the party's philosophy on issues.

Moral Patriot Masterfile: The Moral Majority's contributor list. These people care about the state of our nation—morally, politically and strategically. They are: Conservative, Moral, Religious, Patriotic, Republican, and Charitable Donors. They will give and continue to give generously through the mail to appeals relating to the issues in which they believe. Call Atlantic to ascertain what is the best select for your appeal.

Gray Go-Getters: This list is a rare find! These direct mail–generated energetic older Americans are liberal to moderate, progressive, "cause conscious" donors who don't let age get in their way. They are the perfect market for your "cause"— retirement/insurance offers, membership appeals, etc.

Figure 5.1
Sample Rate Card

MORAL PATRIOT MASTERFILE
ATLANTIC
LIST MARKETING
A Division of Atlantic List Company, Inc.

1,044,591	TOTAL DONORS	$85/M
	Charitable Fundraisers	$75/M
828,509	Oliver North/Religious Donors	$85/M
228,717	Political Donors	$85/M
258,879	Donors with Phones	$105/M

The Moral Majority's contributor list. These people care about the state of our nation—morally, politically and strategically. They are: Conservative, Moral, Religious, Patriotic, Republican, and Charitable DONORS. They will give and continue to give generously through the mail to appeals relating to the issues in which they believe.

Call Atlantic to ascertain what is the best select for your appeal.

SUGGESTED USE: Civic Appeals ●
Health and Welfare Fundraising Organizations ●
Religious Appeals and Organizations ● Family
& Conservative Social Interests ●

USAGE/CONTINUATIONS include:
National Right To Life Committee
Coral Ridge Ministries
National Republican Senatorial Committee
Republican National Committee
Rutherford Institute
Christian Family Renewal
American Bible Society
Campus Crusade for Christ
Christian Coalition
American Family Association
Salvation Army
Concerned Women for America

20% Commission to Recognized Brokers

------------date------------
Spring 1992
----------unit of sale----
Average Gift: $24.00
-----------source-----------
100% Direct Mail and/or
Direct Response
----------addressing---------
4-up Cheshire labels
Mag Tape: 9track, 1600 or
6250 bpi
P/S Labels @ $7.50/m
----------selections--------

$5/M	SCF or State
$25	Zip Tape Select Set-Up
$6/M	Zip Select
$2/M	Keycode
$7.50/M	P/S labels
$25.00	No-refund Mag. Tape

--------restrictions--------
Sample Mailing Piece required with each order; All rentals subject to owner's approval.

Maildate to be reserved in advance by phone.

TERMS: Net 30 days from mail date. $50/Flat cancellation fee on orders canceled prior to mail date. Cancellation after original mail date will require payment in full.

Minimum order: 5,000

1525 Wilson Blvd., #1225 • Arlington, VA 22209-2411 • (703) 528-7482 • FAX (703) 528-7492
900 Ethan Allen Hwy., #108 • Ridgefield, CT 06877 • (203) 431-3266 • FAX (203) 431-3624

While fund-raising is the principal reason a campaign likely would contact a list broker, there are other reasons worth the extra cost for these highly targeted databases. A campaign may wish to cultivate a stable of opinion leaders with desirable demographic traits—people with standing in a community or among members of key voter groups. The characteristics one might expect from a list are suggested by its title. Consider Superior Senior Citizens, Texans for a Conservative Supreme Court, Country Club Republicans: some of the many databases accessible through Atlantic and other list brokers. The candidate's ideology and the campaign's objectives could be served by support from people who may be persuaded to assist, if not with money, then by lending their names to an effort or by making important contacts within their circle of friends.

List brokers and the well-developed lists to which they have access can be of value mostly for the specialized communication and fund-raising efforts of a campaign. Because of their costs, they are not best suited to develop or append general lists. For these purposes, campaigns typically purchase voter registration lists, to which we now turn.

Voter Registration Lists

Dr. Thomas Hofeller, redistricting director for the National Republican Congressional Committee, says that if he could have only two categories of information with which to plan a targeted communication campaign, he would want a voter's turnout records and three personal statistics: age, gender and address. These details, he argues, provide the essential information for any targeting effort.

The turnout record reveals the person's commitment to the political process and to voting. Regular voters are more likely to be consumers of political information. If they vote regularly, polls indicate, they also are more inclined to read, listen and analyze news and campaign information.

Work by Everett Rogers (1983) and other specialists in information dissemination reveals that information consumers are more likely to be opinion leaders who set the tone and provide information for others making up their minds about how to vote. So, from voting history alone, something is known about a person and the likelihood s/he will pay attention to targeted communications. As a bonus, regular voters may sway the votes of less committed people.

To voting records, Hofeller adds the indicators of age, gender and address. Age and gender are obvious categories—appreciated, no doubt, by the classical Greeks. Younger voters are more likely to be concerned with education and job prospects. Some will be attracted by issues concerning child care and home buying. Seniors, understandably, are drawn to social security and medical issues, as well as to high interest rates on savings. Men respond to defense and crime issues, women to abortion questions and career opportunities in a changing work force. Age and gender provide the azimuth and the range for targeting.

Addresses are more than a place on the map; they reveal a voter's political leanings. Tim Roper, president of the Washington-based political consulting firm of Odell, Roper and Simms, Inc., said he finds geographic information to be a key in voter categorization. "Where people live gives us an idea of how they vote. We have a lot of precinct data, and the address ties a voter into a precinct. Quite simply, we have found that people tend to vote the way their neighbors vote." This is easy to see. People living in Beverly Hills vote Republican; people living in low-cost developments vote Democratic—at least those are the generalizations of precinct data.

It is a stroke of good luck that voter registration lists conveniently provide all the information prized by Hofeller; most states offer even more. These lists, updated continuously in most states, contain data obtained directly from voters, usually under oath. This is about as accurate as data gathering is likely to get.

There is considerable variance by state in the amount and variety of data collected. Here is a list of all the items that appear on voter registration questionnaires throughout the country. None of the states requests all of this information, although some, like South Carolina and Tennessee, ask for most of it. Others, like Iowa, Vermont and Virginia, ask for very little.

Name	Prior voter registration
Address	Race
Telephone	Height
Date of Birth	Weight
Place of birth	Hair color
Age	Eye color
Gender	Occupation
Social Security number	Criminal record
Party	Mental state
Citizenship status	Aliases

See Table 5.1 for a state-by-state table of information requested on voter registration forms.

In some cases, the use of voter registration lists is restricted to political campaigns and to nonprofit organizations. Usually, when there are restrictions, states must approve users and in some instances confirm their intended use of the data. The State Board of Elections in Virginia, for instance, must qualify all purchasers and will sell its voter registration lists only to the following (Fitz-Hugh 1983):

• Candidates for election or political party nomination to further their candidacy
• Political party committees or officials thereof for political purpose only
• Incumbent office holders to report to their constituents
• Nonprofit organizations which promote voter participation and registration—for that purpose only
• Courts of the Commonwealth and the United States for jury selection purposes

Many states have similar restrictions. These limitations and costs for voter registration lists are included in Table 5.2 (Limits on Information Release and Costs).

The costs of voter lists are nominal, usually a few cents or less per name to offset the cost for preparing the files. Thus, not only are these databases valuable—because they identify the most likely voters, have age, gender and address and reveal voting information—but they are a real bargain. This is evident particularly when compared to the cost of commercially developed lists obtained through list brokers.

For all their value, however, voter lists are not perfect. In many states, they offer little more than the bare essentials outlined by Hofeller. Conspicuously missing in many states are phone numbers. Only twenty-one states request these; the rest make them optional or make no provisions for them at all. Campaigns in the majority of states, therefore, need to fortify their voter lists, and this can be difficult with the growing popularity of unpublished numbers.

Low-budget campaigns can make do with voter registration lists, adding phones and other staff-developed information. They can append voter lists with information from in-house files and add data gathered by volunteers canvassing the neighborhoods. As long as there is time and manpower, voter lists can be fortified with additional information useful in targeted communication.

For campaigns without the time or the staff, or those interested in information that cannot easily be generated from local sources, there are specialists for hire who can do the job. Companies such as CACI, CLAR-ITAS, Donnelly and TRW append voter lists and upgrade the information they contain.[5]

The process is simple. Campaigns pack up their voter lists (on computer disks or tape) and ship them off to a service facility. They instruct the company to add the items they need to help with targeting efforts and other campaign activities. The facility then matches campaign files with company master files and appends the requested information.

Dr. Alex Norsworthy, a database specialist and independent consultant in Washington, D.C., sees two general categories of database upgrades. First, for general voter files, where only a moderate level of detail is necessary, he says campaigns can turn to companies that provide categories

Table 5.1
Information Requested on Voter Registration Forms

	Tele	DOB	POB	Age	Sex	SSN	Party	Citiz Status	Prior Reg
AL	Yes	Yes	Yes	No	No	Op	No	Yes	Yes
AK	Op	Op	Yes	No	Yes	Op	Op	No	Yes
AZ	Yes	Yes	Yes	Yes	Yes	No	Yes	Yes	Yes
AR	No	Yes	Yes	No	No	No	No	Yes	Yes
CA	Op	Yes	Yes	No	Op	No	Yes	Yes	Yes
CO	Op	Yes	No	No	Yes	Op	Op	Yes	Yes
CT	Op	Yes	Yes	No	Yes	No	Op	Yes	Yes
DE	Yes	Yes	Yes	No	Yes	Yes	Yes	Yes	Yes
DC	Yes	Yes	No	No	No	Op	Yes	Yes	Yes
FL	No	Yes	Yes	No	Yes	No	Yes	Yes*	No
GA	Op	Yes	Yes	No	Yes	Yes	No	Yes	Yes
HI	Yes	Yes	No	No	Yes	Yes	No	No	No
ID	Op	Op	No	Yes	Yes	Op	No	Yes	Yes
IL	Op	Yes	Yes	Yes	Yes	Op	No	Yes*	Yes
IN	Op	Yes	Yes	No	Yes	Op	No	Yes	Yes
IA	Op	Yes	No	No	Yes	Op	Op	No	Yes
KS	Yes	Yes	No	No	Yes	Op	Yes	Yes	Yes
KY	Yes	Yes	No	No	Yes	Yes	Yes	No	Yes
LA	Yes	Yes	Yes	No	Yes	Op	Yes	Yes	Yes
ME	Yes	Yes	No	Yes	Yes	No	Yes	No	Yes
MD	Op	Yes	Yes	Yes	Yes	No	Yes	Yes	Yes
MA	No	Yes	No	No	No	No	Yes	Yes	Yes
MI	Op	Yes	Yes	No	Op	No	Op	Yes	Yes
MN	Op	Yes	No	No	No	No	No	Yes	Yes
MS	Op	Yes	No	No	No	Yes	No	Yes	Yes
MO	Op	Yes	Yes	No	No	Op	No	Yes	Yes
MT	Yes	Yes	Yes	No	No	No	No	Yes	Yes
NE	No	Yes	Yes	No	Yes	No	Yes	Yes	Yes
NV	No	Yes	Yes	No	No	Yes	Op	Yes	Yes
NH	No	Yes	Yes	No	No	No	Op	Yes	Yes
NJ	Yes#	Yes	No	No	No	No	No	Yes	Yes#
NM	No	Yes	Yes	Yes	Yes	Yes	Yes	Yes	Yes
NY	Yes	Yes	No	No	Yes	No	Op	Yes*	Yes
NC	Yes	Yes	Yes	No	Yes	Op	Yes	Yes	No
ND	N/A	N/A	N/A	N/A	N/A	N/A	N/A	N/A	N/A
OH	Yes	Yes	Yes	No	No	Yes	No	Yes	Yes
OK	No	Yes	No	No	Yes	No	Yes	Yes	No
OR	Op	Yes	Yes	No	No	No	Op	No	No
PA	No	Yes	Yes	No	Yes	No	Yes	Yes	Yes
RI	Op	Yes	Yes	No	Yes	No	Yes	Yes*	Yes
SC	Yes	Yes	Yes	No	Yes	Yes	No	Yes*	Yes
SD	Yes	Yes	No	No	No	No	Yes	Yes	No
TN	Yes	Yes	Yes	No	Yes	Yes	No	Yes	Yes
TX	No	Yes	Yes	No	Yes	Op	No	Yes	Yes
UT	Yes	Yes	Yes	No	No	No	No	Yes	Yes
VT	Yes	Yes	Yes	No	No	No	No	Yes	Yes
VA	Op	Yes	Yes	Yes	Yes	Yes	No	Yes	Yes
WA	Yes	Yes	No	No	Yes	Yes	No	Yes	Yes
WV	Yes	Yes	Yes	No	Yes	Yes	Yes	Yes*	Yes
WI	No	Yes	Yes	Yes	No	No	No	Yes	No
WY	No	Yes	No	No	No	Op	Yes	Yes	No

Op = Optional; * If foreign born, naturalization info required; # On mail registration forms only.
Source: Brian Hancock, "Fast Facts on State Registration and Election Procedures," *National Clearinghouse on Election Administration*, February 1992.

Table 5.1 (continued)

	Race	Hgt	Wgt	Hair	Eyes	Occ	Crim Rec	Ment Rec	Other Names
AL	Yes	No	No	No	No	Yes	Yes	No	No
AK	No	No	No	No	No	No	No	No	Prev
AZ	No	No	No	No	No	Yes	Yes	Yes	MMN FN
AR	No	No	No	No	No	No	No	Yes	MN
CA	No	No	No	No	No	Op	Yes	No	No
CO	No	No	No	No	No	No	No	No	No
CT	No	No	No	No	No	No	Yes	No	No
DE	No	Yes	No	Yes	Yes	No	No	No	No
DC	No	No	No	No	No	No	No	No	No
FL	Yes	No	No	No	No	No	No	No	No
GA	Yes	Yes	No	No	No	No	Yes	No	MMN FN
HI	No	No	No	No	No	No	No	No	No
ID	No	No	No	No	No	No	No	No	No
IL	No	No@	No	No@	No@	No	No	No	No@
IN	No	No	No	No	No	No	No	No	No
IA	No	No	No	No	No	No	No	No	No
KS	No	No	No	No	No	No	No	No	No
KY	No	No	No	No	No	No	No	No	MN
LA	Op	No	No	No	No	No	Yes	No	MMN
ME	No	No	No	No	No	No	No	No	No
MD	No	No	No	No	No	No	No	No	No
MA	No	No	No	No	No	Yes	No	No	No
MI	No	No	No	No	No	No	No	No	No
MN	No	No	No	No	No	No	No	No	No
MS	No	No	No	No	No	No	Yes	No	No
MO	No	Yes	Yes	Yes	Yes	Op	No	No	MMN
MT	No	No	No	No	No	No	No	No	No
NE	Yes+	No	No	No	No	No	No	No	S
NV	No	No	No	No	No	No	No	No	No
NH	No	No	No	No	No	No	No	No	No
NJ	No	No	No	No	No	No	No	No	No
NM	No	No	No	No	No	No	No	No	No
NY	No	Yes	No	No	Yes	No	No	No	No
NC	Yes	No	No	No	No	No	Yes	No	No
ND	N/A	N/A	N/A	N/A	N/A	N/A	N/A	N/A	N/A
OH	No	No	No	No	No	No	No	No	No
OK	No	Yes	Yes	Yes	Yes	No	No	No	No
OR	No	No	No	No	No	No	No	No	MMN FN S
PA	Op	Yes	No	Yes	Yes	No	No	No	No
RI	No	No	No	No	No	No	No	No	No
SC	Yes	Yes	Yes	Yes	Yes	Yes	Yes	Yes	No
SD	No	No	No	No	No	No	No	No	No
TN	Yes	Yes@	No	Yes@	Yes	Yes	Yes	No	No
TX	No	No	No	No	No	No	Yes	No	S MN
UT	No	No	No	No	No	No	No	No	No
VT	No	No	No	No	No	No	No	No	No
VA	No	No	No	No	No	No	Yes	Yes	MN PLN
WA	No	No	No	No	No	No	No	No	No
WV	Yes	Yes	No	Yes	Yes	No	No	No	No
WI	No	No	No	No	No	No	No	No	No
WY	No	No	No	No	No	No	No	No	No

MN = Maiden Name   FN = Father's Name   PLN = Prior Legal Name(s)
MMN = Mother's Maiden Name   S = Spouse's Name   + Ethnic Orig; @ If unable to sign

Table 5.2
Limits on Information Release and Costs

	State Voter Regis. Card.	Required at Polls	Limits on Release of Information	Price of Info
		Registration Procedures by State		
AL	Yes	No	Published in Newsp.	----
AK	Yes	No	Pub. Disp. Cpy to Myr	----
AZ	Yes	No	Pol. activity only	$2 Print Fee
AR	No	--	No Limits	Copy costs
CA	No	--	Court decision pending	.50/1,000
CO	No	--	No Limits	Reasonbl Fee
CT	No	--	No Limits	Free
DE	Yes	No	Only party & candts.	$5 set up
DC	Yes	No	No Limits	Copy costs
FL	Yes	No	Limited release	----
GA	Yes	No	No Limits	.01/Name
HI	No	--	Election use only	Copy costs
ID	No	--	No Limits	Copy costs
IL	County	No	No Limits	Copy costs
IN	No	--	Pub. Inspec./No release	----
IA	County	No	No Limits	Copy costs
KS	Yes	No	No Limits	Copy costs
KY	No	No	----	Cost/LT .50 pp.
LA	Yes	No	Request By 25 or more	Copy costs
ME	No	--	No Limits	Reasonable fee
MD	Yes	No	No commercial use	State/County
MA	No	--	No Limits	Copy costs
MI	Yes	No	No DOB or Driver ID	Copy costs
MN	Yes	No	No DOB	Copy costs
MS	County	No	County by County	Copy costs
MO	Yes	Yes	No Limits	Reasonable fee
MT	Yes	No	No Limits	Copy costs
NE	County	No	Only to Parties	.01/Name
NV	No	--	Pub. in Newspaper	----
NH	Twn/Cty	No	No Limits	$5-$25
NJ	No	No	No Limits	.25/dist
NM	No	--	Name/Pty/Gend/Prec	$4/1,000
NY	Yes	No	No Limits	Copy costs
NC	County	No	Selective/Reqst	Copy cost
ND	N/A	N/A	N/A	N/A
OH	No	--	No Limits	Free
OK	Yes	No	No Limits	.25/pp.
OR	Yes	No	No commercial use	Copy costs
PA	County	No	No commercial use	Set by county
RI	Yes	No	Pub. Inspec. Cpy to Pty	----
SC	No	--	Pub. Inspec.	Set by county
SD	Yes	No	No Limits	Copy costs
TN	Yes	No	No Limits	Copy costs
TX	Yes	No	No commercial use	Copy costs
UT	County	No	County by County	Copy costs
VT	No	--	No Limits	Copy costs
VA	Yes	No	Pub. Inspec./No Copies	----
WA	County	No	No DOB	Copy costs
WV	Yes	No	No Limits	----
WI	No	--	No Limits	Copy costs
WY	County	No	Pub . Inspec./ Pty use	$1.50/$1.00

Source: Brian Hancock, "Fast Facts on State Registration and Election Procedures," *National Clearinghouse on Election Administration*, February 1992.

based on block groups used mostly for marketing purposes. These sources do not use data specific to one individual, but to a small group to which the individual belongs. If you live in Beverly Hills, for example, there's a high probability you earn more than $250,000 per year, so everyone in Beverly Hills is tagged as earning over a quarter million. That's the logic of the broad brush. Such sweeping generalizations will be accurate for most individuals, although some will be misidentified. Not everyone in a Republican neighborhood is Republican, nor does everyone who lives around a military base favor high defense spending. But given the cost-detail trade-off, Norsworthy says this approach will deliver information suited to general voter contacts.

On the other hand, the second type of upgrade is very specific, offering details rich enough not only for letter-writing campaigns, but for phone calls and even personal visits by the candidate and the staff. These specific targets get special attention. For them, the information can be thick with details, like membership, hobbies, spending habits, even stock portfolio contents!

Naturally, the more details you buy, the higher the cost. Therefore, campaigns must do a cost/benefit analysis to reduce the size of the lists for which they obtain such high-power details. How? Develop the most promising prospects by choosing certain geographic regions or selecting characteristics that identify a high proportion of people likely to respond to the special appeal.

This list, now reduced in size, can be appended by a service facility with information such as income, home ownership, automobile ownerships, stock and bond ownership, club membership and an impressive, some would say meddlesome, variety of other information obtained from many sources. These companies acquire data from driver's registration forms, real estate records, brokerage houses and insurance claims forms, to name a few. Sometimes, the service houses purchase the databases; sometimes they create them from public records and even newspaper accounts.

Like a tiny farmhouse whose owners expand, update and modify it over the years, voter registration lists, properly managed and appended, provide the database core for a campaign. That core provides a listing of all the active voters in a defined geographic region and includes their basic characteristics. Some states provide a meatier voter dossier; the data are almost always accurate, given the controlled conditions under which they are collected. Furthermore, the voter files are easily processed by standard campaign computer equipment, which means they can be linked with other databases, appended by outside firms and manipulated to apportion the list into useful target groups.

Campaigns also can obtain fortified voter registration lists from outside vendors. Washington-based Aristotle Industries, a computer services firm, offers information on CD–ROM (Computer Disk—Read Only Memory) for every registered voter in the United States. Campaigns can obtain voter lists for any geographic region and either use their own or Aristotle software (Campaign Manager II) to process the information. A voter record contains name, address and usually phone. It also has voting history, age, gender, party affiliation and information about other household members. According to company literature, in most cases, all this information can be packed onto a single CD for each state. Each costs around $1,000.[6]

John Phillips, president of Aristotle, told me that the company also offers a database containing the names and vital statistics of every person who ever has contributed to a federal campaign. Such a list could help in fundraising activities without incurring the higher costs of list broker services and other costlier sources of donor information.

The key to Aristotle's large-scale database collection is the use of CD–ROMs. Phillips noted that his sixty-disk national voter data set would fill hundreds of floppy disks. He said that as campaigns come to rely on more information for their targeting activities, the CD will occupy a larger place in the technology repertoire. His company has staked everything on this prediction. The old philosopher who demanded moderation in all things would stand speechless before this extraordinary volume of data.

Census Data

Every ten years during the past two centuries, American citizens, willingly or not, have yielded personal statistics to the federal government as it fulfilled its constitutional obligations to conduct a national census. Over the years, data collection techniques have changed, new questions and categories have been added and sampling methods have been updated, but the availability of the results has remained pretty much unaltered. The government has tabulated responses, published key statistics and made the information available in formidable volumes which droop library shelves all over the country. This vast wealth of information had remained locked in endless bound tables like the bones of a mammoth frozen tight in a glacier.

It was a dramatic, revolutionary decision by the Census Bureau in the late eighties that broke the lock on this treasure chest of information. Beginning with the 1990 census, the government said it would make available all of the census data on CD–ROM. Each CD–ROM can store nearly a quarter million pages of data—that's about five hundred hefty volumes contained on a light, plastic disk smaller than a tea saucer. Data, once physically restricted by its volume and format, now is available in a highly transportable, vastly more accessible medium.

The government's CD–ROM decision was joined by several collateral decisions that have had remarkable consequences. The Census Bureau has made the information openly available. Large businesses, small businesses, nonprofit organizations, political campaigns, even private citizens have access. Census Bureau Director Barbara Everitt Bryant described the program as "the democratization of census data." In fact, it also has become the ambitious retailing of census data. The government sees the numbers as money-makers and is aggressively marketing the data and associated products.

Furthermore, the Census Bureau entices its customers with support services and with the many veins of its rich data lode. It provides retrieval software (called "Go") to access the data, and it offers guidance in selecting other software for more aggressive data manipulation. It also offers a release known as the TIGER/Line files that transform the statistics into digital maps. Where are high-income (say, over $100,000) strongholds? Where are older homes (those over, say, 30 years)? Where are homes heated by natural gas? Any of the census data can be displayed instantly on maps that reveal concentrations. This converts census results into graphic displays at any geographic interval down to the block level.[7] At a glance, the user can assimilate patterns and pockets of statistics that otherwise would emerge only after enormous effort spent on countless tables scattered through many printed volumes. (See chapter 6 for more information on mapping.)

The Census Bureau also promotes the considerable richness of its data. There are dozens of reported variables. Here are a few from the 1990 census:

Household relationship

Sex

Race

Age

Marital status

Number of units in structure

Number of rooms in unit

Tenure (owned or rented)

Value of home or monthly rent

Education

Language spoken at home

Veteran status

Occupation

Income

Heating fuel[8]

It is no mere coincidence that the Census Bureau decided to release its data in electronic form at this time. By 1990, there were enough businesses, organizations, campaigns and individuals equipped with the necessary hardware and expertise for the CD–ROM project to have a sufficiently large constituency and thus be cost-effective. This would not have been so only ten years earlier, when the technology was too primitive and the market too underdeveloped for such an undertaking. It was a remarkable ten years in which computer technology grew in sophistication and acceptance and, on both counts, passed a threshold that allowed the widespread dissemination of this bountiful national biography. Only now, through technology, can average citizens enjoy easy access to data that heretofore were beyond their reach. Bryant was right: This technology has "democratized" the dissemination of the census data.

It would be a mistake to believe the preparation of census data on CD–ROM is simply a means to improve the logistics of the data release. Sure, a thin, half-ounce, plastic disk is easier to ship, to lift and to store than a ton of unwieldy tomes. It is more portable, more accessible and more convenient. It is more pleasant to work with, it costs less—a lot less—and it is easier on the environment. But advantages go far beyond the physical properties of a plastic disk.

The medium permits manipulations of the data not possible—or at least not possible without extraordinary effort—with printed tables. The software allows you to juxtapose various pieces of information for easy inspection. Suppose your campaign is concerned about pay scales in your district. You can compare the earnings of your 50- to 65-year-old white-collar workers with those in New York and Chicago and arrange data from the three settings on the same page. If, after inspection, that doesn't provide the information you need, you can expand the age range to include 45- to 65-year-olds. You can bring in data for Los Angeles, Houston, Detroit or smaller communities surrounding your own district. You then can separate the statistics by gender and display them on the same page for easy inspection. The computer gets the data you request, compiles it according to your specifications, then dutifully assembles it in a format you prescribe. The whole process, in the hands of someone familiar with the easy procedures, may take only a few minutes. Try that with a stack of printed census books!

Since the data can be exported to other programs, it can be used as you would use any other raw data. You can export data to statistical packages—for instance, SPSS and SAS. You can use them in graphics programs such as Freelance and Harvard Graphics. Export them to dBase, Q&A or word processors, such as AMI Pro, Wordperfect and Microsoft Word. You also can export the data to special campaign software for integration into the other information you have collected in-house from other database sources.

Remember one thing: To protect privacy, the data go no lower than the block level. There are no individual statistics. You will not be able to find out how much John Sledgehammer earns or whether or not he served in the military. You will be able to find out, though, the percentage of people earning designated incomes and the percentage of veterans in Sledgehammer's neighborhood. In fact, you can learn a great deal about his neighborhood and, thereby, a lot about Sledgehammer because of where he lives. Remember Thomas Hofeller's advice about the value of voters' addresses in determining their demographic profiles and their likely views on candidates and on key issues.

Further, you can append block information to individual data files as we described earlier. Political campaigns do this all the time; in fact, they spend a great deal of money adding general information to specific files. We noted that this can result in inaccurate information for some individuals, but statistical averages often are accurate enough for campaign activities, and they may be a lot better than no information at all.

Even if a campaign chose not to graft block information onto individual files, it would find the breadth and depth of information on these disks invaluable. The mapping features alone would benefit most campaigns as they conceptualize the mosaic of their population. Mass-media targeting strategies surprisingly can emerge from color graphics, whereas they once remained hidden in a gray table of numbers. Counties in these regions have larger concentrations of Hispanic voters; these have higher incomes; these concentrate female heads of household; and so forth. Details that pop up in colors reveal the density of any trait or combination of selected traits. Again, try this with a stack of printed census books.

Not only are the disks rich with detail, but they are inexpensive—if you buy just what you need. The going rate now is $150 per disk, and there is a good chance that, for most state and local races, one or a few will be sufficient. There are several files, each containing a different combination of statistics (these are described in footnote 8). You will not need all the disks, so the selection and purchase is not as daunting as the formidable list may suggest. Also, even though CD–ROMs hold huge quantities of information, you must consider the vast size of the census information stockpiles. For instance, in one file alone, Summary Tape File 3A—tabulations from the long-form questionnaire—there are thirty thousand megabytes of information! That is nearly four dozen CD–ROMs. In pages, it's around 10 million; in books, around 25,000. You will not want the whole set, so buy the few disks you need.

In summary, the Census Bureau has unleashed a resource that is just now creeping into the political campaign market. Its value soon will be discovered on a wide scale. As campaign workers become more comfortable with the data-access technology, they no doubt will come to rely more on the data.

Shelf life may become a problem. Ten-year data collection intervals were adequate for the first two hundred years of this country, but a decade is just too long in these days of instant communication. People move in this transient population, and their life-styles are ever changing. Consequently, by mid-decade, the census numbers will lose much of their sharp edge, and their usefulness will decline. Interim surveys can whet the numbers, however, and a Census Bureau decision to release these data on CD–ROM will ensure the data as a perpetual information resource for campaigns. The continued adoption of computers and now the inexpensive CD–ROM drives will guarantee a growing market for this very valuable high-tech resource.

CONCLUSION

In order to demystify the subject for this chapter, I started by comparing electronic databases with the file card databases of a bygone era. You saw how they both contained voter data and were at heart the same. True, but practically, this so understates the real differences that the comparison is misleading. Electronic databases hold more information, work a vastly greater range of sources and are immensely more malleable because they allow instant additions, deletions and modifications. This capacity for change and adaptation grants them an organic quality.

The greatest differences between electronic and hand-scrawled databases, however, are found not in what they contain, but in what they allow a campaign to do with them. Campaigns can now sort and select among tens of thousands of entries to form target groups for communications and other activities. They can analyze population characteristics and display them in ways unknown to the old files. They can integrate database information directly into personalized information dispensed from a campaign—a task possible with three-by-five cards, but not practical for any large-scale operation.

However clichéd it may sound, we are entering a new era of information retrieval and use. Campaigns are constructing databases with such sophistication that, by any realistic measure, they possess an instrument unknown to earlier campaigns. With the software to create impressive in-house files, vendor list supplements and voter registration lists in electronic form, campaigns, for the first time, have the capacity to generate a holistic view of a target population. As we have seen, this view is not limited to simple demographic mainstays. It can include highly detailed information about family, profession, finances, personal interests and purchases. Add to this the census data available for the first time in 1990, and you have a resource whose dimensions are almost incomprehensible. Imagine population data with such an expanse and depth that, if published, would consume 25,000 volumes. All of this and over 75,000 additional volumes are available to any campaign—to any citizen, for that matter—with a department store computer and simple reader that costs less than $300.

At the heart, electronic databases and index cards are akin. Forgive anyone, though, who, at first blush, misses the likeness.

NOTES

1. Richard D. Schlackman is president of the Campaign Performance Group, a direct-mail company. His statement was quoted in: Ben Smith III, "Your Vote's Your Secret, but Open Voting Lists Tell a Lot about You," *Atlanta Journal and Constitution*, August 11, 1992, p. A1.

2. We have taken liberties with the use of terms that, for database specialists, have precise meanings. Anyone writing for general audiences makes decisions about where to use exact terminology and where to substitute close terms. Nonspecialists may be more comfortable with familiar terms whose meaning is a close enough approximation. For example, data item—an element in a record—is more precise in database parlance than variable, although variable makes sense and is not too far afield. Also, in the strictest sense, data is not the same as information. A computer stores data, which are numbers or letters totally devoid of meaning. These data become information only when we attach a reference—and then only to us, for the computer sees only data. For instance, the number 270 is data and means nothing in particular. However, 270 electoral votes have considerable meaning, but only after we have affixed the reference. In some contexts, the data-information distinction is important; for our work, it is not critical. We will use the two interchangeably.

3. Note that in the Worthington entry, one of the commas is enclosed in quotation marks. Since the computer looks for commas to identify the end of one variable and the beginning of another, any comma that is part of the variable itself (as in the address) must be set apart from the true delimiters. Most software packages use quotation marks for this purpose. You may also use specific semicolons or other delimiters that are less likely than commas to appear in the text.

4. The *Washington Post* reported that this plan was dropped for now because of an outcry about privacy. The privacy issue, of concern to the government and citizens' groups alike, has been looming over the list—or database—industry. This time, it stopped Lotus, but as technology improves and the demands and markets for data increase, can such innovations be forever sidetracked?

Information sharing, amalgamation (called appending) and use in direct-marketing campaigns have raised the specter of Big Brother. They evoke images of a society where every purchase, phone call and personal statistic is hawked to those who would use it to their own advantage and, perhaps, the disadvantage of the target individuals. The cry has been about privacy, and it has appealed to many sympathetic ears. As the *Post* reported, Lotus dropped its plan in the heat of objections by citizen groups and state attorneys general, but the issue is far from closed.

5. These are a few of the many companies that append voter lists and other databases with individual-level information:

CACI Marketing Systems
1100 North Glebe Road

Arlington, VA 22201
(903) 841–2926

CLARITAS/NPDC
201 North Union Street
Alexandria, VA 22314
(703) 683–8300

Donnelly Marketing Information Systems
70 Seaview Avenue
Stamford, CT 06904
(203) 353–7227

TRW Marketing Systems
505 City Parkway West, 8th Floor
Orange, CA 92668
(714) 385–7500

   6. Information obtained from Aristotle Industries promotional literature, 1992.
Aristotle Industries, 205 Pennsylvania Avenue, S.W., Washington, DC 20003–
1164, (800) 243–4401.
   7. The Census Bureau Public Law 94–171 Files are available for the following
geographic areas:

United States
Regions
Divisions
States
Metropolitan areas
Urbanized areas
Congressional districts
Zip codes
American Indian and Alaska Native areas
Counties
Minor civil divisions and census county divisions
Places (such as cities, villages and census-designated places)
Census tracts and block numbering areas
Block groups
Blocks

   8. (Information from "Census, CD–ROM, and You!" U.S. Department of
Commerce, Economics and Statistics Administration, Bureau of the Census, 1992.)
This information is taken from a promotional document prepared by the Census
Bureau titled, "CD–ROM 'Democratizes' Dissemination of 1990 Census Data"
(1992).
   The following 1990 files are (or will be) available on CD–ROM:
   Public Law 94–171 Data: Counts of all persons and persons 18 years and over;
by race; of Hispanic origin; and not of Hispanic origin by race; total housing units.
Data are available for States, counties, county subdivisions, places (or place parts),
census tracts/block numbering areas (BNAs) (or census tract/BNA parts), block
groups, blocks, State and/or county parts of American Indian and Alaska Native
areas, and voting districts for the District of Columbia and selected States.
   Summary Tape File (STF) 1A: Includes population and housing counts and
characteristics (age, sex, race, Hispanic origin, marital status, household relation-

ships, value of home or monthly rent paid, number of rooms in unit, etc.) from the short-form questionnaire for States and their subareas in hierarchical sequence down to the block group level. Also has summaries of the State portion of American Indian and Alaska Native areas, whole places, whole census tracts/block numbering areas, whole minor civil divisions in 12 States, and whole block groups.

STF 1B: As extract of the tape file—12 tables instead of the 100 on STF 1A and 1B (tape)—will be available on CD–ROM for the full geographic hierarchy for States, to the block level. There are about 7 million census blocks. Among data items included are: race and Hispanic origin, some age ranges, housing units, and occupied housing units. It will be on 10 disks.

STF 1C: Same tabulations as in STF 1A presented for the United States, regions, divisions, States (including summaries such as urban and rural), counties, places of 10,000 or more inhabitants in selected States, metropolitan statistical areas, urban areas, and American Indian and Alaska Native areas.

STF 3A: Includes population and housing characteristics from the sample or long-form questionnaire (education, ancestry, language, disability, occupation and industry of worker, income in 1989, year moved into residence, number of bedrooms, etc.) for States and their subareas in hierarchical sequence down to the block group level. Also has summaries for the State portion of American Indian and Alaska Native areas, whole places, whole census tracts/block numbering areas, and whole block groups.

STF 3B: Same tabulations as in STF 3A summarized for 5-digit ZIP codes within each State, including county portions of the areas when a ZIP code falls in two or more counties. Available in 1992.

STF 3C: Same tabulations as in STF 3A presented for the United States, regions, divisions, States, counties, places of 10,000 or more inhabitants, minor civil divisions of 10,000 or more inhabitants in selected States, American Indian and Alaska Native areas, metropolitan statistical areas, and urban areas.

Census/Equal Employment Opportunity Special File: Provides sample census data to support affirmative action planning for equal employment opportunity. Detailed occupation and educational attainment data by age, cross-tabulation by sex, race, and Hispanic origin for counties, metropolitan areas, and places of 50,000 or more inhabitants.

County-to-County Migration Special File: Summary records for all intrastate and substantial interstate county-to-county migration streams (including codes for the geographic area of origin and the area of destination) and selected characteristics of the persons who made up the migration stream. Issued by State.

Readers may obtain additional information from: Customer Services, The Census Bureau, Washington, DC 20233, (301) 763–2074. On-line data systems also are available through CompuServe (800–848–8199) and DIALOG (800–334–2564). CENDATA, available through these on-line systems, provides up-to-date statistics on many subjects including population, housing, business, industry, income and foreign trade.

Chapter Six

Data Analyses

Marshall McLuhan spoke of communication technology that would level everyone across state and national boundaries, creating one vast global village. But the next generation of communication technologies—custom-tailored, personalized technology—may leave not a global village but a global vacuum—and a global cacophony.

—David Shaw[1]

INTRODUCTION

Before industrial pollutions turned all rivers gray, you could stand on the water's edge in downtown Paducah, Kentucky, and watch the merging of ·two great rivers, the Ohio and the Tennessee. Amazingly, the merging was not immediate. The Ohio waters were dark and the Tennessee light, so the observer could see a line of separation that took miles to dissolve into a mightier flow.

Audience analyses are similar. Like the Ohio, one river of survey data charts the views and activities of a population. Like the Tennessee, another river of individual statistics flows from population databases. Together, the two form one powerful information stream, which enables a campaign to know its voters.

Analysis of survey data, like a scout's analysis of the terrain ahead, provides a campaign with intelligence information. Targeted communication thrives on feedback and audience surveillance data, and there is no better source of such information than surveys. The analyst's chore is to hammer out every detail in order to understand the audience, recognize relevant subgroups and plan persuasive messages. Good survey data yield their treasures through good analyses.

Database analysis, the other merging stream, follows the course plotted by the surveys. Surveys tell you about population subgroups: how they think, how they behave, how they can be moved. Database analyses give you the members of these subgroups, separating them one from the other, allowing you to reach them one at a time or in small clusters.

During the past decade, campaigns have witnessed remarkable changes in both phases of audience analysis. Computers have allowed survey data to flood the political marketplace, opening the information to every campaign, no matter how small. Computers gave birth to the database. Whether you know it or not, you live today in the database era. There are more sources of personal information and more users of information than ever before. Computers facilitate the collection, dissemination and use of database information, and now that most campaigns have the hardware, the database marketplace has expanded like a suburban shopping mall. The old mom-and-pop stores have been replaced by info-centers of larger volume and more sophisticated techniques. The new merchants of survey research and personal databases have flooded the information market in American politics.

Computers have made audience assessments faster and more accurate—just as they have improved word processing and tax preparation—but they have done more than improve efficiency. Computers have struck entirely new data analysis tools. There are statistical techniques available today that were unthinkable to most campaigns before the mid-eighties. Multiple regression analyses, cluster analyses and other techniques disclose things about an audience that never could be known before. Computers enable analysts to explore the data, sort out audience combinations and plot new paths that may lead to fresh insights and productive discoveries.

Computers are the engines that make the databases work. They grind the gears that churn through millions of audience details. They search through an audience member by member, placing each one in the proper category the way a high-speed coin sorter places dimes in one pile and quarters in another. The computer, however, makes dozens of piles based on many characteristics: not just any old pile of pennies, but each penny grouped according to when it was made, where it was minted, how worn it is.

Such things can be scary to the old practitioners. I've talked with those who fear computers the way auto workers fear robotics. They're the latest thing, sure, but over time, won't they take too many decisions away from "our" control? Is there too much information, too much intrusion into the human decision process? Such questions mostly betray a fear of the unknown. Will computers replace us as the old campaign hands? Some people need to be reminded that computers are just another tool, a powerful tool, but still a tool that responds to what the human brain proposes.

A more valid fear about computers in audience analyses stems from the fact that voters have become so abstracted as survey numbers and database statistics, that the human element has been wrested from the process. Some fear the flesh and blood of voters and staff alike have been squeezed out of modern campaigns. This is a legitimate concern, but not a realistic threat. There is still audience contact, pressing the flesh, even televised town meetings, a case in point being the Clinton/Gore bus trips. The very subjectivity of campaign decisions precludes the loss of human judgment, although information feeding into the process requires some examination. So, it isn't the numbers; it's what the numbers mean and what they personify that concern us.

A cheerful thought is this: Even when campaigns involve computers extensively, all plans must pass the "Inspector 12 Test." Sweet, matronly Inspector 12 held a very important job at the Hanes undergarment factory, as seen in a television commercial several years ago. Her job was to stand by while the quality-control machines on the assembly line stretched, squeezed and pummel-tested each undergarment. At the end of the day, however, in the last 10 feet of the line, after the machines had done their mechanical best, it was Inspector 12 who lovingly examined each T-shirt and pair of shorts. So, at least for now, making underwear and analyzing audiences have something in common: Both still require the human touch.

THE FIRST SORT

There are as many ways to conduct an audience analysis as there are audience analysts, but most start with an initial sorting to identify friends and flag foes. In *The Next Hurrah*, Richard Armstrong compares the sorting to what goes on in an emergency room triage, where doctors examine the conditions of arriving patients to determine a priority for treatment. As the term *triage* suggests, patients are assigned to one of three groups: (1) those who do not require immediate treatment, (2) those who are so badly injured, there can be no hope for recovery and (3) those for whom immediate treatment can make a difference between life and death. Under conditions of scarce resources, this division allows a logical allocation of facilities and medical expertise.

Political triage campaigns divide voters into: (1) supporters, (2) opponents and (3) undecideds. *The Next Hurrah* notwithstanding, I argue for the division of people into five groups (call it pentage): (1) strong supporters, (2) moderate supporters, (3) moderate opponents, (4) strong opponents and (5) undecideds. Why five and not three?

The strong supporters will remain in your camp unless you do something grievous and unforgivable. Ross Perot's copout in the 1992 race turned many loyal Perotistas into instant Democrats or Republicans. Even so, he rewon his most fervent supporters when he jumped back in. So, the rule of thumb is, don't spend much time on strong supporters, except for an occasional pat on the back and a periodic expression of thanks, as Bill Clinton did to sure-thing California.

Sadly, the strong opponents are lost, so save your resources. Only the rare campaign with abundant reserves could justify a run at this group. George Bush avoided the surely Democratic California for the opposite reason Clinton stayed out of the state. Bush's polls told the ex-pilot he had not a wing nor a prayer on the West Coast.

The moderates, both supporters and opponents, require a lot of coddling. Moderate supporters need shepherding, lest they stray. Moderate opponents are votes within your grasp. None of the moderates has committed firmly to a candidate, and so they can shift back and forth with the natural movement of the political tide. Campaigns seek out these groups in order to solidify the soft support and attract the soft opposition. It's always a scramble to lock in this group as early as possible in the race.

The true undecideds are special cases. Most polls attempt to discover some inclination among these fence-sitters by asking if they are leaning toward one candidate or another. Those with no preference—the real, die-hard undecideds—often settle a race, and so they become the bull's-eye for all candidates. Look at how Bush, Clinton and Perot—and their armies of pollsters—worked the swing states through the eleventh hour of the 1992 campaign. The need for information grows with the power of these voters to resolve a nip-and-tuck race. This is not unlike a personal encounter, where attention to another person increases proportionately to the importance of the relationship. Critical relationships demand better communications, and better communications require better information.

Let's look more closely at why this important, undecided group may straddle the fence. First, they may not have adequate information. Some ignore the media because of demanding schedules, lack of interest or a preference for entertainment media over news media. It is helpful to know which to determine how to intervene. Others have no interest in politics. Find out why. Some can't make a distinction among candidates because they "all look alike." If differences are blurred, put them in focus.

Other undecideds remain neutral despite great efforts to settle on a candidate, and this indecisiveness becomes a fertile ground for research. What persuasive approach will work best? Imagine a street confrontation with an undecided voter. In order to know how best to discuss the virtues of your candidate and the vices of the opposition, you would ask this fence-sitter to describe her views about the issues and the candidates and to explain why she felt nobody seemed worthy of support. What questions would you ask or not ask? What information would help you frame a knock-down response? How would you classify this person's response and organize your strongest arguments?

Project those questions onto the public communication scenario, where there are many undecided voters, all potential supporters. Wouldn't you want to know from the masses as much as you would from that lone voter? Campaigns may think in large numbers, but people still make decisions and vote one-by-one.

Ironically, the undecideds get more and better attention than political friends, although campaigns don't confine their efforts to fence-sitters alone. Voter pentage is a practical way to sort the voters and define the target groups. It prompts an allocation of effort according to the probability of support, much as medical triage apportions resources according to the probability of patient survival.

The initial polls make initial audience classifications, but nobody expects voters to run in place. Throughout the campaign, they are impacted by a blizzard of persuasive messages, and they shift like topsoil in a Kansas windstorm. From the start, audience analysts face a dynamic group, some voters drifting from pillar to post, some finding their place and staying put—for a while. To affect the voter population, campaigns need a lot more than five piles of names. They need to know how voters think and act, and for this they need to plow the fields deeper.

PATTERNS AND PARCELS

The secret to transforming data into information is the discovery of patterns and parcels—patterns of voter alignment on the issues, parcels of voters with similar traits. Patterns use an issue to define the population; parcels use the population to define the issues.

Take first the patterns. All the talk about an increase in the national gasoline tax has crescendoed in the nineties because of press stories about crumbling highways and bridges. Stump speeches during the 1992 presidential campaign added to public misgivings. Here's an issue that touches everyone, although its features strike different segments of the population disproportionately. For one thing, rural drivers are on the highways more than city drivers, so they would pay more. For another, low-income people would pay proportionately more than wealthy people, making this a regressive tax. On the other hand, the tax looks fair because it hits those who use national highways and bridges the most—it thus has the appeal of a user's fee.

The analysts' task is to disclose how the population breaks down on this issue, or put another way, to reveal the subgroups that form around the gas tax issue. Who understands it and who does not; who is for it and who is against it; who feels it is fair or unfair; who feels it is needed or not needed? The answers reveal patterns of alignment within the population, and these, in turn, suggest a logic for audience stratification and the consequent development and delivery of targeted messages. The analysis uses an issue to define the patterns of voters. (If your ethical Geiger counter is buzzing—because nobody asks whether the increase is in the best interests of the nation—you are sensing something noticed by a lot of other Geiger counters. The large national perspective often is lost in all of this.)

The analysis of parcels, on the other hand, starts with the audience and works toward the issues. Begin with demographic groups determined in advance, perhaps by logistic considerations (e.g., ready access through newsletters, targeted media or available databases) or previous research. Age is often used to break down a population, as is party affiliation, geographic division, group membership, income and occupation. Use these categories to partition the population accordingly, then examine the agenda and the leanings of each group individually. For instance, what issues are on the minds of older Republicans? How do they rank these issues? What are their concerns about each issue? Their answers develop the parcels— a lineup of issues for each subgroup.

Analyses in both cases—the formation of patterns and of parcels—configure clusters of voters who hold reasonably uniform views on key issues. Both yield demographic characteristics, and both yield a set of issues. This is the heart of communication targeting: the identification of audience segments and the exposition of the issues that relate to each.

A WAY TO ORGANIZE THE ANALYSIS

Researchers know that an analysis does not begin when the data have been neatly stored in an SPSS, SAS or some other file. Like a carpenter, the data analyst does not lay in supplies, then decide what to build. You start with an idea before a trip to the lumberyard. The end should be in sight from the beginning, because all the intervening steps accommodate those final objectives, whether it's at a workbench or CATI station. Organization has as much to do with data analysis as it does with survey planning and instrument construction. Ask the right questions to get the right data. Specifically, what information will lead to a useful audience analysis?

First, the great differences among campaigns prohibit a checklist of specific questions or analysis categories. There is a matrix, however, that helps campaigns decide which categories to include and ensures against information gaps that can blindside a campaign.

The matrix is formed by the intersection of two well-known communication tools: source, message, channel and receiver (SMCR) and knowledge, attitudes and behavior.

Source   Message   Channel   Receiver

Knowledge
Attitudes
Behavior

Remember communication scholar David Berlo's shorthand for communication: "A Source creates a Message which is carried by a Channel to the Receiver—SMCR." The choice of SMCR in the analysis matrix is important because political campaigns are communication campaigns. They seek to explain and to persuade, and this is accomplished by the power of ideas and the force of words. Naturally, campaigns seek the strongest themes, the most appealing presentations and the most efficient distribution of information. The messages are then tailored for target groups, and their aggregate effect is a demonstration that effective communication is effective politics. It is fitting that a communication model drives the search for audience information. SMCR is ideal for the task.

When colleagues and I do polling, we alter Berlo's SMCR by assuming the receiver's perspective in analyzing the source, message and channel. Why? Because this leads us to the only information that really matters: What is the Receiver's view of these features? What do the people we plan to address feel about the source, message and channel? This is all that really matters. The candidate may be smart, congenial and eminently more qualified than the opposition, but if the voters don't know him or don't believe him, all the objective measures are useless and misleading. Thus, we move the receiver above the three other features as follows:

Receiver

Source   Message   Channel

Knowledge
Attitudes
Behavior

Look at the difference between the questions, "What are the important issues?" and "What do voters think are the important issues?" Contrast "How trustworthy is the candidate?" with "How trustworthy do viewers believe the candidate is?" Although the logic of putting the receiver first is compelling, it is surprising how many campaigns miss its significance.[2]

On the vertical axis put knowledge, attitudes and behavior. These elements describe a voter's responses to information. Knowledge relates to a voter's awareness of and familiarity with candidates and issues. Attitudes deal with emotional loadings. Behavior describes observable responses.

The three are conceptually related, even if the relationship is not always clear. For instance, it is common to assume that knowledge precedes attitudes and that both precede behavior. You cannot like or dislike someone unless you first know s/he exists. This much is generally accepted. People who have heard nothing about a tax reform proposal or about endangerment of the spotted owl cannot form impressions about these issues. They may have general thoughts about taxes and ecology, but they cannot assemble issue-specific attitudes until they are introduced to the specific issues.

The attitudes-behavior relationship is trickier. Conventional wisdom says that attitudes drive behavior. If you like a candidate and you approve of her style and convictions, there is a good chance your behavior will align with your attitudes and you will vote for her.

Other scenarios exist. Psychologist Daryle Bem (1970), for instance, suggests that behaviors sometimes precede attitudes. Take the Yellow Dog Democrats—those die-hard Southern voters who would rather vote for a yellow dog than for a Republican. For many, voting behavior precedes attitudes. Once they have voted for the Democrat—because they always vote for the Democrat—they would face uncomfortable "cognitive dissonance" if they didn't align their attitudes with those of the person for whom they voted. Even Yellow Dog Democrats believe they are rational thinkers.

Others have proposed scenarios for a random order among the three elements. Behavior may come first, attitudes second (à la Bem) and knowledge third. Or, attitudes may come first, behavior second, then knowledge and so on.

In the 1992 presidential campaign, millions of voters formed first an attitude about Ross Perot. Many joined his fan clubs before knowing much about his views, plans or personality. Knowledge came last—or at least later. So, the combinations of knowledge, attitudes and behavior are not as simple as they first appear.

Although knowledge, attitudes and behavior can be arranged interchangeably like boxcars on a freight train, there is a probable order that political communicators must consider. They know they can best intervene by affecting voter knowledge, which leads to a change in attitudes, which, in turn, influences desired behavior. Thus, they nearly always must start with knowledge.[3] It is important to remember that, ultimately, success is measured by voter behavior—at the polling booth—and nothing more. Like a hanging, a win/lose scenario marvelously focuses the mind.

Thus, the norm: A voter's knowledge of the candidates and their issues precedes the formation of attitudes, which precedes hoped-for behavior. Voters will know before they feel before they behave.

USING THE MATRIX

Finding organization and structure at the beginning of an analysis is an important and demanding task. The riddle is knowing what you need to know, and in solving this riddle, campaigns are twice challenged: first, not to chase after meaningless information; second, not to overlook features critical to the audience portrait. Common sense helps, as does a sixth sense about human behavior and familiarity with a given population.

Turn next to the matrix for an orderly approach to audience analysis. Each of the nine cells addresses a critical set of questions that analysts should study. Start by thinking about the source as the candidate, the message as the campaign issues, and the channel as the media—mass, narrow and individual. For instance, candidate Louise is running for Congress on an environmentalist platform. She is using television and direct mail to get her message across. Candidate Bob is running against her and is stressing economic austerity. He uses lots of radio and telephone solicitations.

Sources: Candidates Louise and Bob.

Messages: Environmental and economic topics.

Channels: Television, direct mail, radio and telephone.

Now, consider these items (note: the checklist items correspond to the number in each cell of the matrix):

	Receiver		
	Source	Message	Channel
Knowledge	1	4	7
Attitudes	2	5	8
Behavior	3	6	9

Cell   **Questions for Analysis**

1. What do voters know about the candidate (source) and about the opposition candidate (source of competing messages). [What do they know about Louise and Bob?]

2. How do voters feel (what are their attitudes) toward these information sources?

3. What behaviors (past, present and anticipated) do voters enact toward these sources? [Did they vote for Louise or Bob last time? Do they plan to vote for Louise or Bob this time? Have they contributed to either candidate? Would they consider contributing?]

4. What do voters know about the issues (message)?[4] [What do they know about environmentalism and about economic matters? What other issues, not addressed by either candidate, do they find of interest?]

5. How do voters feel about these issues? [Do they like Louise's environmental stand? Why do they feel this way? How about Bob's economic arguments? Why? How do they feel about other issues?]

6. What behaviors do voters enact toward these issues? [Do they practice environmentalism? Do they vote for environmental propositions? Would they join a protest about budget cuts? Do they write letters about the deficit to local newspapers?]

7. What do voters know about the availability of information (channels)? [Have they heard of radio station WWWW? What about cable station WXYZ? Do they know that they can get candidate information from Project Vote Smart at (800) 786–6885?]

8. How do voters feel about these channels? [How do they feel about station WWWW? What do they like/dislike about personal letters from candidates?]

9. To what channels (media) are voters routinely exposed (behavior)? [What television stations do they watch? Have they received campaign mail? What radio stations do they listen to? When? Have they talked with campaign workers on the phone? What media do they usually follow? Which do they avoid?]

This series configures a targeted communication analysis. It lays out the major elements of audience alignment on the candidates, the issues and the information-bearing channels. It accommodates the formation of audience patterns and parcels by defining strata according to shared views. Furthermore, questions in each cell examine the agendas of the candidates, of the opposition and of the voters and thus provide a comprehensive view of audience perspectives.

Analysts begin with a wide-angle view, then partition the image the way an insect's compound eye separates the landscape. Analysts subdivide the audience into patterns and parcels—into audience clusters—on the basis of empirical data.

(Note: Appendix A contains additional information on the matrix approach to audience analyses.)

ANALYSIS TOOLS

Survey Data Analysis

Unlikely as it sounds, data analysts and chili cooks have something in common. Both search tirelessly for the perfect combination of ingredients, and each works differently from fellow analysts or cooks. You can teach both the basics, but when you let them loose, you know they'll tinker with different techniques and develop their own styles.

And so, in a review of data analytic techniques, it makes no sense to offer a recipe or to describe a routine with which to unwrap the many layers of audience information. Even if analysts did not cultivate personal styles, conditions in most races rarely would adapt to cookie-cutter methods.

Analysts and analyses differ from case to case, but most draw from a repertoire of techniques that sort, sift and crunch numbers to seek the meaning of polling data. Let's review the most common.

Frequency Distribution

Frequency distributions are simple counts of respondents offering each answer. For instance:

Response	Frequency		
	All Respondents		Without Don't knows
	Number	Percent	Percent
Excellent	480	40%	58%
Good	180	15%	21%
Fair	120	10%	14%
Poor	60	5%	7%
Don't Know	360	30%	--
	1,200	100%	100%

In this case, 480 people, or 40 percent, said the congressman is excellent, 180 (15%) said good and so forth. Several other bells and whistles can be added. For instance, remove the "don't knows" from the base, and predicate percentages only on people who volunteered an opinion. In this case,

Response	Frequency		
	All Respondents		Without Don't knows
	Number	Percent	Percent
Excellent	480	40%	58%
Good	180	15%	21%
Fair	120	10%	14%

Response	Frequency		
	All Respondents		Without Don't knows
	Number	Percent	Percent
Poor	60	5%	7%
Don't Know	360	30%	--
	1,200	100%	100%

Crosstabulations

This procedure is the second most often reported statistic. A crosstabulation (or crosstab) is nothing more than a frequency distribution for each element of a subgroup—males and females; young, middle-aged or older respondents; or Republicans and Democrats. A simple crosstab would look like this:

	Total Sample		Gender			
			Male		Female	
	N	%	N	%	N	%
Excel	204	30%	94	27%	110	33%
Good	238	35%	112	31%	126	39%
Fair	136	20%	80	23%	56	17%
Poor	102	15%	65	19%	37	11%
Total	680	100%	351	100%	329	100%

Data so displayed makes it easy to compare and contrast the responses of subgroups. In this case, women rate Congressman Gabby more favorably than do men. Thus begins the analysis—the pentage that sorts a population into groups of supporters, opponents and undecideds. Much more will be necessary, but simple crosstabs give a first-blush review of the data and flag paths that campaigns may later track.

An examination of crosstab tables provides a helpful first review of the data, but simple eyeballing does not allow an analyst to declare that there are meaningful and material differences among the elements. For instance, are there real differences—significant differences—between the responses of men and women? Does gender cleanly separate this sample into distinct, independent clusters or strata?

Such questions are answered through tests of significance; the chi-square test, for crosstabs, is most common. Chi-square is a test of independence, which means that it evaluates portions of a sample for independent responses or behavior patterns. For instance, do men and women hold significantly different views about a candidate or about policies? Do they have truly different voting or volunteer behaviors? Chi-square answers such questions about the association among subgroups. Most statistical packages can be instructed to calculate chi-square results separately or along with the preparation of crosstabulation tables.

Cluster Analysis

An inherent part of the search for patterns and parcels is the identification of audience subgroups (or clusters). Analysts look among the total population for the aggregation of like-minded souls who are likely to hold similar views and respond alike to marketing and persuasion appeals.

Cluster analysis refers to techniques that classify people into strata based on a collection of attitudes or behaviors. A cluster analysis may group survey respondents by their views on abortion, the environment, foreign policy and the deficit. It can group them on voting behaviors, contributions and volunteer activities—as long as there are such patterns within the sample.

These processes involve the identification of the strength (or nearness) of clusters. Analysts build larger clusters from smaller ones (agglomerative hierarchical) or break down larger clusters into smaller ones (divisive hierarchical). It is a step-wise process involving subjective judgments at each level—assessments made in part on the targeting capacity and plans of a campaign.

Cluster analyses, without computers, would be impossible. With the rapid improvement in hardware and statistical software, though, they are coming into popular use, particularly among the sophisticated and detail-oriented campaigns seeking to squeeze the last drop of information from their data. Of course, today's breakthroughs quickly become tomorrow's standards, so it is not unreasonable to believe that cluster analysis will become a familiar fixture of audience analysis within the near future. It also would not be surprising to find cluster analysis routines in future versions of campaign-in-the-box software.

Regression Analysis

Analysts predict voter attitudes or behaviors by evaluating characteristics related to those attitudes or behaviors. They may predict whether someone is for or against a tax referendum by knowing his income, education and occupation. Analysts can predict the occurrence of a dependent (or criterion) variable by examining the relationship of that variable to independent (or predictor) variables. One process that leads them to understand this relationship is called a regression analysis.

Based on what you know about voter income, education and occupation, suppose you wish to predict voter support for a tax hike. You have the key demographics on all of the voters in your district, and you wish to determine which people are most likely to support and which are most likely to oppose the referendum. You can approach this by conducting a poll that includes at least four items: the likelihood that a respondent will support the referendum (measured through one or a combination of questions) and the demographic data for income, education and occupation. Then, armed with a regression package, your analyst can derive an equation that explains the relative contribution of income level, education and occupation (independent variables) in predicting support for the tax hike (dependent variable). The equation tells you how to weigh the scores of the predictors to best estimate the criterion variable. From income, education and occupation, you will be able to determine the likelihood that subgroups will support the tax referendum.

Furthermore, from these results, you can assess the logic of retaining all the predictor variables or dropping those that contribute little to the overall explanation. For instance, occupation may explain little about preference for a tax hike, in which case you disregard it and concentrate on the remaining two demographic features.

Regression thus flags the key elements on which campaigns should logically focus communication efforts. If education and income are strong predictors of how people will vote on any given issue, you can concentrate targeted messages on appropriate voter segments within these categories. You can ignore occupational subgroups and, perhaps, other designations that do not explain much about how people feel. Regression benefits communication analysis by accenting voter characteristics most likely to yield positive results. It establishes a priority and contributes to decisions about the allocation of scarce campaign resources.

Like cluster analysis, regression analysis would not be possible without computers. There are too many mathematical calculations for even the most volunteer-blessed campaigns, and what would take a millennium for the human mind takes but a moment for the silicon chip. Technology has indeed contributed regression analysis to campaign investigations and decisions.

Other powerful multivariate techniques—whereby several voter characteristics are considered simultaneously—include factor analysis, discriminate analysis, analysis of variance and path analysis. The analyst's quiver is filled with an assortment of data assessment techniques, all of them possible because computers process millions of calculations in the time it takes an average reader to scan this sentence.

The speed and capacity of computers have made it possible to store data once warehoused in notebooks and on scraps of paper. In this storage capacity, computers have streamlined a function that, while possible, would be a backbreaking task.

In their analytic role, however, computers have added something entirely new. Never before could campaigns run the kinds of sophisticated, multivariate analyses used in today's races. As a result, political communicators enjoy a sixth sense about the electorate. With growing numbers of voters and the increasing speed of communications—which greatly expands the repertoire of issues with which voters and candidates alike must deal—computers will be necessary to keep pace in twenty-first-century campaigns. Exhaustive data analyses are essential to disclose all that surveys and databases have to offer. Although such data investigations were launched only a few years ago at most campaign levels, there is every indication that the processes will grow more detailed through the next decade and become more rigorous with every campaign cycle.

Survey researchers explore voter populations the way an army lookout explores an unknown hillside. They both keep a head up for clues and signs, and they both seek to learn all they can about the lay of the land. They look for the best course and flag the worst quagmires. When their work is done, the troops know the terrain and have a sense for the course ahead.

Database work follows on the heels of survey analyses which have charted the course. Polls describe the friends and foes of a campaign, and databases yield the names and addresses of people who fit the profiles. Polls reveal how voters cluster around given issues, and databases yield the fitting demographic matches to form specific targets. Among identified subgroups, polls tell which issues are hot and which are not, and databases lend the specifics that put campaign communicators on the trail of individual voters. Databases are the link between the abstract calculations of survey results and the voters who make concrete decisions on election day.

Database Analysis

If surveys are the engineering laboratories, air-conditioned and squeaky clean, then databases are the steamy assembly plants where voters are sorted and selected into prepackaged clusters. Database work is remarkably efficient: It instructs a computer to assemble groups of voters, compile the lists and send them to the loading dock.

Suppose a survey analysis showed that a tax referendum was strongly supported by people over 50 with higher incomes and educations. Low-income, younger voters, meanwhile, were uncertain about the matter. Accordingly, you draw from campaign databases a group comprised of 50 and older, college-educated voters earning over $55,000. Then, draw one of 35-and-under voters earning less than $22,000. That separates supporters from undecideds. Now, with a few simple commands, database programs can sort among voter lists and assemble the two groups into individual files. With the two targets clearly in focus, staffers can have the computer insert the names and addresses (and a lot more personal information) into targeted letters and integrate the names, phone numbers and other specifics into personalized telephone solicitation programs.

Since databases also show addresses, revealing geographic clusters of voter groups, your campaign can guide the placement of billboards, the distribution of handbills and the visitations of volunteers. Efficient, isn't it? And, since polling data and published media statistics reveal the media habits of these two groups, you also know how to place broadcast and newspaper ads.

But wait, there is one flashy innovation in the database business that will drop your jaw. Imagine this: Poll results for a senatorial campaign reveal large blocks of uncommitted voters among middle-aged, blue-collar registered Republicans. It's a hot group both campaigns will stalk early in the campaign. All very well, but where are these people located throughout the state? By no means a trivial question, it matters because geography offers direction for media buys, volunteer efforts, personal campaign visits and the allocation of scarce resources.

The candidate could examine voter address lists, summary charts by county, frequency counts within metropolitan statistical areas, or pen-and-ink maps painstakingly drafted by interns and bleary-eyed volunteers. But, besides being a headache, abstract lists require a lot of inventiveness and provide little intuitive information. Handcrafted maps take enormous staff time and offer only fragmented information about limited geographic areas.

The jaw-dropping solution? In the early nineties, a treasure trove of visual information became available through a generation of computer mapping programs. This sophisticated, tabletop computer software—developed first for land and forest analysis—draws addresses from any standard database and projects them onto national, state, regional and local maps. The software found an instant home in political campaigns. MapInfo, by Mapping Information Systems, for instance, was used extensively in the 1992 races.[5]

How do mapping programs help the senatorial candidate who wants to examine the location of middle-aged, blue-collar Republicans? With a few simple keystrokes, campaign workers instruct the program to display the location of all such voters on a state map. The density of these households appear in different colors—say areas of 10 to 20 percent concentration in blue, 21 to 30 percent in green, and more than 31 percent in red.

But, the state is a large platform. Look closer. With another keystroke, MapInfo flashes a single city. The screen fills with neighborhood concentrations of middle-aged, blue-collar Republicans displayed in living color. Zoom in on just one neighborhood? Why not? A keystroke, and a preselected neighborhood fills the screen, the blocks glowing with concentrations of the targeted group. Finally, zoom down to the block level to see which sides of each street have middle-aged, blue-collar Republicans. Instantly fly over other blocks and neighborhoods, cities, regions or any geographic area. Look at any combination of traits, refine the range (e.g., from 40 to 60-year-olds to 40 to 50 and 51 to 60-year-olds), alter the density of the categories in which they are presented (e.g., from 10 percent concentrations to 5).

The program can project any voter characteristic contained in the database. It can display voting history, income, education, strength of candidate support (a different color each for strong and moderate supporters, another for the undecideds), who received a personal call, who got a campaign letter (and which version). Run combinations and permutations of variables—the possibilities are endless. And, as Al Jolson shouted, "You ain't seen nothin' yet!"

Sensing the value of geographic images, and confirming the merit of this data display technique, the U.S. Census Bureau has configured its massive 1990 databases to integrate easily into commercial mapping programs. It bills the TIGER/Line (T/L) files as a special product with "geographic coordinates and codes, enabling you to create maps for a variety of areas" ("Census" 1992, p. 20). The T/L files are organized by state and display a great range of population data down to the block level.[6]

Mapping, of course, is not limited to use by political campaigns. In fact, the largest users are commercial companies, municipalities, law-enforcement agencies, universities, the media and nonprofit organizations. With new users and new uses, mapping companies are now scrambling to evolve new products along with new client needs. Imagine what lies ahead.

CONCLUSION

Imagine, indeed. In a handful of years, the analyses of voting populations have gone beyond the dreams of the canniest campaign professionals. The computer has expanded the range of analytic options to the point that no campaign can ignore its techniques. The wealth of a campaign matters little, since equipment costs are so low. Moreover, simplicity of the software has lowered the threshold of expertise, so even the nonexpert has easy access to these extraordinary machines.

Computers allow campaigns to pick the lock on the treasure chest of audience information. Audience views and behaviors, once sealed away from all eyes, now are laid bare for all who would spend the time to analyze the data. There is little about an audience today that a campaign cannot uncover.

The many databases available today complete the process. These individual files dovetail with polling analyses and allow campaigns to apply intelligence information to specific voters. With more computers and more analyses, there is an increasing need for more databases. Private merchants are increasing their inventory, and individual campaigns are building their own. Bought or homegrown, databases are a growth industry.

And yet, behind the brass bands and the cheers for a brave new world, one can hear the distant sirens of caution. It is difficult to sate an appetite for information. As campaigns add facts and figures to their databases, they find a need for yet additional facts and figures. The need grows with the capacity to use the information.

The analysis of an audience is good for a campaign, but what does it do to the subjects whose views and behaviors go under the microscope? What about the voter whose personal information is scanned, sorted, bartered, traded and fortified with yet other personal information? How does all this affect individual voters?

How does this mega-information affect the press, whose job it has been since the birth of the republic to serve as unofficial observers and moderators in political debates? Have the communications that flow from these analyses become too targeted, too directed to individuals and small groups for the fourth estate to access and evaluate? If the national press is being replaced by the pop culture of Larry King, and if volunteer campaign workers are being instructed by the Hals of *2001*, what hath the computer wrought?

These fears shake the timbers of the political system itself and the government that ultimately forms from the political process. Are audience analysis and voter segmentation and laser-guided communication society's worst nightmare come true?

These are haunting questions for the chapters ahead.

NOTES

1. David Shaw, "Inventing the 'Paper' of the Future," *Los Angeles Times*, June 2, 1992, p. A1.

2. Conventional survey research also tends to impose a candidate's agenda on respondents, as they ask questions dealing with a closed set of issues. This discussion attempts to modify that approach although it, too, suffers some of the same problems.

A project now on the drawing boards approaches audience information from a very different perspective. It gives the respondent complete control of the topics, while promoting productive discussions. This American Conversations project is planned for the 1996 presidential campaign.

3. There are clever ways to cultivate environments supportive of desirable voter

attitudes, which then allow the introduction of information about program details (knowledge). For instance, it may be helpful to foster a public attitude toward environmentalism, and more specifically recycling, and then introduce specific re-cycling programs. In this case, the specific attitude does not precede the knowledge of a particular program; an attitude conducive to reception of the specific proposal is created.

4. Messages, of course, can be about any subject. Many are about the candidate (source) covered in the first column. We take a narrower view here and interpret the message to concern non-candidate issues.

5. These companies also offer mapping software: Intermap Inc. (product name: Descartes), GeoQuery (product name: GeoQuery) and Strategic Mapping, Inc. (product name: Atlas Map-Maker).

6. The U.S. Bureau of the Census reports that the complete set of U.S. digital map data is contained on forty-four disks. They are organized by state and cost $250 per disk. The T/L data are presented in ASCII format, and each disk contains technical documentation, the census codes and a name reference file.

Part II

Effects of the New Technologies

From one perspective, the use of technology has closed the gap between the voters and the candidates. Computers, polls and databases combine to chisel out a reasonable likeness of individual voters. This "personal knowledge" has enabled candidates to acquire again a sense of intimacy once cultivated through interpersonal settings. But, instead of notes scribbled on the backs of envelopes, the information today is coded, categorized, classified and presented in a form that can be assembled into snapshot views of any chosen subgroup, even individual voters.

Individual-level information allows individual-level communication. Building on the blocks of personal facts and traits, campaigns craft messages that match a voter's profile the way one side of a DNA molecule matches the other. Young parents are matched with child-care information, the elderly with information about a candidate's defense of social security, hunters with news of NRA endorsements. Voter characteristics and voter-directed communications are matched then fastened into one seamless weld that bonds contemporary political campaigns with voters.

This has all the appearance of a twenty-first-century answer to a twenty-first-century condition. Nobody—not politicians, not salespeople, not even the clergy—retains the rapport once known when life was slower, before television, before jet transportation, before two-worker families and the other trappings that separate and isolate us all. McLuhan's world may have imploded, but that hasn't brought us closer together. The Global Village, wired in and totally in touch, is not a more intimate place.

By any technical measure, communication has never been faster or better. But, one could argue that the effects are not nearly as impressive as the advances.

This is not another indictment of modern media. A lot of ink has been spilled to describe television as a virus, breeding its ills of shallow-mindedness and vulgarity throughout society. Ever since hometown newspapers became chains, say the critics, they have lacked their former depth and insights—and besides, nobody reads them anymore.[1] *USA Today*, not the *New York Times*, has become print journalism's symbol of the future. There was a time when we could wait until the morning papers to learn who won an election; now, the media tell us before the polls close.

Well, as some sage once said, the future is not what it used to be, but it is foolish to argue for a return to the good old days, which were never as good then as they seem now. My sense is that real human communications—even on a mass scale—can be as effective and efficient as communications ever have been. But, one thing is certain: The greater the power of modern communications—especially the intrusive ones—the greater the pitfalls. Lord Acton said of politics: "Power tends to corrupt, and absolute power corrupts absolutely." Surely the marriage of computer power to political power should alert us to the possibilities of corruption.

Today, campaigns amass an impressive file of facts and figures about voters. They always have, but while we have identified similarities in information collection and maintenance between campaigns past and present, there really are differences. Two stand out.

First are the methods used to gather voter information. Information collected in former times, sometimes scrawled on the back of a napkin, but generally organized in a notebook or on file cards, usually came from interactions with the subject. The process was tactile and personal and involved one-on-one exchanges. The information was contextual and it was shaded, if ever so slightly, from one subject to the next. By contrast, contemporary data gathering is rarely personal, tactile or contextual. It is often assembled from a mosaic of sources whose bits and pieces are fastened together electronically.

Second, the notion that current data files are merely electronic correlates of pencil-and-paper files may be a helpful description, but it is misleading. In pre-computer days, candidates could develop a sense of familiarity with voters. Is it possible for a candidate—or anyone—to know the voters by reading today's compilation of dry statistics? Summary data, polling results, even verbatim comments collected in focus groups and telephone interviews are synthesized information bites that only index voter thinking. They provide categories and clues, but they cannot develop individual thinking nor can they unfold the nuances of concerns and interests. The use of such abstract information allows only a quick rendering of voter views and public passions; it does not provide the detail necessary to paint a fine portrait.

Nevertheless, we must deal with the reality of the world in the 1990s. With tens of thousands and tens of millions of voters, it is no longer possible to "work the crowds" for personal, flesh-and-blood impressions. What polls can do is acquire representative voter information more complete and more revealing of individual impressions than the old pols could dream of. So why knock it? Constructing even these modest files consumes enormous energy and represents a courageous effort by political campaigns to understand their audiences. What more would we have them do, given the realities of mass society?

In the past twenty-five years we have gone from one-size-fits-all political mass communications to targeted political mass communication. Hasn't the progression been good, and isn't the current approach of focused, selected, directed information better than the shotgun deliveries of bygone days when one portion of an audience was treated pretty much the same as another?

It would be difficult to deny the improvements in political communication for information senders and information receivers alike. The focus is on the individual, there is less clutter with irrelevant messages and there is more efficiency in the analysis of target audience needs. One could argue that routine audience monitoring contributes to a more efficient form of representative government, since the voters are routinely polled for their views.

But there are also onerous consequences of the process. First, individual voters are affected when their personal information is bought, sold and traded in the database flea market. Individual privacy is assaulted throughout the political season. Personal statistics, laid bare, render voters vulnerable to manipulation, and this simultaneously attacks the individual and, thus, the political process at its most elementary level.

Second, campaign press coverage is affected in subtle, but substantive ways. Several leading national political journalists interviewed for this discussion expressed frustration at the pigeonholing of information. It is not possible to monitor dozens of individual messages fired at dozens of individual voter groups, and so the capacity of the press to trace the candidate's communication salvos has been greatly diminished.

The spoon-fed syndrome is also at play. This occurs when campaigns give reporters select information tidbits while they quietly distribute different information parcels to important voter blocks. It is easier to report the releases and the leaks than it is to pound out a story based on information acquired from an arduous ten rounds with tight-lipped campaign staffs. Such extraordinary effort saddles additional demands on already burdened reporters, whose numbers are being reduced by an industry-wide belt tightening.

During the 1992 campaign, candidates at all levels and from all parties discovered how helpful fax machines were in this effort to spoon-feed reporters. National Public Radio (NPR) described the vastly popular technique of "power faxing"—the procedure of sending a single message simultaneously to hundreds of media—which allows campaigns to initiate communications and to respond instantly to charges by the opposition. NPR described how power faxing accommodates those reporters who wish to write impressive charge-response-countercharge stories without making a call or leaving their armchairs. This makes for good copy because it projects a sense of closure, it showcases a reporter's research abilities and it denies the competition a coveted scoop. Of course, it also standardizes campaign coverage, it loses the rich shades and colors brushed by different reporters working with different sources and it allows campaigns to control a bit more the information they release. None of this benefits the readers, viewers and voters, some of whom seek a less packaged, standardized truth.

In all fairness, National Public Radio was quick to note that many reporters refuse to be seduced by the power fax or to let the information blitz interfere with their aggressive data gathering techniques.

The question is, will diminishing resources in the industry allow the best intentioned reporters to continue their research unfettered by these convenient distractions? As NPR suggested, many reporters already have been tainted. The hope is that journalism schools and the media will compensate quickly enough to deny the influences of tempting, hermetically packaged, high-tech campaign communications.

Finally, the electoral process has taken serious hits. Recent demands for system reform portray office seekers who have become Lone Rangers, abandoning the party and escaping the moderating influences the parties once imposed on candidates. There are benefits to unlocking party shackles, but do they outweigh the drawbacks now surfacing?

Furthermore, campaigns are fixating on single issues. In the process, the emerging image of the candidate may not represent his true character and breadth. The sum of the visible parts may not equal the whole of the candidate's beliefs. There is more to know about a candidate than the simple addition of his views on an assortment of hot topics.

As a result of campaign events, government itself is affected. Campaign promises have a life beyond election day. Pledges and IOUs, scattered like wild seed among constituents, sprout in due time, and these often affect the way officials govern. Political leaders may become trapped by conflicting vows or hamstrung over promises made to narrow-interest groups in the heat of campaign battles. By appealing to an antitax constituency in the 1980 campaign, Ronald Reagan started and George Bush was compelled to continue a policy that contributed to a massive debt frustrating all government operations. Promises to unremitting antiabortion groups positioned the Bush administration awkwardly before a population clearly in favor of a woman's right to choose. Had Michael Dukakis, Walter Mondale or, years earlier, George McGovern prevailed, their captivity to liberal, but warring special-interest groups could have undercut the ability to govern for the common good. Bill Clinton tiptoed away from many traditional liberal traditions during his campaign and struck out on a more moderate position. He may have done this to win back the "Reagan Democrats," but the approach also kept him from making too many promises that could return to haunt him.

Major national-level campaigns have used computers and survey research for several decades, but these technologies have been in the hands of local and regional campaigns for only a few years. It wasn't until the mid–1980s—when the IBM XT and 286 machines hit the streets—that the equipment came into popular use. Before that, hardware didn't have the capacity and software didn't have the flexibility (or intuitive ease of use) to be of much value to mom-and-pop campaigns. Computer power expands every year, and software becomes better and easier to use. All this and "user-friendly" to boot means the inevitable acceleration of high-tech campaigning.

Three chapters in this section discuss implications of the new technologies for political communications. Given the paucity of empirical research, I will draw from case studies and from the reasoned opinions of professionals. Political consultants, journalists, media analysts and others give their opinions. You can evaluate their wisdom for lessons on how the technologies affect individual voters, media coverage and, finally, the political system and government.

A NOTE ABOUT CULPABILITY

Theodore Tronchin once said that the sins of commission were mortal and the sins of omission venial. Both are sins, only one is worse than the other. There should be such a distinction of magnitude in these discussions by noting the differences between what political candidates mean to bring about and what they actually bring about.

There is no evidence that anyone in the political arena wishes the disturbing side effects of the new technologies. Most don't even recognize the problems resulting from their activities. Tronchin could find no mortal offenses.

Still, there is this matter of the victims: the voters, the press, the political system, the operations of government. Can harmful ends be derived from noble intentions? Of course. People drive automobiles because it serves their transportation needs. The environment suffers nonetheless from these joint decisions. Individually, people indulge in innocent practices that collectively deplete the ozone, erode the soil and sour the waters. One need not wish to harm for the ends to be harmful.

A small but growing number of candidates may suspect developing side effects from the technologies, but for now, even these will find peace in the innocence of their intentions. They mean no harm and feel no guilt.

The "diffusion of responsibility" rationale also can salve a conscience: If everyone is guilty, then everyone is innocent. Everyone pollutes the environment, but we disperse the blame and the guilt among millions of offenders. Where is the personal guilt for the collective violation?

Such thinking figures in many discussions of political ethics. It is particularly evident in considerations of the new technologies. In the 1990s, candidates must accept the high-tech campaign tools. If they choose to join the political battle, they must bear the political swords and shields.

Thus forms the resolution of dissonance and the dispersion of guilt. Intentions are noble. The ends justify the means. Ill effects are the fault of everyone and of no one.

In the final frame, we will be left with this frustrating irony: Polling and computer technologies, so helpful to a political campaign, are damaging the political system and menacing the voters. At the same time, few political candidates may see the problem. Those who do escape a sense of personal culpability through soothing rationalizations.

NOTE

1. Newspaper readership statistics are not encouraging. Philip E. Meyer, at the School of Journalism and Mass Communication at the University of North Carolina, reports that 73 percent of the population read a daily newspaper in 1967. The figure dropped to 51.5 percent in 1991 (Jones 1992).

The real problem is in the demographics. Older Americans, steeped in a newspaper reading tradition, are dying off, and young people are not picking up the habit. Citing work by Jon Katz, a writer for *Rolling Stone*, John Leo writes, "This is a generational issue: 'The people watching and reading are aging and dying, and the young no longer take their place' " (Leo 1992).

Chapter Seven

Effects on Voters

With all the electronic computers . . . and the flashing numbers and percentages, one can lose sight of the essential fact of any election. And that is the mind of the voter.

—Eric Sevareid,
CBS News Commentary,
November 2, 1958

By definition, a democracy demands more of its people than do other forms of government which look to the elite. Lincoln's words "of the people, by the people, for the people" have more than poetic appeal. They express his abiding hope for the active involvement of citizens in government. John Adams, one of the principal architects of the Constitution, made this early appeal for the "people to erect the whole building with their own hands, upon the broadest foundation . . . by conventions of representatives chosen by the people."

The founders further guaranteed the public access to information. The Virginia Declaration of Rights, a seminal document for the American Bill of Rights, described citizens not only as the benefactors of government, but as custodians of it as well.[1] The Virginia document recognized that this custodial function required an uninhibited public access to information and accordingly affirmed a free press.[2] This provision was echoed by the Pennsylvania statement on individual liberties which furnished the companion right of free speech. Both guarantees—free press and free speech—became fixtures in the first amendment to the U.S. Constitution.

Thus, in the deepest foundations of this democracy lie the stones of liberty and obligation. The liberty to produce, distribute and access information fundamental to the democracy sits squarely on the citizens' custodial obligations to the government. From the beginning, the liberty and the obligation were understood to be mutually dependent. The years have proven this to be a valid expectation.

We also have come to believe that if citizens enjoy free access to information, they will have the good sense to make the best choices. This is a central tenet of a democracy. It speaks to our faith in the informed wisdom of the masses (moderated by the republican vision of representative power) which we always have believed is sounder than the isolated judgments of a crowned ruler.

This thinking reflects confidence in the hearts and minds of individuals to choose representatives (free to vote their consciences), while it settles a weight of responsibility firmly on their shoulders.[3] It also ensures a largely unqualified right to information which fuels the system. It expresses a trust that people will discern the good from the bad information, the useful from the useless, the reliable from the frivolous, and at the end recognize the best solution. Through the informational cacophony, the founders trusted that the people would hear the sweet tune of reason and, for the good of the republic, elect the best representatives to arrive at the wisest judgments.

This ideal, of course, does not always work out in practice. Indeed, it sets the stage for cynicism. In the free marketplace of information, the truth does not always get equal time. The blend of facts may be distorted, the priority of items on the public agenda may be turned on its head. The true and best information may be crowded out.

The legendary *New York Times* publisher Arthur Hays Sulzberger once said that a person's "judgment cannot be better than the information on which he has based it." Sulzberger saw his newspaper as an instrument for better public judgments, but we see a condition evolving in political campaigns today that prevents even the toughest investigative reporters from presenting "all the news that's fit to print."

Where journalists once easily monitored the political exchange between a candidate and the voters, it now is becoming increasingly difficult or, in many cases, impossible to do so. The recognition that campaign information can go without press scrutiny understandably makes many reporters nervous.

The inability of the watchdogs to sniff out each message does not suggest the messages in each case are foul. Lack of scrutiny does, however, increase the chance that a tainted message can slip through unnoticed and so tempt some campaigns to take liberties that they otherwise would avoid.

When that happens, new technology-driven communications merely increase the potential for inaccurate and incomplete campaign information—so subtly, sometimes, that it may not even be recognized by a campaign as distorted. The temptation is there to make the case more persuasive.

Accordingly, campaigns are known to present unimportant details in life-and-death terms, they assault the opposition to dodge discussion of their own weak record—that is the smoke-screen strategy. They can invert the priority of public issues.

Recent campaigns have been filled with these tactics. Despite the Soviet collapse, right-wing groups continue to flail the dead horse of communism, warning against its reincarnation in other forms and in other places. Left-wingers see plots against every minority, and anyone who disagrees with their demagoguery is racist, sexist or politically incorrect. A candidate's experimentation with marijuana, involvement in check bouncing, service in Vietnam, conduct of extramarital romances are hyped and elevated among certain groups, while discussions of the national debt, environmental disasters, poverty and crime go begging for attention. While these distortions can and do sprout even in the most sun-drenched public forums—in open debate and in major media—they blossom in the dark shadows of the information pigeonholes where candidates meet the voters one-on-one.

Sulzberger's cautions about the quality of information on which public judgments about political candidates are made must be taken to heart. If the computer-driven, targeted campaign communications throw dust in people's eyes, will voters have the wisdom to clear their vision, to sort out the right information, the salient bits and pieces, in order to make the wisest decisions?

As with most public questions, two goods collide. On the positive side, technology-driven communications may invite into the process peripheral voters who otherwise would choose to keep politics at arm's length. Even with no inherent interest in the general political process, they may be tempted by an appeal to their special interests. The threat to control guns, fear of losing the right to an abortion, anger over a decision to strip-mine national parks may be just the lures to attract some political outsiders into a race.

On the negative side, voters may fix on a single panel while failing to broaden their concern for the full patchwork quilt that makes up a campaign. A limited interest may be better than no interest at all, but one also could argue that such parochialism distorts the political process.

The new communications create real problems for voters. First, they may trample an individual's right to privacy as campaigns slog through files looking for revealing personal traits. In order to distinguish between what society has come to accept as a "normal" level of revelations and a more serious intrusion into personal lives, we will need to consider the size and use of a data stockpile. We also must consider the means by which this information is obtained. The shifty nature of some data gathering is alarming.

There are other risks. Sophisticated data gathering and analysis allow campaigns to manipulate individual sensitivities by means of million-dollar strategies that play on emotions. The techniques take aim at segmented and isolated groups and aggressively pitch voters with one-on-one communications.

BRINGING IN THE VOTERS

Sandra Haskins went to college, got decent grades, participated in the student government association but never became involved in politics. She didn't vote, didn't follow the issues, didn't care about who won or lost. Most of the time, she didn't even know the candidates' names. She graduated in the early 1990s, got a job at a large brokerage firm and, for the first time, enjoyed life as a single working woman with a few dollars in her pocket. Politics meant less to her than sun damage to the paint job on her new BMW.

During the congressional election of 1992, Sandra got a letter from a candidate who spelled out the personal implications of the Supreme Court's decision on abortion. It was very personal. It noted specifically her college education and her new professional status. It said that, as a single woman, she should be concerned about the Court's decision and its implications on her right to choose in such matters. It described how options now were withering from a process that began under Reagan in the eighties and ended at the hands of a Reagan/Bush Supreme Court in the nineties.

The sender of the letter promised to do something in Washington about a woman's right to choose, and he asked for Sandra's help—help with her vote, help with her check.

Sandra sent $25 and thereby ensured her continued relationship with the campaign. Throughout the election season, she received additional information about developments on the abortion issue, notices about abortion rallies, announcements for abortion discussion groups and a stream of information about the candidate's stand on the abortion issue.

Unbeknownst to Sandra, database searches had identified her as a primary target for the candidate's special abortion appeal. There were other special packages—on health care, child care, foreign competition—but Sandra fit the demographic profile for the abortion pitch, and her early response earned her a subscription to follow-up mailings and calls.

As a result, Sandra became interested in something political. This had never happened before. Throughout the campaign, she followed the abortion issue, even met with others concerned about it, and she carefully watched the stock of her candidate with the hope that his election might affect the Washington power balance on abortion. She became another citizen brought into the political fold. Score one for democracy, right?

Yes, and also wrong. This is good, yes, but is it all good? What about the other issues in the campaign? Through targeted communications, the candidate discussed abortion matters with Sandra, but he didn't talk about much else. He had positions on a dozen matters, appealing to other voter blocks with other special interests. What about the whole picture of the candidate? The answer is prudential. Some of those positions might have repelled her as solidly as abortion had attracted her. Was Sandra affected by these other issues? If so, she would have had to look beyond the candidate's one-on-one, abortion-specific communications. Finally, there is a matter of proportion. Promoting abortion as THE issue serves only to reinforce a voter's narrow focus. It overshadows the other topics.

Although this is a fictitious account, it is not an unrealistic description of a common event in contemporary political communications. For individual voter blocks, campaigns often drive home one issue to the exclusion of the others. In the process, the voter is offered an agenda that may not reflect either the range or the importance of issues relevant to an election. Voters are pigeonholed and pounded with specific, directed messages, and over time, they come to fix on a single concern.

What about all the other media, all the other candidates with their directed communication campaigns and all the other opinions found within the voter's circle of friends? Doesn't the net effect of these provide a more accurate range and balance of information?

For many people, it does, but for a sizable portion of the electorate, it does not. Some people would rather listen to a single message, particularly if it is designed just for them. That is where the strength of targeted communication really lies. The lack of exposure to political stories in this, the most media-soaked, information-rich society ever to occupy the earth, can be seen in recent surveys. Newspaper readership is down considerably. The average person spends less than one hour per week reading a newspaper, compared to 2.5 hours in 1965 (Robinson 1990). Moreover, only about half the population takes the time to read a paper, whereas three out of four did so in 1965 (McLeod 1992). Researchers at Young and Rubicam report that "the decline in newspaper reading over the last three decades has been one of the steadiest and most pronounced trends in the free-time behavior of the American public" (Robinson 1990). Not only is the audience and the time spent with newspapers diminishing, but a troubling pattern of readership became evident as early as a decade ago. "The readership pattern is clear. Most people turn to the least taxing, most entertaining sections first, glance at the front page and then stop . . . most newspaper readers are not very interested in news" (Sandman, Rubin and Sachsman, 1982, p. 263).

In the mid-sixties, television replaced newspapers as the primary news source for most Americans—reducing complex issues to sound bites—but even this medium no longer holds sway with the rank and file. Writer John Leo (1992) reports in *U.S. News & World Report* that the decline in newspaper reading is matched by a similar decline in viewing patterns for television news. With cable choices so abundant, people are turning away from news altogether and, instead, watching nonnews alternatives. So many choose "I Love Lucy" and "Gilligan's Island" over Peter Jennings and Dan Rather. Media experts make the point that, since Americans do not immerse themselves in the rich information environment, they become particularly vulnerable to the single-issue, direct-impact messages generated in targeted political campaigns.

Targeters first discover, then fix on your special interest. For people like Sandra without a strong visceral interest in politics and in foreign and domestic issues, there may be some appeal in following a single, highly charged and well-defined issue. For them, the other topics may not much matter. Even in the 1992 election, with the upswing in voting nationwide (a surrogate measure of voter interest in politics), the public did not show great interest in the candidates' or the press' serious discussion of the big issues. The *Columbia Journalism Review* examined this issue for the 1992 campaign. It says there was a

crushing consensus about what is, and what is not, subject to political debate. George Bush can be attacked for proposing a capital gains tax cut, and Bill Clinton hailed (or assailed) for proposing a tiny increase in the top rate, without any sustained reporting on the overall tax burden in the U.S., on how little Americans get for their taxes, or on how none of the candidates proposes to do anything about the widening gap between the rich and the poor.[4]

This is one way of saying that many voters are disinterested in the big issues confronting society.

One of the goals of technology-driven communication programs is to find those people, identify their passions and hit hard the issues that really stimulate them. That does not cultivate a well-rounded voter, but it may be enough to attract someone to the polls. Such voters may not listen to the whole orchestra, but they lend a close ear to the fiddles playing their tune.

Sandra's case pinpoints the effects of single-issue targeting. To one degree or another, the lessons from that example carry over to most other "persuadable" voters typically sought by targeted communication campaigns. Although many of the persuadables may read the papers, watch television news and form general political opinions from the panoply of information that blankets American homes, they are not sufficiently committed to any candidate or position. Thus, they are "persuadable." In these cases, targeted strategies can make a difference. They can clarify an issue and plant it at the top of a voter's agenda.

A Washington political consultant told me that campaigns count on aggressive targeted programs to find the buttons that, once pushed, get "persuadables" to fix on a topic. By virtue of the targeting concept, that means different agendas for different voter groups. The purpose of a campaign, the consultant said, is not to offer a broad education for voters, but to focus them on the issue that will land their votes.[5]

The verdict? Flip a coin—one side is shiny, and the other is tarnished. On the shiny side, citizens disenfranchised from politics may be stimulated to participate in a system they otherwise would avoid. Voters uncommitted to a candidate or to a position may discover a newfound interest in an issue hit by the targeted campaign. Clearly, these effects are beneficial to the democracy. They can stimulate citizen interest in government, and they can expand the base of the democracy. Remember Sandra's disinterest before abortion caught her attention.

The tarnish forms from the distortion of voter perceptions. No campaign, and certainly no public office, involves just a single issue, and yet these targeted approaches often focus on only one. This can dominate voter concerns the way a toothache dominates your feelings. Even when the voter's agenda is more complete, these strategies can distort issues by looking at only one side of a discussion or amplifying the significance of trivial items. It is an easy political hit, for instance, to strike at the salaries of federal workers, even though the small cuts a candidate may propose would be insignificant in dealing with the colossal budget deficit. A candidate's draft status during the Vietnam War, personal relationships and religious beliefs are trivial in light of the weighty issues facing the country. Yet, federal pay, the draft, family life and religion are easier and more effective in targeted communications than dealing with the demanding and difficult subjects about which the candidate may have not a clue or only painful solutions. Is it selling the Sandras short to say, a priori, that her interest in the right to choose precludes any wider concern, any broader vision?

The trouble with this distortion becomes apparent when the campaign is over, when the newly elected official must deal with the real slate of issues. How important are all the little matters that preoccupied the targeted campaigns? Even the significant topics now become part of a blend that compels the official's attention. Will the officeholder's preoccupations match the expectations generated within each group? That often is a tall order, and when it cannot be filled, people feel betrayed.

Candidate Ross Perot was right about one thing. He pointed out that in 1988, when Democrats and Republicans were mudslinging on flags and wimps, the savings and loan scandal was a known fact. Today, every American can look at that $500 billion river of debt and ask, "Why didn't somebody tell us?" So, what about all the demanding issues never discussed in a campaign? Did voters know where the candidate stood? Is there confusion about why the official now must deal with them and not with the flashy but narrow topics so hot during the campaign? These matters sow deep seeds that, in time, germinate into voter anger and contempt for the system.

PRIVACY ISSUES

Candidates' privacy is a casualty of an open society. The courts allow no limits (outside of libel) on intrusion into the lives of the well known, but what about the rest of us? Have we no rights, no control over the personal details in our lives? The answer is, not much. Never before has so much information about so many people been known to so many computers. For pocket change, a candidate can rent a stack of lists, join them with voter registration information and other data and amass a substantial personal portfolio for every individual in a region. Without an individual's permission or even awareness, intimate details are bartered and traded among list brokers and political operatives. There are no practical limitations to these information swap meets, nor are there adequate safeguards to govern the use of the personal data.

What does it mean when scattered information is assembled into a unified database? Do bits and pieces of data, when joined into a single frame, reveal an image that people have a right to keep secret? These questions are neither trivial nor academic. They tap a fundamental right to privacy and the privilege to be known only by those we choose to know us. Where does the unbounded acquisition and assembly of personal information fit into these protections? Does the need to improve political communication justify this violation?

Years before computer technology was known, Ayn Rand wrote, "Civilization is the progress toward a society of privacy. The savage's whole existence is public, ruled by the laws of his tribe. Civilization is the process of setting man free from men" (Rand 1943).

Clearly, the unregulated use of computers does not suggest a civilization progressing toward privacy. In an effort to improve the efficiency and effectiveness of political campaigns, the people who write the laws are involved in a process that challenges the security of private citizens. Whether or not the process chips away at the foundations of civilization envisioned by Rand is another matter. In less than a decade, technologies have reached an alarming level of sophistication, and they are rapidly evolving.

An ethical concern for personal privacy begins in the data collection process itself. It asks these questions: Should political campaigns be permitted to collect, aggregate and act on the growing volumes of data now becoming available? At what point does the activity intrude on the right to privacy? When does a database reach a critical mass and become so complete that it imposes an unacceptable threat, not only to individuals, but to the common weal?

Do people know their dossiers are being assembled in order to render them better targets of political messages? Would they choose to have their voting records, purchasing activities, life-style characteristics and demographic data accessed then mapped, charted and outlined for campaign workers and persuasion strategists? Should they be given a choice? News magazines, "60 Minutes" and other television investigative shows have begun examinations of such intrusions in commerce—as with TRW's master dossier on the American consumer, especially the matter of credit ratings— but no one has blown the whistle on politics.

The first step in dealing with these ethical concerns is to raise the issue for public discussion. Not enough has been written or aired about the topic in the popular press. One or two TV shows will not alert Americans to information about their unwitting participation. The recipient of a political letter, phone call or visitation is unlikely to understand what complex technology has made it possible for the communication to be so extraordinarily convincing and precise. Maybe people are flattered that Ed McMahon and their congressman know their names. Before new developments permit further refinement and improvement of targeted persuasion techniques, it is time to let the public in on the process. Voters should be told about the databases, their origins, contents and applications. They should understand that important features of their lives are being used to make them more susceptible to campaign merchandising.

Notification will require legislation, since it is unlikely that any political candidate would choose to inform voters about such activities without assurances of similar disclosure by opponents. It may be necessary to require bona fide candidates to inform potential subjects about a plan to compile and manipulate personal data. This may be accomplished by direct mail, newspaper notices or some other recognized public communication technique.

At some point, it also may become necessary to consider legislation governing the assembly and use of aggregated databases. There must be some determination of what constitutes a critical mass of personal information. Then, accordingly, campaigns (and commercial interests, for that matter) should be limited in the amount of personal information they may collect and use in communication activities. This may curtail the effectiveness of targeted strategies, but the violation of personal privacy is worth talk and strong measures.

It is difficult to predict the chances of such legislation. At this time, there is no public outcry (because there is little public knowledge) about privacy invasions by public office-seekers, and it is unlikely motivations will rise from within the institutions whose members are the primary benefactors of the technologies. But as computers accommodate larger and more intrusive databases, public pressures are likely to increase. The unknown at this point is the tolerance level of a population growing more accustomed to and comfortable with institutional maintenance of personal information. Again, the race is on between the advances of technology and the human tolerance of technology's effects.

VOTER MANIPULATION

Although campaigns set their agendas, in part, by weighting issues and ranking them for their vote-getting properties, they are really setting out to tell voters what to think about. The idea is to direct attention to an issue to set the agendas of the candidate's choosing. Let's say it's successful, and the audience commits energy and involvement to an issue. Given that two ideas like two stones cannot be in the same place at the same time, the campaign simultaneously diverts audience attention from competing topics. In other words, agenda setting both focuses and distracts attention and thereby affects priorities.

Political campaigns manipulate when they set different agendas for different voter subgroups, directing the attention of some on one set of issues, and of others on different issues. Targeting techniques, refined by polling and computer technologies, expand the opportunities for such strategies. As with Sandra, a candidate may identify his antiabortion stand with concurring voter groups. Campaign letters, phone calls and media messages plainly identify the candidate's position for kindred thinkers. Good targeting!

At the same time, other voters who are not likely to agree with the candidate on abortion will be treated to a different set of issues—by the same candidate, of course. These letters, phone calls and media messages will deal with, say, the candidate's more agreeable position on environmental matters, veterans' concerns, the savings and loan bailout, whichever demonstrates a convenient alignment of views. Again, good targeting. It directs the fitting issue to the proper group. It focuses, aims and shoots with pinpoint accuracy the right bullet at the right bull's-eye.

Remember, an officeholder cannot narrow his concern to one or two issues unless running for dogcatcher. Mayors, state legislators, members of Congress and presidents must deal with a host of issues. Yet, through the pigeonholing techniques of targeted communication, voters are led away from issues on which they may oppose the candidate. Different agendas for different people. When the net effects of these divide-and-conquer strategies are measured, the candidate will have been successful in reaching isolated groups with congruent images, while concealing from all groups the total picture. Voters thus are manipulated by the process. Each group has a vision of the candidate, but few have the full view.

Another characteristic of such targeted strategies is a bit more sophisticated: It is easier to ply psychological strategies on well-defined homogeneous groups than it is on heterogeneous mass audiences. In targeted mailings during the eighties, for example, the Moral Majority hurled fire and brimstone at the apostates to inspire the faithful. The letters and fliers discussed godless Communists, backsliding Christians, menacing liberals and the murderers of unborn children. These blistering references, buttressed by appropriate rhetoric and pictures, made a compelling pitch for contributions and political action. They worked their psychological magic on many recipients. The tactics would have had little effect on broader audiences, but they tugged the right strings for this special group. Moral Majority coffers swelled, and elected officials were made to feel the pressure.

Similar manipulations directed at targeted groups are used by supporters of environmental positions, abortion advocates and others. People for the American Way uses evangelical excesses to panic its liberal constituency. Consider the alarms they sounded during several of President Bush's Supreme Court nominations. There are no monopolies on the tactics, right or left. The point is, when groups or candidates wish to persuade a narrow voter segment through targeted channels, there is considerable opportunity to exploit persuasion techniques calculated to have maximum impact on target-group biases and views. Polling and computer techniques compress audiences and thus expand opportunities for and improve the effectiveness of targeted communications.

CONCLUSION

Technology-driven, targeted communications hit the political system at its most vulnerable level—the individual voter. They seek to unravel the strands of voters, one-by-one or in small groups, then cultivate the appeals most likely to affect these segmented parts. From one viewpoint, the process has merit. It draws in the disaffected, the voters who otherwise might sit it out. Different fish require different bait. Find the right issue, and the great congregation of American voters will grow by one more.

The plain fact is, this process harms voters. Many people come to adopt the agenda set by targeted campaigns. Voters fix on the one or two matters driven into their consciousness and, in the process, lose sight of the full campaign spectrum, and eventually of the full range of issues that will occupy the winner of an election. This can lead to frustration and anger, as voters see their important issue blended into the large mixture of issues when the campaign songs have ended and the confetti is swept from the floor. They see their concerns watered down when consensus demands compromise.

Individuals are affected in other ways. Building databases ruffles their privacy, as personal information is chiseled from their records and the chips reassembled in new forms by people to whom they likely would not volunteer such information. We have a thing about privacy in this country, and at some point, database building behind closed doors is likely to stir a nasty public response.

People also are affected because, culled from the rest of the group, they are subject to magnified manipulation. A good deal of research goes into the focused appeals and pitches that work in private settings but would not catch on in larger forums. There are political communicators who ply tactics and tricks against unsuspecting, scattered individuals.

The ongoing exploitation of voters would be less an issue if we could count on our faithful media watchdogs to prowl these back channels for mixed messages and distortions. As it turns out, they are kept well back by campaigns not interested in sharing private communications with public representatives. We take up this issue in the next chapter.

NOTES

1. The Virginia Declaration of Rights also contributed substantively to the French Declaration des Droits de l'Homme et du Citoyen and the United Nations' Universal Declaration of Human Rights.

2. Writings of the founders often reference the importance of a free press to the functioning of the government they were attempting to forge. Thomas Jefferson is one of the more colorful writers on the subject. Consider his line in a letter to Colonel Edward Carrington in 1787: "The basis of our government being the opinion of the people, the very first object should be to keep that right; and were it left to me to decide whether we should have a government without newspapers, or newspapers without a government, I should not hesitate a moment to prefer the latter."

3. Adams, Madison, Franklin and even Jefferson feared the passions of the masses; thus, they favored a republic, not a true democracy. The belief—and maybe more accurately, the hope—was that the president and Congress would make the best judgments and not follow popular enthusiasms. The Supreme Court was included to put a governor on the people, the president and Congress.

4. This passage is cited in Molly Ivins, "The Media and the Election Press Asks Itself, 'How Did We Do?' Sins of Omission Count," *Atlanta Journal and Constitution*, November 28, 1992, A17.

5. Washington political consultant who requested anonymity.

Chapter Eight

Effects on the Press

We [journalists] tell the public which way the cat is jumping. The public
will take care of the cat.

—Arthur Hays Sulzberger,
Time, May 8, 1950

INTRODUCTION

When politicians and government officials catch cold, the press sneezes.
Throughout history, there hasn't been a better example of symbiosis, each
institution so totally dependent on the other, even if most often it is a
puzzling love-hate relationship. This mutual dependency is not just a splen-
did coincidence. The founding fathers knew there could be no democracy
without a free press, and so they planted firmly in the Constitution a hard,
blunt safeguard ensuring against laws abridging freedom of the press.

Only occasionally have free press protections been challenged, and these
most often have been in head-to-head clashes with other constitutional
guarantees. The press nearly always has come out on top, and that usually
was due in large part to the moxie of battle-toughened journalists willing
to defend the larger matters of press freedom that loom heavily over individual cases.[1]

Elected officials are constitutionally bound to abide a free press, and
because of sunshine laws and regulatory demands that have sprouted over
the years, they must grant reasonable access to government business by
the people and the press. But, there is the tension of a fiddle string between

government officials and the press and a palpable antagonism very much anticipated from the beginning. It was anticipated because, regulations and convention aside, over time, elected officials would shut out the press, were they not dependent on the fourth estate to carry their messages to the voters, to project their images, to buff their halos every now and then. When the press is the only channel to the people, officeholders tolerate and accommodate the strain because they have no other choice. Government officials thus suffer the paradox of the press as an institution they can't live with and they can't live without.

Press coverage in more recent times has been only one of two major information streams from campaigns to voters. The second is paid advertising, which uses media channels that avoid the interpretive machinery of news departments. Traditionally, the two message flows—press coverage and paid advertising—have comprised most of a candidate's communication with voters. Whistle-stops, rubber-chicken dinners, church gatherings and Labor Day parades—dutifully reported in hometown newspapers—have been the bread and butter of campaigning for two hundred years in America. But, starting with FDR in the thirties, the main link to voters became broadcasting, which uses the old techniques as props and backdrops only.

Beginning in the eighties, two new categories of communication channels opened up. Both are targeted, both are less dependent on journalists or interpreters of the message and both are under tighter candidate control. The first is cable TV, and the second is direct-contact media.

Cable television and the dozens of smaller narrow media permit access to clusters of like-minded voters. These are more efficient at delivering targeted messages, and because they cost less, they permit a greater number of messages and a greater repetition of them.

 By direct-contact media, I mean mail, telephone and computers. Direct mail and telephone are nothing new, but in the past decade of computer enhancements, they have become truly targeted, personalized media—on a large scale. Electronic mail (EMail) communication, just pulling out of the blocks, will leap forward in the next decade, as personal computers and network linkups are brought into increasing numbers of American homes.[2]

Advances in communication technology confront the press with two challenges. One is the expanding repertoire of political communication options that do not require the intervention of journalists and other message filters. Using these channels, political candidates circumvent the press and go directly to the voters. They can do this both via the budding technologies and conventional media. The challenge for journalists is to stay in the loop. An even greater challenge may be to justify that need.

The second challenge has to do with the conduct of political coverage. As campaign communications splinter, reaching different groups through the many channels—both established and forming—coverage of messages becomes more difficult. A greater effort is required to access a greater number of messages, to review them and to analyze them in the larger context of a campaign. Of these three tasks, obtaining the messages is the most difficult. Journalists have described how the thick blizzard of messages has impeded their task of tracking campaign communications. The job is particularly difficult now that so many messages travel on back channels (e.g., direct-mail and telephone communications) not easily accessed by the press.

And yet, the content of these messages is critical in assessing a candidate. The press is in a unique position to evaluate claims and diagnose implications for larger campaign themes. But in order for political reporters to echo, much less interpret, evaluate and synthesize candidates' communications, they must have access to the raw material. Reporters today find themselves caught in a frustrating game of hide-and-seek. Campaigns hide their messages among the many tiny audience fragments, while the press seeks a way to uncover them.

CHANGES IN CAMPAIGN COVERAGE: THE TELEVISION BACKDROP

Thirty-year UPI veteran Wes Pippert, now director of the Washington Reporting Program for the University of Missouri School of Journalism, described how reporters in the sixties and seventies piled into buses and followed candidates from stop to stop. "We spent our time on the road and never let candidates out of our sight. The speeches were repetitive, but every so often something would break, and we would be there to get it."

Speeches during the "boys-in-the-bus" days were the meat and potatoes of political campaigns. They were the vessels for the grand themes, positions and statements. They fed the press, and they furnished source material for paid campaign advertisements. Those speeches and news stories spread thickly over the population, all voters covered by the same arguments and proposals. There was minimal audience segmentation, and message distinctions were only a matter of emphasis on different features of the same picture.

The big breakthrough in the early sixties were live TV news and the big ad campaigns on the three networks. The result: Orators like Adlai Stevenson, who wrote his own speeches, gave way to speech writers, spin doctors and sound bites. Today, speeches are still important in campaign communications; press coverage and big media advertisements continue to magnify the grand themes. But, two relevant changes have occurred in the past decade and a half: Campaigns approach media differently, and the media approach political news differently.

First, candidates have become less interested in the primary impact of their road shows than they are in the secondary effects achieved through media and, in particular, television coverage. Television has changed the composition and the consequences of political stump speeches. Addresses now are written for television audiences and not the faithful gathered to hear them. Cheering crowds are convenient props, nothing more. Speeches have instant national reach as their messages are telescoped by clips and fragments, sandwiched snugly between short narratives and sometimes a reporter's interpretation. Often, a speech, and even a day full of speeches, come down to a news editor's selection of which seven seconds will best draw an audience. Sound bite politics has blossomed. Candidates have learned the value of spiking one or two key images into the consciousness of fidgety audiences fatigued easily by compound ideas. The meat of a speech has become less important than its sizzle, because only the sizzle makes the seven o'clock news.

The press has obliged, and this is the second important change in campaign coverage. For one thing, there has been a sharp reduction in the coverage of political events. No network covered President Bush's prime-time press conference in June 1992. That was a first. Convention coverage was whittled down to a mere sliver in 1992, NBC even joining its efforts with Public Broadcasting rather than shouldering the expense alone. Also, despite the high drama imposed by Ross Perot, the religious right, the *National Enquirer*'s watch on Clinton's morality and the sad stumblings of an incumbent president, networks cried when they faced the prospects of six debates, then grumbled over the revenue losses imposed by the four that finally took place.

Television accommodated the candidates by running night after night the pithy slogans, granting viewers their ersatz "actual moment" experience of a political speech. Television nudged candidates forward to recite their own lines and withdrew traditional analyses further into the background.

Larry Grossman, former president of NBC News, sees this as an abdication of journalistic responsibility. "Edward Murrow has been replaced by cameras," he told me. The reporting, the interpretation, evaluation and synthesis of political news cultivated by the pioneers of broadcast journalism, has been supplanted by technology. "People think they are getting a better view of the issues if they see the candidate for themselves. They have come to believe there is no need for interpretation and explanation of events if they can see the candidate with their own eyes."

Seeing is believing, and television seduces its viewers into believing they can observe the objective reality of an event. Viewers regard more their own snap judgment of a flash-fried, seven-second clip than a journalist's simmering review.

This approach draws from televised sports, where only the moment really matters. It has evolved through news stories that delivered great visual components—a lunar landing, exploding volcanoes, bombs bursting in an Iraqi desert. Here, seeing is believing, or at least people believe it is. Sound bite and visual-nip exposures, in no small measure, contribute to the process through which people reach judgments about candidates and events.

Marvin Kalb, former CBS newsman and current director of the Joan Shorenstein Barone Center on the Press, Politics and Public Policy at Harvard, said that he feared the public would not always recognize the difference between technology and reality. Uncensored footage of an event does not provide reality, and yet it is remarkably convincing with its in-your-face displays.

Nonetheless, television news has chosen the sound bite format, because it feeds public desires to "be there" and because it is easier and less risky than analysis and evaluation. TV news chiefs defend this shorthand by pointing to the millions who read newspapers about the same event. They say, "We introduce the subjects, let newspapers pick up the details." Newspapers, they correctly state, are expandable, taking as many pages as necessary to report an event. Network TV (CNN et al. are another matter) has twenty-two minutes each evening and that's it—for politics, business, human events and human interests. Nevertheless, while time limitations and story compressions are a reality, most people who follow the news get most of their information from network television, not from newspapers. People have turned to the most abbreviated news form for their routine information.

Journalists may be on hand to select the sound bite of the day, but even that judgment is aided by the campaigns, which make it painfully obvious which clips to showcase. In this process, there is little synthesis and evaluation and only occasional integration of an event into the larger tapestry of a campaign. Reporters intro and "outro" a clip, but they spend little effort assessing the implications of its message. This says nothing about information lost in the unseen scraps of film lying on the cutting room floor.

Uninterpreted clips may be what the people want because they believe they offer the best political news, but something is missing, and Kalb put his finger on it when he said, "Technology can become a substitute for political thought." That is precisely the problem. Technology—of the camera, in this case—has made it easy for news organizations and attractive for audiences to supplant abstract thought with concrete images. This highly visual and video-oriented society invests more in the illusion of television images than in the substance of reasoned analysis. This is a function and a failing of the medium, and one not likely to be resolved anytime soon—this side of C-Span.

Television is best when it is active, alive with pictures and movement, when it puts viewers and the event belly to belly, without the encumbrances of an intermediary. This is why people ran first to television during the

Challenger disaster in 1986, the San Francisco earthquake in 1989 and the Los Angeles riots in 1992. These were acutely visible events, and the people did not want to read about them or hear about them; they wanted to see them, and television made that possible.

Missouri may be the "show me" state, but we have become the "show me" society. As visuals capture an event, they seize human interest and satisfy curiosity at a primary level. Visuals reveal the kind of reality that satisfies, and it satisfies because it beguiles us into believing we know what we need to know about an event. In this view of reality, *what* has occurred becomes more important than *why* it has occurred. The what is empirical, tangible and clear; the why is often subjective, complicated and muddy. Voters and viewers like their politics neat, and television delivers; technology tells the what very well and leaves its customers satisfied. Thoughtful analysis tackles the why and goes begging for an audience, at least by television standards.

This pummeling of television is not just from the fists of media critics, but from the very media bishops who nightly deliver the news. In a June 1992 conference at Harvard's Shorenstein Barone Center, news anchors from the three major networks, PBS and CNN analyzed the state of campaign coverage, and they conceded it was not good at all. Howard Kurtz of the *Washington Post* (1992, p. D1) reported: "Jim Lehrer called the press 'arrogant.' Dan Rather said campaign reporters have shown 'a lack of guts.' Tom Brokaw said the media were engaging in 'voyeurism for the sake of voyeurism.' "

The anchors considered the charge that their 7.3 second sound bites constituted superficial coverage, and some offered a defense. NBC's Tom Brokaw said he timed a few network news campaign clips and found they lasted an average of 8 to 10 seconds—not 7.3 seconds. Let that put rest to the notion of short sound bites! He defended the use of flash quotes, saying that most of the time, candidates don't say anything worth much more than that. "On most days, most candidates are not going to say something [so] pithy that it's going to go more than ten seconds." How revealing about a professional who daily judges, for millions of viewers, what is and what is not important to know about political candidates! In this view, only the glib one-liner merits airtime. Dan Rather, anchor for CBS, explained the practice, noting, "The fear is that you'll wind up being serious but dull" (Kurtz 1992, p. D1). The last thing television journalism wants is to be dull and run the risk of driving viewers to "I Love Lucy" reruns or, worse, to another network news program.

Robert MacNeil, of the "MacNeil/Lehrer News Hour" on Public Broadcasting, challenges the network policies, saying, "It takes courage to be dull." The "News Hour" format is at variance with network approaches, offering a full hour's coverage on only a few topics. The show customarily offers long segments and even marathon-length clips from stump speeches.

In all fairness, PBS does not suffer commercial pressures, as do networks, nor does it have an audience with an acquired taste for sound bite nuggets. Its viewers are eager consumers of information and news—print and broadcast—and they have the tenacity to sit through long segments. But this audience also typically is small, rarely breaking a 5 share, whereas the networks routinely garner a combined share of over 50 percent.[3]

The Harvard conference revealed a discomfort among the anchors with their skip-the-stone-across-the-surface treatment of political and campaign news, yet it also confirmed the networks' commitment to an attractive formula that may romance viewers, but does not do much to enlighten them. Maybe a better analogy comes from the circus. The networks' peek under the tent gives voters just enough to believe that they have seen the show, but it fails miserably at providing them front-row seats for all the events under the big top. Network formats, by the anchors' own assessments, do not assemble the events, they do not interpret the meaning of these events nor do they engage in the political thought necessary for a real understanding of a campaign.

In the derivative sports model, distinctions between an event and the meaning of that event are small and of no consequence. This is not so in government and politics. Events define larger issues and policies, and, in aggregate with other cues, render a total view of a candidate.

Uninterpreted events—sound bites and disjoined footage of speeches and campaign appearances, which form the heart of contemporary television news coverage—lie like loose threads on a floor. It takes skilled political thought and analysis to pick up these issues scattered about and to weave them into useful cloth. When the choice news source for most voters—and the only news source for many—fails to spin the threads, voters are left with a frayed understanding of campaign agendas and of the candidates' views on national matters. Issues are not joined, and the public looses perspective and a sense of direction. Kalb is right: Technology can become a substitute for political thought, and a prominent example is television sound bite journalism.

Television is not the only news source. There is a palette of media from which to paint the political picture, and voters need only pick and choose from the many options to obtain their personal portrait of a campaign. The fact is, voters just don't do it. Since the mid–1960s, most voters have turned to television for news, abandoning newspapers and magazines and using radio for sports and information about weather and traffic jams. During an election, the serious voters turn an eye toward the papers and an ear to National Public Radio's "All Things Considered" and "Morning Edition."[4]

Most people do not invest the energy necessary to assemble a comprehensive view of the issues or the candidates. Only half the population reads a daily newspaper (Jones 1991), and even television news, which replaced newspapers as the primary source, now is being abandoned for cable entertainment by large audience segments (Leo 1992). People will seize on a few topics, follow the sound bites and, if they vote, it is often without a fundamental understanding of the range or the implications of critical issues.

Richard Kimball, board president of the Center for National Independence in Politics and director of Project Vote Smart, says two trends have developed that lead to political ignorance. First, candidates have learned to use polls, surveys and high-tech media to create images. The images have little context and are designed not to educate, but to manipulate. They don't create an informed electorate, just a sensitized one. Second, the "traditionally stable institutions that once helped educate voters—communities, churches, schools, local newspapers—became less stable as American society became more mobile."

CNN's Bernard Shaw said at the Harvard conference that "most Americans are underinformed. . . . Many American voters don't do their part" (Kurtz, July 13, 1992). Most voters with an interest in news have settled on television news, they are comfortable with it and they are unlikely to give it up or to fortify its coverage by seeking out other media. It is largely this truth that makes the next discussion more important.

PRESS COVERAGE AND THE TARGETED CHANNELS

While most voters who seek political information seek it on television, political campaigns seek voters on the targeted and direct media—the communication back channels. Political communicators have been at it steadily since the early eighties, and they are getting good. Meanwhile, newspapers, the once mighty icons of political reporting, are tripping badly as the population outgrows the reading habit.[5]

Wes Pippert noted that two forces in the newspaper industry have converged to reduce political coverage. The first is rooted in the economy, the second is high-tech mailings.

Newspapers have not escaped the economic virus infecting companies nationwide. In 1992 alone, more than fifteen daily newspapers suspended operations, merged or became weeklies. This happened to nineteen others in 1991 and to sixteen in 1990 (Boisseau 1992). "Newspapers' ad position is being eroded by competing media, especially direct mail. Newspapers had a 24.1% share of the $125.4 billion ad market in 1991, down from a 25% share a year earlier" (Fisher 1992). With ad space down and competition up, Draconian budget cuts have struck at the operational heart of newspapers, reducing the number of reporters and staff whose beats once focused on political fact-finding and analysis. "There are empty chairs and silent typewriters all over Washington," said Pippert. "There are far fewer professionals than there needs to be to cover the complex stories arising in this town and in state capitals around the country."

"Moreover," Pippert said,

there has been a real shift in focus. It's a chicken and egg story, and I don't want to get into which came first, but papers are offering less political news to a public less interested in reading about it. Research shows people want high school sports scores and local news. Any local story, no matter how trivial, will push out a Washington story. So instead of investing their scarce manpower resources in Washington and in state capitals, they leave reporters home or they don't hire them at all. It saves money. Washington bureaus are greatly understaffed, and that means political news goes underreported. I don't see a push from the readers to change that.

Not only have newspapers axed political reporters, but in the current spirit of austerity, they have not kept pace with advancing computer facilities and other resources necessary to cover today's high-tech political campaigns. Pippert's concerns about a shrinking force and an inadequate arsenal for political news coverage take on a special significance in light of the next issue.

Pippert's second reason for the decline in political coverage echoes our treatment of computerized, targeted, personalized mailings to voters. The advances in polling, database building and computer analyses serve the growing, targeted information needs of political campaigns. These tools have seeded a field of innovative communication techniques that have presented journalists with new challenges. As we noted at the beginning of this chapter, it is not enough anymore to cover stump speeches and monitor candidate-sponsored television ads. The new technologies have opened a number of channels, and these are unlike anything we have seen before. They are direct and focused, and they have the capacity to route messages to one receiver alone—and, paradoxically, to do it on a mass scale. They thrive on feedback, gulp huge quantities of voter information and profit greatly from the benefits of personalization. But, they are also illusive and easily dodge the notice of would-be observers outside their intended circle of recipients. This is the feature that gives journalists the morning-after sweats. Stealth messages moving from campaigns to voters fly quietly beneath the journalist's radar and, by the dozens, slip through unnoticed.

Covering this rich new crop of voter communications requires a more tenacious, creative and skilled press corp and a new assortment of tools—first to harvest the information, then to process it. Unfortunately, just when resources are most needed, they are least available. Manpower shortages and the scarcity of technical facilities necessary to bird-dog campaigns hamper coverage and throttle press efforts to engage in the kind of political thought Kalb found so necessary for good campaign coverage.

The next discussion focuses on specific problems the press face when covering communications borne of the new technologies. Several journalists interviewed for this chapter have been exploring techniques to deal with these problems. Specialists at the Poynter Institute, for instance, have foreseen the impediments campaign technologies impose. They have been studying and addressing these matters in seminars and classes. We will review some of their activities and a cross-section of other work underway.

THE JOURNALISTS' VIEWS

Among the nationally ranked print and broadcast journalists interviewed for this discussion,[6] there was not much doubt about two things. First, the proliferation of computer technologies in political campaigns has fomented a surge in back-channel, targeted communications. Each has seen an increase in targeted mass media—including radio and small cable channels—and a greatly expanded campaign use of targeted direct mail. Second, they have seen that press access to these communications is becoming increasingly difficult. A handful of messages and channels has been replaced by dozens or more as campaigns segment and target, and this increases the logistics effort required for routine press monitoring. Reporters know that the difficulty of screening these communications is not with the number of messages involved, but with the inaccessibility of them. Campaigns simply have not made it easy for journalists to get their hands on a cross-section of targeted messages.

Reporters looked first at the increased use of directed media channels. E. J. Dionne of the *Washington Post*, for instance, said he listens to many hours of small, narrow-audience radio, where he finds a very different collection of messages from those carried on the mass-market stations. He said that when he travels, he also makes a point of watching local cable stations to get a sense for political news and for paid announcements. These, too, he noted, deliver an information inventory different from the offerings of mass-market channels.

David Broder, also of the *Washington Post*, said there now are so many smaller stations, each with the capacity of releasing select, targeted information, that it no longer is possible for the press to monitor all or even most of the information reaching voters. The number of channels has overwhelmed the resources of the American press. Radio has become more targeted, and cable, not in existence twenty years ago, now offers viewers a great sea of options.

More important, though, are the highly targeted mail and telephone campaigns. These are messages by invitation only, and they cannot be monitored by just anyone who wants in. Recipients are selected because they meet demographic, ideological or membership criteria and pass the morning muster held by campaign computers. Consequently, direct messages often slip by quietly without notice by a press that traditionally has monitored the stream of policies and pledges flowing from a campaign.

Edward Miller, an associate at the Poynter Institute, noted that he and others at Poynter have been monitoring computer uses in political campaigns. He said the targeting technologies have "imposed a fog bank that journalists must get through. Messages are hidden in radio and direct mail and in telephone appeals. These increase the difficulty of access to campaign communications, and they require a new approach to political coverage."

Howard Kurtz noted that technology today hits journalists twice. First, the press never again will be able to monitor the full range of campaign communications. "We see only a fraction of what campaigns are putting out. There just are too many outlets carrying too many messages to too many small, specialized audiences."

Kurtz also expressed concern for the volatility of campaign messages. "These technologies allow campaigns to turn around a message with incredible speed. In twenty-four hours, they can read a poll, then write, film, edit and package a message and distribute it nationally or just to a few selected states." Campaigns similarly can respond to audience feedback through radio, mail, phone or fax distributions. The dizzying result is the rapid creation and dissolution of messages sent over a profusion of channels, many of which are beyond the reach of the press. Thus, the monitoring function of the watchdog becomes ever more difficult to fulfill.

The journalists saw and felt the information lockout and expressed frustration at not being in on all that candidates were saying to voters. It is an understandable frustration, given that information is the mother's milk of this profession. David Broder, often called the "dean of American political journalism," was particularly annoyed that campaigns shield the full range of information distributed to voters. He lamented the lack of "public monitoring and the absence of standards by which campaigns conduct their voter contacts."

Poynter's Edward Miller, too, expressed frustration with voter communications conducted out of press view. "I think press scrutiny of all voter-directed communications is critical to press coverage, and when reporters are blocked from access to this information, we realize an accountability problem."

Wes Pippert shook his head at back-channel communications and contrasted these with the time when candidates used the big media easily tapped by the press. "They targeted to some degree, but their media options were limited. They used television, radio and even direct mail, but these messages always were laid bare for everyone to watch and to hear and to read. That isn't so today. The fact is, we just can't get our hands on many of the messages that go out in the name of a campaign."

The problem is clear, a solution is not, in part because the target moves. Technologies, like flowers, unfold each day with new features. The speed and capacity of computers have grown mightily in only a half-dozen years. Software, once awkward and dull, has blossomed into brilliant, full-service, easy-to-run campaign aids. All the while, prices have dropped, so even a threadbare, outpost campaign can be armed to the teeth with the best computers. Political communications transform with every election cycle, as computers absorb more information, increase analytic capacity and automate the rote tasks that personalize voter contacts. How does the press draw a bead on such a thing?

Journalists and media observers have put a few suggestions on the table. Let's dispense first with an obvious but obviously implausible solution: Candidates all could agree to place reporters on each of their mailings lists, thus ensuring that no communication leaves campaign headquarters without the press on board. Candidates also could send along their media and telephone solicitation scripts. Fat chance. Maybe that's too taxing. Instead, they could compile the same information in a notebook and place it on a shelf at campaign headquarters for reporters to come by and study. Never happen—even though that approach would demand more of the press but less of the campaign.

The truth is, it isn't the inconvenience that deters campaigns from facilitating press and public access to this information. Campaigns stand little to gain by reporters poring over their communications, comparing one message with another, one promise against the next, one spin alongside another. Even campaigns careful about consistency among their messages fear a gap or contradiction that might bubble up under the heat of close press scrutiny. If reporters want access, they had better work at it, because the campaigns will not oblige them. They need to cultivate their own sources and arrive at their own solutions if they want to stay even with the emerging high-tech campaigns.

Journalists know this well, and they know also that they must configure their investigative procedures to complement the computer-driven campaigns. David Broder said campaigns "will not put out a daily summary of all their communications, nor will they even provide an index of the campaign audiences or messages. They would claim it is too much trouble for overburdened campaign staffs and too much of a logistics effort. They just would not do it."

E. J. Dionne agreed. He said he has tried that approach, and despite requests for campaign mailings, he has yet to get any. None of the other journalists thought there was a wit of a chance campaigns would comply. Slam the door on that idea.

Perhaps the problem could be solved if reporters somehow quietly entered their names onto candidate mailing lists and blended unnoticed into the gray background of voters. Thus, these journalists, cloaked in plain

voter's clothing, would receive a steady diet of specialized campaign communications, and the campaigns would not be any the wiser. Reporters
could compare mailings and phone solicitations and, thereby, review and
analyze the complete array of campaign-generated communications.

Given the development and current use of databases, this could never
work. Reporters could not systematically assert themselves onto voters'
lists largely because they never could guess all the demographic combinations that form the nuclei of campaign mailings. Also, people do not
self-select into target groups; they are placed there. At best, the drive
would be a wasted effort of hit and miss, and in the end, there would be
little to show.

Reporters could employ surrogates for the job, and this is just what
Miller and his Poynter team in Charlotte did during the 1992 campaign.
As part of a much larger campaign reporting field test, Miller enlisted
voters who matched a carefully developed demographic profile. These
recruits agreed to pass along all letters, brochures and other material they
received from any campaign, national or local. Their selection followed
probable combinations of traits campaigns use to stratify voting populations, giving Poynter a reasonable cross-section of voters and a net fine
enough to trap most campaign messages distributed in Charlotte.

Miller said reporters involved with the project "analyzed the communications and compared variances in major positions across groups." The
team also examined mass-media advertisements in light of these targeted
messages to clock the spin and determine contradictions and inconsis-
tencies.

E. J. Dionne and his colleagues at the *Washington Post* have used this
technique among swing voters. With limited resources, it makes sense to
follow these undecideds who clearly would be the most popular targets for
all campaigns. They typically are pursued first and last and receive the
largest volume of direct-mail and telephone attention. An alliance with
swing voters allows the press to obtain the greatest volume of back-channel
communications for the least cost.

The planted-voter technique may disturb some reporters. First, it is a
departure from conventional campaign reporting. The lone wolf reporter
loses some control. S/he must initially rely on help—probably from a computer specialist—to determine the personal characteristics of the voter
cohorts and then to select specific recruits. Much of the work takes place
up front. Voters must be selected, then contacted, then convinced to co-
operate. Many of the chosen later will forget or have a change of heart,
and these must be cajoled and persuaded back into the fold or be replaced.

Then there is the matter of relying on this untested, unpaid, uncontrolled
group. Of the voter population, the undecideds may be the most fickle and
least likely of all to possess the necessary endurance to see the plan through.
They likely are least committed to politics and have little time for such

things. Reporters, confident in their own skills and wit, can lose patience with the insouciance of these summer soldiers.

Some reporters may be uncomfortable with the surreptitious nature of the plan. After all, they are planting confederates among the voters—conspirators whose function it is to hand over communications to those who would find fault in discrepancies and misstated facts. It is understandable, too, that participating voters may be burdened by guilt at the thought of turning over material "personally signed" by a candidate. Reporters may be uncomfortable putting someone up to the shadowy task of passing along information, unbeknownst to the author.

The fact is, candidates running for public office traditionally ran public campaigns. Their speeches were on the stump, their messages on trees then television screens. Messages were out for all to see. Even early targeted communications were comparatively generalized, and the few versions of a message almost immediately became public knowledge.

Computers have enriched the back channels, and now public campaigns contain greatly expanded private components. But they remain public campaigns, and anything a candidate does in pursuit of a government office should be open to public scrutiny. There always have been and will be dark corners in American politics, but the press has worked tirelessly to flood the process with light. Now that computers have introduced new communication techniques, the press must rely on new data gathering activities. It does matter that a candidate will promise one thing to one group and something else to another. It does matter that agendas expressed in private do not match those stated in public. If the press is to fulfill its watchdog responsibility, it must stay even with the candidates and employ techniques that make this possible. It is critical that reporters observe campaign communications, and because some campaigns appear not to oblige requests that facilitate this effort, other solutions should be sought. Inviting voter participation is a sound way to approach this problem, and it is likely to become a technique common in campaign reporting during the years ahead.

We noted earlier that reporters and computer specialists would form an alliance in the effort to prepare selection criteria and to choose and contact voters. As computers become further integrated into campaign activities, they also must become more prominent in reporting activities. By now, most newspapers are using word processors and computer typesetting facilities, but computer use must extend beyond these simple functions. It is not possible for a slow chase plane to keep an F–15 in view for very long. Journalists must develop the same or better expertise and sophistication than the institutions they cover. Reporters should understand enough about computer use in a campaign to see through the smoke and past the mirrors and understand just how a campaign can manipulate the growing body of rich and elaborate data. They may rely on resident specialists to perform data manipulations, but they should understand the procedures and the capacities of contemporary high-tech activities.

The Poynter Institute offers professional journalists several courses in computer-based reporting. They look at data storage and manipulations, and they examine the range of techniques called computer-assisted reporting. "Reporters have to use the same tools available to the people they cover," said Miller. "They have to understand how to manipulate public databases and, when necessary, to follow the various computer trails of campaigns, businesses and the government." He admitted that this is a heady task requiring rigorous training and work for people who never before may have been exposed to computer operations. But, he said, Poynter sees the critical need for a press corp equipped to fly with the skill and equipment of the institutions they cover. Poynter is joined by several of the nation's larger journalism schools in offering courses and seminars on computer-assisted reporting techniques.

Campaigns may balk at handing over their own back-channel communications, but they take pleasure in turning over private messages from the opposition. David Broder confirmed that campaigns are a primary press source for such information. They assiduously scout the opponent's information, and they eagerly retrieve messages they feel unfairly disparage their candidate. Campaign workers, friends of friends, and networks woven invisibly through the population have access to messages not available to reporters. When the opposition picks up something unsettling or unfair, the staff is quick to forward the information.

"Private messages about explosive issues or which conflict with a candidate's public positions are most likely to find their way to us," said E. J. Dionne. This is a benefit of the adversarial system in American politics, each side keeping book on the other, serving as a watchdog for the watchdog.

It is a system that has worked since the early days, when someone first slammed on a newsroom desk a tattered handbill ripped angrily from a public post. Adversarial surveillance continues as one of the primary tools to monitor campaign information. Even Poynter's 1992 Charlotte project, with its cadre of chosen message monitors, counted on campaigns to keep reporters tapped in to the back channels.

Opposition-assisted information gathering is critical, but we should cast an eye toward other techniques in this changing environment where messages are becoming more targeted, more narrowly focused and more directed to ever smaller groups. At some point, that opposition net will be too coarse to catch the targeted messages. It is a matter of selectivity and probability. A greater number of messages will be disseminated to a larger number of select groups, and these groups each will be smaller in size. That is what targeting does. Messages in increasing numbers will slip through unnoticed by the opposition. Friends and families will not find themselves among the targeted audiences; campaign networks will not cross the many communication strands planted deep by the opposition. Reporters should encourage campaign assistance but, at the same time, shore up their own information networks.

Other suggestions to gain access to back-channel communications are on the table, and each helps tighten the grid just a bit. Consider this one: Throughout an election, papers and broadcast media could ask readers to send in interesting campaign mailings. Inspiring appeals to a lively readership will yield a truckload of letters. Most will be duplicates, but some will bear surprises. Interns can sort the catch, and they just might find back-channel traffic that otherwise would slip by unnoticed. There is no guarantee that the most interesting information will find its way to the newsroom, but no other technique can ensure that either. The cost-benefit ratio of this technique argues for a try.

Even if this approach yields only disappointing scraps for the journalist, it is likely to contribute much to the political system. The bugle blasts summoning voter assistance will sound as sirens to political campaigns. The notices will remind candidates that someone is listening to everything they say. Howard Kurtz believes that the thought of surveillance may be enough to keep campaigns from mischief. He said it is the perception of risk that matters to many campaigns, and if they feel they may be caught in a discrepancy, they are less likely to take liberties with which they otherwise would feel comfortable.

More on the Need for Computers in Reporting

Reporters increasingly will face difficult analytical and warehousing chores as they become successful at collecting and assembling campaign communications from the front and back channels. It will take a cataloging system of some sophistication to keep track of the messages, to learn how campaigns divide up audiences and parcel out information. Journalists always have carefully watched and evaluated the communications of political campaigns; it is important now that they adopt techniques to keep up with the campaigns they follow. It is hard to see how journalists can accomplish this without the aid of computers. Compared to the campaigns, journalists have a more difficult task, one of assembling the pieces and inferring a strategy, measuring message differences and discovering the tactics used to draw the votes from small groups. With analytic techniques and database building of their own, journalists can match the campaigns they shadow. Computers make the impossible task possible.

Many computer-based innovations require an expertise not so easy to grasp. Reporters already wear many hats. Daily, they cover a waterfront of issues, maintain an expertise in politics and policy, cultivate sources and stay abreast of who-did-what-to-whom, so they can be forgiven for not embracing the complex tools of the new political communications. I found many of the journalists interviewed for this book perfectly happy to keep an arm's length relationship with computers. They faced a dissonance familiar to many professions: Computer involvement in their line cannot be denied, but the thought of personal involvement cannot be accepted. Such is the pattern of adoption for major innovations. People have faced this discord since the first bronze knife was cast, only computer development has been so rapid that there has been little time for the human element to adjust and integrate new tools into old customs.

No doubt, there will evolve a subfield of computer journalism, where the "beat" will not be city hall, but the computer files of city hall; not the Pentagon, but Pentagon databases; not the campaigns, but campaign computer records. Specialists who practice this hybrid form of journalism will be part computer master and part journalist. Likely, many will join small reporting teams whose members will collaborate on the research and development of a story. Thus, traditional investigative reporting will be augmented by computer journalism (computer-assisted reporting). Reporting teams will triangulate on developing a campaign, just as campaign team efforts triangulate on developing a campaign. Many professions have summoned computer specialists into their midst; it is critical now that investigative teams embrace them also.

In the meanwhile, as Ed Miller and Wes Pippert counsel, it is a good idea for practicing journalists to become familiar with the array of computer investigative tasks. Journalism students should be encouraged to take courses in database building, computer analysis and survey research. Computer skills will become every bit as valuable to investigative journalists of the next century as interviewing and news writing. This new skill will arm American journalists with the same tools used so well by the subjects of their investigations.

A CHALLENGE TO DEMOCRACY—AN ISSUE FOR THE PRESS

The effects of technology might be more than an inconvenience to the press, an intrusion on individual privacy, a tampering with personal sensitivities. Some scholars believe, and Marvin Kalb among them, that technology could have serious effects on the deep fibers of this democracy.

More than a mere annoyance to the political system, Kalb suggests that technology can generate a fundamental change in the voters' role in the electoral process. We look first at Kalb's thesis then at an expanded role for the press in dealing with the challenge.

A Challenge to Democracy

Eric Sevareid once remarked that one walked away from a conversation with Edward R. Murrow "with the impulse to write down what he had said, to recapture his phrases so that one could recall them and think about them later" (Sevareid 1946, p. 83). Marvin Kalb leaves that impression. When asked to summarize his views about press coverage of technology-driven political campaigns, he said off-the-cuff, "With the increasing sophistication of technology, there is a danger of democracy losing its vitality. Technology may be substituted for dialogue, and voters will become the targets, rather than the participants, in the process. I believe the use of technology can contribute to the growing irrelevance of the voter and, therefore, to the weakening of the democratic process."

Kalb's statement illuminates several points raised earlier in the book. First, databases and polling technology provide the details once gathered directly from voters. Candidates and their surrogates in years past routinely engaged in face-to-face encounters with voters—to talk, but also to listen. We noted how the ward-and-precinct system established a formal face-to-face information network—again, providing an active voter role in campaign dialogue.

By contrast, polling technology, which has become the primary data gathering tool of campaigns, probes a population without actually engaging voters in dialogue. Surveyors enter an interview with a set, directed agenda, and while they hear the respondent, they rarely listen to him. But, even if this wafer-thin cross-section of respondents is treated to a real discussion of the issues, such scattered, selective events do nothing for the vast majority of voters who go begging for substantive involvement. Information gathering today is not designed to measure public views so much as it is to measure public vulnerabilities. That is clear from the directive methods used to gather voter information.

Still, the process looks like dialogue. At least it appears that serious dialogue took place, given the dizzying display of facts and figures proffered as the thinking of voters. Campaigns claim to know how voters feel about foreign affairs, education, the environment, abortion, the deficit and all the rest. They describe it all with four-point scales, one-line squibs, bars, charts and computer maps that display in living color the facts as though they were a synthesis of deep voter thinking. They are not. They are a reflection of public thinking, but like any reflection, they disclose only the thinnest surface. The polling methods just do not allow the kind of dialogue that permits voters to engage substantively in the political debate, to introduce their own concerns, to explain their own feelings and to elaborate on their expectations for their government and for their leaders. This feedback is watery thin, and while it serves the purposes of computer analysis and, thus, the campaigns, it does little to accommodate the voters and to assert their role in the political dialogue. Jefferson said that the people themselves are the only safe depositories of the government, but it is the people who are being quietly wrung from the system.

The feedback mainstays today are surveys and databases. Focus groups offer some substance, but these are inadequate for several reasons. First, they, too, generally are arranged with fixed campaign agendas. They gather people to review and comment on campaign messages or themes or to discuss hot-button topics that fit campaign itineraries. They involve limited population segments, not representative of all voters. Focus group discussions often are dominated by a vocal few who assert positions and establish norms for ensuing interactions. This further distances the focus group scenarios from the environments of average voters whose political views are developed and expressed in less intense settings. None of the current methods—including focus groups, surveys, database analyses—gives voters a real chance in the discussions. They are not meant to do so. Voters are invited into the process the way a spider invites in the fly. The role one plays when asked to dinner makes a difference.

The fact is, current feedback gathering methods fail the voter and ultimately fail the political process. Kalb had it right. Technology is being substituted for dialogue, and in the process, voters are not participants, but targets. The problem is, it's tough to see and to understand, and so it's tough to shake a fist at the process, much less find a solution.

At the end of the day, what does it all mean for voters, for the political process and for the press? Kalb feels the role forced on voters leads to their irrelevance in the process—a valid argument for several reasons. Democracy must be participatory by definition, and this participation must go beyond the physical act of pulling a lever. It demands a substantive role. It assumes a two-way interaction between the government and the governed, and it requires channels that allow ideas, concerns, disgruntlements and suggestions to be directed to the leaders. Much of the voter frustration witnessed during the 1992 campaign came from a sense that nobody in government was listening to the people. Democrats protested that George Bush "just doesn't get it." Republicans claimed the Democrats "just didn't get it." Ross Perot said nobody got anything. Each party accused the other of not listening, not paying attention, not heeding the people. Both were right and both were guilty. One elderly woman interviewed by a local television station put it well. She said she felt frustrated and abandoned by the political process, which gave no sign of noticing her concerns. She said she felt like "a voice crying in the wilderness."

Voters are not being heard. Unemployed workers in 1991 winced when the president proclaimed the recession had ended. Didn't he know? Millions of people who once worked in America's factories and offices were turning their pockets inside out and facing needs that never before had concerned them. Their shouts went unnoticed. The poor always may have faced these problems, but the sense of invisibility has crept deeply into the middle class. Tens of millions live without health-care insurance, and only recently, through shocking news accounts about cases of preventable death and dying, has Washington taken notice. People ask what it takes to be heard. Clearly, the mechanisms now in place neither require nor seek substantive and regular dialogue with the voters. Such dialogue is not essential. It is necessary and sufficient for the technology-driven political campaigns to rely on the highly specific, directed, quantifiable information derived from polls, databases and scattered focus groups. More substantive feedback is neither needed nor sought.

This is the point where democracy weakens—where one participant in the two-way relationship is relegated to a tenuous role, not as a participant in the system, but as a target of it. The old mechanisms for substantive dialogue have rusted, and they have been dismantled. The ward-and-precinct system is gone; the neighbor-politician is growing scarce as lifelong congressional members use their districts as mail drops. Sensitivity to the depth and breadth of public concerns—which can be obtained directly only from nose-to-nose dialogue—is less evident than it ever has been. Public input has been limited. It has become sterilized and quantified, and it has become reactive in a top-down system of information gathering and dissemination. This does not bode well for a democracy that thrives on rich public input, voter-generated concerns and agendas and significant public participation in the give-and-take of political dialogue.

An Issue for the Press

What can be done? An answer may lie with the journalists whose views were gathered for this chapter and with the other reporters and media practitioners who link the government with the people it serves. The value of the fourth estate to this democracy is nothing new. The tenacity of the *Washington Post* and other media disclosed the Watergate transgressions and saved the country from a frightening assault on the democratic process. Daniel Schorr of CBS (and now Public Broadcasting) informed the people of foul government dealings through his release of the Pentagon Papers in 1976. The press did much to keep alive public (and thus official) concerns about circumvention of checks and balances during the Irangate violations and other schemes that followed in the aftermath.

Now the press can perform two functions to ensure the public is not left out of the political dialogue. First, it can hold the politicians' feet to the fire. The press has unique access, power and responsibility. It can get into government doors that others cannot. Few constituents can initiate a half-hour discussion with a congressman or a president, but the press often can. Once inside, the press has the power to focus attention and to compel a response. At the same time, it can impart lessons and assert agendas.

Reporters can confront an officeholder with direct questions about the public's views and concerns, and it can approach questions with the public viewpoint in mind—a viewpoint that demands recognition. There would be great value in asking direct questions that draw from these perspectives:

Would you describe the range of views borne by your constituents on this matter?

Do you understand why people feel this way?

Would you tell me how they want you to solve the problem?

What are the people's thoughts on your decision to act as you did on this matter?
   How do you know this is so?

Specific answers, thorough answers, complete with references to exhaustive discussions—as well as to the statistics—on the matters will reveal an interest in sustaining the essential public dialogue.

The power of the press can back the chutzpah of investigative reporters. Weak answers, based on a fragile understanding of public views, will draw public attention. Stories will reveal which officeholders and candidates draw from the wisdom of the people and which do not. They can demonstrate which decisions appear to have arisen from information developed through a real interaction and involvement of the public. This is not the same as quoting statistics from a survey report, and the distinctions should be proclaimed.

Author William Greider asked, "Who will tell the people?" We ask, who will tell the politicians? The answer may have to be the press, through its reporting and coverage techniques and the stories it writes about campaigns and government.

Second, the press can assert the public view directly and attempt to compensate for the inadequate job of campaigns and officeholders. Much of this is already done. David Broder has for years conducted and written about his exhaustive face-to-face discussions with average voters. In "cold calls," he knocks on doors and asks people to talk about how they feel and what they see in the political issues around them.

During the 1992 presidential election, National Public Radio interviewers began a series of in-depth discussions with a preselected panel of voters. Their technique suffers from several methodological difficulties, but theirs is a heroic effort to reignite the dying embers of political dialogue.

The Poynter Institute has built into its Charlotte project a substantial public dialogue component, and reporters who participated in that field study worked to integrate public views more conspicuously into their stories.

In all of these approaches, the press does well what the campaigns have not been doing at all. They seek out the voters, cultivate the dialogue and, on a small scale, feed the thoughts of common people into a system starving for public input. The press, though, cannot and should not be the agent to ensure public representation in public campaigns. That is the responsibility of the candidates and officeholders, and at some point, it is they who should assume the task. In the meanwhile, the press must do it for them, if it can.

We may have traveled too long down the electronic road to reinstate the ward-and-precinct system or to return candidates to the old ways of information gathering. But, what technology takes away, it also can return. In Appendix B, we describe a solution that combines the best of human interaction and computer technology. We look at a data gathering technique that has been endorsed by leading journalists, news organizations and academic institutions. It provides a forum for average voters to express their thoughts in ways they have not been encouraged to do in recent times. It gives voice to the public agenda and brings forth the stories and human experiences that exemplify the views and the thinking of average voters.

At the same time, it uses scientific principles of representative sampling and data reduction. Computers are used to flag and quantify the thoughts for quick digestion and conversion of energy for the political system. It is not the solution, but part of a solution, and its products can be of great use to the press, to candidates, to officeholders and to the people themselves, as they reflect on the thinking of fellow voters.

AFTERTHOUGHT

We have been preoccupied with the impact of targeted mass media, mailings and phone solicitations, and in the process, we have stepped around several budding technologies that lie in wait. Larry Grossman cautioned us with this sobering thought:

Do you realize that we are on the edge of something revolutionary? Just ahead is a communication system of enormous complexity, and when it takes off, it will make everything we've seen so far look simple. Even now, we have people standing in line for computer bulletin boards and signing up for EMail and other computer-based systems. With these technologies, people have instant news and highly personalized information. Moreover, they have an enormous potential to change the very dynamic of political communication.

Computer-based communications allow fast, personalized, user-involved, interactive communication, not just from a candidate to a voter, but from a voter to a candidate and among voters themselves. "This allows one-on-one, one-on-many, many-on-one communications," said Grossman. "Imagine the possibilities. If you really want to see what's shaping up, toss in faxes and improved telephone communication with 800 and 900 numbers and let your imagination expand for the rest, and you see the complexity we're facing. How does the press cover any of this?"

While looking at candidates' growing arsenal of computers and other technologies, we have overlooked the ordinance stockpiled by voters. So far, technology has worked on behalf of political campaigns, but computer equipment in the hands of citizens will further alter the relationship between candidates and voters.

Earlier in this chapter, we cited the growing popularity of interactive on-line services. Grossman's vision is the natural outgrowth of that trend to weave an invisible communication network where each user is a potential originator as well as a recipient of messages bound for one or many receivers. At some point, this notion of compound political communications will become a reality. It is not here yet. Too few people are on board, and the technology has not yet spread across a wide enough range of voters. But, average citizens will continue to adopt this technology, and at some time in the next decade, their numbers will reach a critical threshold. At that point, campaigns—and no doubt other marketing operations—will move forcefully into computer communications.

Actually, the process already has begun on a small scale. For the first time in history, major, national candidates communicated with voters through EMail during the 1992 campaign. George Bush and Bill Clinton participated in an electronic town meeting sponsored by the Prodigy computer network. Prodigy said Clinton answered about fifty questions and Bush about twenty-five for the 1.75 million subscribers (Castro 1992).

The press will face a new level of difficulty monitoring the back channels and assessing the many promises and promotions of a campaign. It isn't difficult to envision a time not far off when press coverage will become increasingly irrelevant in political communication.

NOTES

1. First Amendment cases usually involve confidentiality of sources. In these instances, the courts or Congress have demanded that a journalist reveal an information source. Failure to comply can result in contempt of court (or contempt of Congress) charges. The courts can imprison the journalist until s/he yields the information and, in addition, impose punitive penalties. Congress can imprison a journalist as a coercive measure to obtain the information, but only until it becomes evident that s/he never will be forthcoming with the requested details. Further imprisonment at this point would constitute a punitive (not coercive) penalty, a sentence Congress is not empowered to enforce. The journalist then must be freed.

The most recent First Amendment case involved congressional demands for information about leaks in the Clarence Thomas Supreme Court confirmation hearings. National Public Radio reporter Nina Totenberg and *Newsday* writer Timothy Phelps broke the story, which they developed from information leaked from a Senate committee. The senators wanted to know where the reporters got their information. The two weren't telling. Despite the Senate bluster, the reporters refused to identify their sources, and the committee searched elsewhere, unsuccessfully, for the information.

2. The potential for EMail can be seen, for instance, in CompuServe, an on-line information services company that has signed up nearly 1 million subscribers, and Prodigy, a joint venture of Sears and IBM, with more than 1.5 million hookups. General Electric's GEnie, a relative newcomer, already has enlisted 350,000 computer users (Goel 1992). The number of participants still is relatively small stacked against the total voting population, but consider that home computers only now are beginning to achieve the status of household appliances. (A dozen years ago, this author's home computer drew attention from visitors who wanted to see and touch an "actual" computer. Today, a home PC draws less attention than a toaster.)

Marketing of home computers did not begin until the mid–1980s, and even the teens just now graduating high school have been exposed to computers for only a handful of years. As prices drop and computers become ever more integrated into daily routines, the importance of computer communication will increase proportionately. With access to networks (e.g., CompuServe, Prodigy, BITNET and INTERNET), not only can users communicate directly with each other, but they easily can be targeted with highly personalized information by campaigns or other organizations.

3. Nielsen researcher Jo Laverde provided the network information in a telephone conversation, December 10, 1992. Michael Roey, producer of on-air programming at San Francisco public station QUED, offered the information on PBS ratings (phone conversation, December 18, 1992).

4. "All Things Considered" and "Morning Edition" are in-depth news programs. They select several top stories of the day and cover them in extended segments that often last five to ten minutes. These programs are popular among political aficionados and people who seek detailed news accounts.

5. Newspaper readership rates have fallen since the mid–1960s. Philip E. Meyer at the School of Journalism and Mass Communication at the University of North Carolina reports the following daily readership statistics of adults (18 and over): 1967, 73 percent; 1988, 50.6 percent; 1991, 51.5 percent. He says that the last two years in his database suggest a leveling of readership. (Reported in Alex Jones, "The Media Business: Press Amid Dark Clouds of Gloom, Newspapers See Some Hope," *New York Times*, December 30, 1992, p. D6.)

A more troubling trend, however, is readership among young people. A *Times Mirror* study found that only 30 percent of Americans under 35 said they read a newspaper. In 1965, this figure was 67 percent. (Mitchell Stephens, "The Death of Reading; Will a Nation That Stops Reading Eventually Stop Thinking?" *Los Angeles Times Magazine*, September 22, 1991, p. 10.)

6. I interviewed by phone seven leading political journalists and news media experts. Three (Broder, Dionne, and Kurtz) are practicing Washington reporters, two are journalists-turned-educators (Miller and Pippert) and two (Grossman and Kalb) are former television news superstars now in media education. I began each interview with a brief description of my thesis—that the use of targeted media was increasing in political communications—and asked each interviewee to comment on the topic. I have exerpted portions of these discussions for this chapter. Here are brief sketches of the participants' backgrounds:

David Broder is a reporter for the *Washington Post* and a syndicated columnist.

He is considered by many scholars and practicing journalists to be the leading political reporter in America. He often is referred to as the "dean of political journalism."

E. J. Dionne is also a reporter with the *Washington Post* and a frequent television talk show panelist. He recently completed an excellent book titled, *Why Americans Hate Politics* (New York: Simon & Schuster, 1991).

Larry Grossman is a former president of NBC News, former president of the Public Broadcasting Service and Frank Stanton Professor at Harvard University.

Marvin Kalb is a former reporter for CBS News, now director of Harvard's Joan Shorenstein Barone Center for Media and the Press.

Howard Kurtz is a reporter with the *Washington Post* and frequent television talk show panelist.

Edward Miller is an associate at the Poynter Institute and was director of Poynter's Charlotte project during the 1992 presidential campaign.

Wesley Pippert was with UPI for thirty years as a political reporter. He was bureau chief in Jerusalem. He currently is director of the University of Missouri–Columbia Washington Reporting Program in Washington, D.C.

Chapter Nine

Effects on the Political System and Government

As the master politician navigates the ship of state, he both creates and responds to public opinion. Adept at tacking with the wind, he also succeeds, at times, in generating breezes of his own.

—Stewart L. Udall[1]

INTRODUCTION

Finally, we come to the institution that is impacted by all the other elements struck by the new technologies. The political system and the government around which politics revolves have changed in ways obvious and opaque. Political campaigns fix on single-issue themes, one or two to a group, and they assert a strong view on hair-trigger issues, easy to divide up, while avoiding the larger, global topics difficult to address.

Single-issue politics is closely related to another victim of high-tech campaigning: the decline of the two political parties. It's like the breakup of a wagon train, each Conestoga wagon going off on its own with individual maps and dead-reckoning navigators. Nobody seems to need a wagon master anymore, and they don't seem to need the discipline and the group focus.

Party loyalty, once viewed by some as a curse on American politics, is viewed nostalgically today by many as a blessing lost. The new technologies have made it possible to cultivate individual constituencies without adopting party lines on sweeping issues.

Some of this is old stuff. Neither Strom Thurman nor George Wallace needed targeted communications to mount third party campaigns. But some things are new. Poll results have recorded a higher level of cynicism and dissatisfaction with the political system than ever before. People have blamed politicians for many of the country's ills—some of them justified, others not. Clearly, the voters rebuked George Bush for what they saw as his contributions to the nation's economic ills. Even though 97 percent of Congress running in 1992 was returned to office, term limits were passed by each of the fourteen states voting on the issue.

Not only voters, but politicians are looking down their noses at the system. During the 1992 campaign, more senators and congressmen chose not to run for reelection than at any time in history. This was due to bank scandals, sex scandals and other factors, but do not overlook the impact of the evolving relationships between voters and elected officials. These relationships influence and are influenced by the way politicians communicate with those who elect them.

Without strong party loyalty and the group consensus that party loyalty once brought about, governing itself has become less efficient and ever more prone to battles over ideological nuances, personality rifts within the legislative bodies and between Congress and the administration.

This chapter examines the impact of changing communication patterns in politics and government, and it considers problems emerging in the process. It would be inaccurate and unfair to pin the patterns or the ills wholly on the new communications, but it is undeniable that they are in the watery broth that has fed the faltering body politic in Washington and in many state capitals.

SINGLE-ISSUE POLITICS

The American identity is derived from two sources. The first is heritage—blood, race, history and culture. We see ourselves as Africans, Europeans, Asians, Latins. We identify ourselves as Catholics, Jews, Protestants, Muslims. We line up as Republicans, Democrats, prochoicers or prolifers. By history and hope, our forebears took to America—unwillingly for some, already here for others—as part of a melting pot. We are a nation of segments; thus, we value our individuality. We revel in the freedom to exist in racial, ethnic and ideological factions, all of which proclaim distinctions but exist as part of the total mosaic.

The second identity is of that mosaic. From this larger perspective, we see ourselves as nationals. We are Americans. We have a common government, common laws, common problems and fortunes that are intertwined. Natural disasters, economic difficulties, threats to one portion of the country affect the rest.

Americans always have held this dual membership—in narrow groups and in the wider collective. Despite periodic tremors that shake society, the delicate balance enjoyed in this country has not been achieved anywhere else on the globe. Radical factionalism in many countries has eroded a sense of national unity and created explosive conflicts. Several former Soviet countries offer a prime example (e.g., Moldavia, Azerbaijan, Armenia). Ireland, South Africa and Yugoslavia provide a few more.

In light of the workable stability achieved in this country (which has the greatest representation of subgroups anywhere on earth), it is worth asking about the possible effects of divide-and-conquer politics. Do strategies that seek to identify and isolate the differences among groups strike at the national community?

Political campaigns often benefit from exaggerated voter differences. Voters like clear choices. They like to know who are the good guys and the bad guys. It is easier that way to pick an issue and to choose up sides.

Communicators, like dramatists, know this, and that's why they target. Targeting strategies have been used to amplify differences among various sides and to play upon yawing factions. It's easier and more effective to talk the in game with each group than to talk one game for all. Private communications with different camps allow campaigns to play off the distinctions, further separate the views and build distinctive coalitions.

Although political campaigns always have engaged in such tactics, it is only during the past decade that the new technologies have given candidates the capacity to dissect the population with such precision. Sorting voters into clearly defined subgroups is an idea whose time has come by way of computerization. The tactics of targeting, refined by every computer advance, are innately divisive. In time, what will they do to the political system and to the society?

Los Angeles Times writer David Shaw (1992, p. A1) offered this: "If everyone is seeing different stories and advertisements, people will often wind up talking about different subjects and having different priorities, and that commonality and sense of community will diminish—a special danger in our increasingly mutlicultural society, where fragmentation is already a major concern."

Over a decade ago, *Washington Post* columnist and syndicated writer Meg Greenfield (1978, p. A13) envisioned it all. She said these tactics "put a premium on identifying yourself with the special subgroup and help to thin, if not destroy, whatever feelings of larger national loyalty various citizens might have." Greenfield's concern, like that of De Toqueville a century earlier, is for community, the perspective of a nation bound by common elements. Will the result of repeated drumming on parochial issues deafen our ears to national loyalty and to national unity? Special-interest agendas obscure larger needs and make legislation more difficult to develop. Look to the budget debates during the upcoming lean years as divided groups become increasingly more contentious, each fighting for its own allotment of the shrinking pie with diminishing regard for broadly shared hungers.

This already is evident in county and state houses across the country.

As budgets weaken from lower tax revenues and cuts in federal contributions, many state and local governments must raise taxes or cut services. Few want tax hikes, while strong, committed coalitions aggressively defend services—education, welfare, medical treatment, libraries, arts and dozens of other special programs—each sacred to a strong advocacy group. Leaders are caught on the horns of a dilemma: They cannot raise taxes, but they dare not cut services. Too many people have bought the line that they can have it all yet pay for only some. Too many people have been led to regard that one issue as sacred, refusing any measure of compromise.

One of the great myths of our time is that poverty draws people together. It does not. The impoverishment of any needed resource divides people and pits them one against the other. Our system is groaning under the stress of competing, unbending interests, and divide-and-conquer political strategies only add greater strain.

Too pessimistic? Do the appeals to ever narrower voter subgroups yield these unhappy effects?

The coin has another side. To be sure, there are some public interest groups that do not fractionalize (e.g., the League of Women Voters). And many "special"-interest groups, while fighting for narrow concerns, see themselves as citizens in a national community (e.g., AARP reminds grandparents that, without restructuring the distribution of entitlements, their children may never enjoy the social security that today's elders enjoy). Yet, the arguments are strong and the consequences of factionalism are so severe that we cannot overlook the balkanization of America. The sands are running out for political professionals who dodge the ethics of their technologically enhanced campaigns.

LONE RANGER CAMPAIGNS

Our grandparents loved the aphorism, "The hand that rocks the cradle controls the world." Today, we see that the person who controls communications controls the political campaign—and through it, the nation. Before the mid–1950s, parties exercised control over campaigns, because they raised the money and fed the press. Today, there are a dozen ways to go directly to the voter. Besides the ever-narrowing television and radio channels, there is a host of one-on-one choices in direct-mail, telephone and computer communications.

One of the great party end arounds came in 1976, when Jimmy Carter (for a while called "Jimmy Who?") entered the national limelight through his surprising victory in the New Hampshire primary. Carter used the media to assert his candidacy without relying on the grinding seniority system that once graduated a select few candidates.

At the senatorial level, Pennsylvania Democratic candidate Lynn H. Yeakel used the media in the spring of 1992 to rise from total obscurity (an initial name recognition of less than 1 percent) to win the primary over her established, party-supported opponent, Lieutenant Governor Mark Singel. Yeakel relied almost exclusively on a combination of media to gain instant recognition. She lost a squeaker in the general election to veteran (and incumbent) Senator Arlan Spector, who knew a thing or two about using media in megadoses.

Party strength and media access are related inversely; media access enhances candidate power, and this reduces party power. The media are growing more plentiful and more targeted and with the increasing opportunity for channel selection and effective message development, the candidate wields yet greater control. The country only recently has become webbed by cable systems that have expanded channel availability to a household average of more than thirty-three stations. This has provided greater voter targeting opportunities. At the same time, candidates have invested heavily in computers and elaborate software that enable them to exploit the new targeted outlets, using high-tech, targeted direct-mail and telephone techniques to add to the communication repertoire. In 1991 alone, Congress spent 14.5 million taxpayer dollars on computers with which to target constituents. Many more millions were spent through the campaigns.

These communication techniques have eroded the parties. House Minority Whip Newt Gingrich complains that the party is losing its grip at the local level (Edsall 1990). He argues for greater strategic planning and coordination by the party to channel the efforts of local candidates. Gingrich's paper-thin victory in 1992 over an obscure opponent, who knew how to use media, simply underlined the diminishing power of the party to protect its own.

But, is this really a problem? Why should anyone lament the decline of political parties? Not long ago, critics complained about political bosses who cut unholy deals in smoke-filled rooms. Wasn't this corruption of the democratic process as offensive as anything that may occur in the party's absence?

That's a tough one. Despite the reduction of political party influence, deal making and logrolling survive. Parties may have institutionalized such activities, but it is naive to think that back-room politics does not go on without strong party bosses. More to the point, the loss of party influence affects the stability and cohesion within political structures. Berkman and Kitch (1985, p. 320) describe some of the problems.

Without parties to provide political focus or forge alliances among the multiple, overlapping, and conflicting interests that characterize the American political scene, the electorate has been fragmented into little pockets of single interest groups. These small narrowly-focused, single interest groups promote a politics of selfishness, intolerance, and zealotry. This kind of politics reopens old wounds, separates rather than unites, and poses a mighty threat to the principles of democracy.

Such a forlorn view may be justified. The Lone Ranger campaign, unrestrained by the balance and discipline of party influence, finds little motivation for cohesive, mainstream strategies. The natural result is a set of disjointed political campaigns in pursuit of hot-button issues among disparate voter groups.

Syndicated political columnist David Broder (1992, p. A23) states the serious fallout of party decline: "The evidence is now overwhelming that government without parties does not work. There is no accountability; therefore, no responsibility; therefore, no incentive for presidents or legislators to make the hard choices." Broder paints a picture of leaderless sheep, ambling about their own square of pasture without regard for where the flock may be heading. The process began with the advent of television and has assumed new dimensions with the arrival of advanced information technologies.

Causes and effects are seldom clear-cut. The relationships among technology, communication strategies, voter isolation, and the descent of parties are woven tight. Technology permits the identification and segmentation of groups, which diminishes party influence, which, in turn, promotes the use of individual targeted strategies. The circle is complete and contracting.

The campaign of former Ku Klux Klansman David Duke of Louisiana provides a good example of party irrelevance. Although this state legislator is nominally a Republican, the national Republican party has publicly disavowed him and exercised no recognizable influence on his U.S. senatorial campaign. Duke ran for the state house using targeting strategies among narrow subgroups receptive to his racist philosophies. He adopted a similar approach in his senatorial campaign (and his run for the presidential nomination in 1992), using focused communication techniques to deal with issues involving affirmative action (e.g., "parasitic welfare recipients and programs for minority contractors," *Newsweek* 1990, p. 37). This campaign is one of the most visible examples of party influence run aground. The maverick Duke's white supremacist campaign would have had little chance within traditional party structures. Duke's bid for the presidency died quickly in the primaries, not because of party intervention, but because his extremist views were unacceptable to national audiences, and because Pat Buchanan drained off far-right voters, who found the journalist a more respectable extremist.

As technology hastens the decline of party influence, Lone Ranger candidates likely will become commonplace.

VOTER DISGRUNTLEMENT

Buffeted by the war in Vietnam, troubled race relations and domestic violence on campuses and in city streets, voters in the 1960s were angry at their government and at each other. That was a decade of pain, change and realignment, the ascendancy of a volatile generation, the push for equality in national life, the examination and conditioning of collective values.

The eighties, too, was a decade of both change and realignment. It was a time notable for its deregulation, tax cuts, high-stakes defense spending, buy-outs, junk bonds, abandonment of energy policies and a score of other short-term, feel-good programs and policies. The country fixed not on a guiding polestar, but on the glittering lights with which Mr. Reagan electrified the nation. It's not surprising that the word "glitterati" was used in the eighties to describe the beautiful people. Not as visible, however, was the decline in wealth for middle- and lower-income groups—the very ones Reagan proselytized from the Democrats.[2] Today, pundits by the brigades are looking back at the destructive effects of the corporate realignment, income redistributions from the poor and middle class to the wealthy and the explosion of national debt.[3]

So, like a bear emerging from hibernation, the public is awakening to the reality of the eighties through which it just slept. Mary McGrory (1992, p. A2) of the *Washington Post* says voters now "sense that democracy has gone astray, that the rich pay less tax while the poor pay more, that corporations pollute and escape fines and merrily represent themselves as guardians of eagles and children on billion-dollar advertising budgets."

The 55 percent turnout for the 1992 presidential election—although weak by comparison with every other major democracy—was good by American standards and suggests a renewed faith in the power of the vote. Still, surveys, feedback to radio talk shows, letters to the editor and other voter measures reveal that driving this surge at the polls was not optimism and a renewed zeal for democracy, but disaffection, anger and fear, many people voting against, rather than for, a candidate. Public disgruntlement remains strong, and it arises from a sense of abandonment by its leaders, the political system and even the press that once represented the people to the establishment.

William Greider (1992) made a case for the isolation of American voters in his book *Who Will Tell the People: The Betrayal of American Democracy*. He described how the old ward-and-precinct system, which tethered representatives to their constituents, has all but disappeared. Ward captains once marshalled local citizens and transmitted their concerns through the system directly to the officeholder. Furthermore, representatives customarily visited their districts every few weeks. This frequent contact kept officials in touch with the people and provided a forum for the people to touch their representatives. That now is gone.

Fading quickly are the once muscular unions that pounded the pylons of middle-class values into the foundations of political party platforms. Their influence and their memberships are shrinking.[4] Unions increasingly are being ignored by management and by politicians who once actively sought their council and endorsement. Cheap labor, open-shop laws, festering internal corruption, shifting world economies and the long, dark shadow of the spectacular PATCO strike in 1981 knocked the wind out of the unions and quieted a onetime powerful voice for American middle-class voters.

Syndicated columnist Mark Shields (1992, p. A19) said that because of the faltering labor unions, the Democratic Party will "be less concerned with economic dinner-table issues and more absorbed with social coffee-table causes. . . . [It will] become more culturally elitist and less economically populist."

According to Greider, elected representatives now transmit messages through the media, and they collect information from polls—or they don't collect it at all. This arm's length relationship is made possible, in part, by the new technologies, which consume polling data by the boxcar full and obviate the "need" for other methods.

How could all of his have happened in a free and open democracy, where the government's business is openly bared to the sunshine of public scrutiny and subjected to the rigors of an aggressive, enlightened press? That is a question about which volumes will be written. The answer, in part, has to do with technology-driven communications. There are several matters worth considering in the mix of explanations.

First, there is the displacement factor. Displacement occurs when the use of narrow channels, with special messages to special audiences, displaces communications on mass channels, with general messages to general audiences. People expect public office seekers to communicate with them. They once anticipated face-to-face contact, as in the ward-and-precinct system, and although today their expectations may be lower, people still expect some contact with the leaders who represent them, spend their money and run their government.

The importance of large, mass-media communications is passing, except, perhaps, in presidential campaigns. Trends now are toward the narrow media: cable television, smaller radio, phone banks and a lot of direct mail. We already have described how these media specialize in homogenous audiences. They provide a forum for the candidate to identify audience-specific issues and to address them directly.

Since broadcasting networks aim at "everybody," they are hardly appropriate for specialized audiences, and so they are used as forums for the large, population-wide topics. The smaller media are the "narrowcasters," the choices for small, homogeneous audiences. The big national topics—the deficit, environmental problems, health care—can be displaced by talk on narrow media about layoffs in local shipyards, regional water-allocation issues, local road and bridge repair, sorghum subsidies, special school programs. These matters are not trivial to people affected by them, but the problem is in the lack of discussion and attention to the large, leather-tough issues that impact the entire population. This is the conclusion of an examination by the *Columbia Journalism Review*.[5] Increasingly, campaigns restrict their communications to specialized topics that wind up displacing the big ones. Politicians are giving people cab rides and leaving the bus in the garage.

When candidates tackle a tough topic, targeted communications allow them to pick and choose which element they will address with each audience. Voters are deliberately cast in the role of the blind men and the elephant. To one group, candidates describe a leg, to another, the trunk and another the tail. No one group learns about the whole elephant, mistaking a specialized part for the whole.

Take energy policy. In an energy-dependent state like New York, a candidate can talk about the need to find less costly, more efficient fuels, better electricity production techniques and conservation programs that lower costs. But, in Texas and Oklahoma, the candidate can talk about oil price stabilization and tax laws favorable to production.

Similarly, environmentalists hear only about a candidate's conservation plank, while coal miners learn about federal encouragement of coal use in power plants. None of the messages conflict, and the candidate never lies—it's just a matter of agendas.

There is nothing wrong with directing specific messages to specific audiences. The problem is the candidate who deals selectively with bits and pieces of an important policy without addressing the entire package.

Where is the gestalt? Oil drilling, home insulation, energy-efficient automobiles, gasoline tax, coal mining, foreign oil imports, smokestack scrubbers and air pollution all are part of a large, unified policy. Together, the various parts fuse into the elephant.

Meanwhile, the Lone Rangers like Perot are chopping the audience into ever smaller parts, giving voters messages with individual interest. You will never hear the Perots, Dukes and Buchannans talk about a platform; they don't have one. They have only hot-button fragments. Voters looking for the complete picture are forced to turn elsewhere for information, and a lot of people never bother.

After hearing from one or more candidates about some special issue or about the special feature of a larger policy, it is natural for voters to believe that their thing is the only thing. This self-concerned attitude is no threat until it is intensified by targeted campaign activities. Smog-engulfed Los Angelenos will believe cleaner fuel burning is the most important part of the energy policy; West Virginians will think consumption of domestic coal is most important. Automobile workers may feel only the abundance of cheap gasoline really matters. People scared to death about the deficit will welcome cuts in entitlements. Environmentalists put spotted owls above the need for jobs; loggers see only the jobs. People believe in the universality of their causes, even without the instigation of office seekers who pander to them. In the process, America is losing its ability to see the grand view that makes the nation one.

It is the role of political leaders to weigh local needs against national priorities, special interests against the public interest. In this calculus, no one gets everything, but everyone gets something. That's the political meaning of the greatest good for the greatest number. Political parties, sewing parochial interests into a broader tapestry, have served that larger view of a national community. Today, individual agendas are becoming more inflexible. Tailor-made communications dealing with specific, narrow issues are threatening our oneness.

Another painful result of technology-driven, targeted communications is the depersonalization of politics. Again, the old ward-and-precinct system sent captains door-to-door, visiting each voter, discussing the campaign and asking for the vote. This personal contact made voters feel like somebodies. They connected, they participated. Voters carried their concerns to captains, then up the line to the candidate. Whatever the problem—and petty corruption was one—it brought people together. Contrast that with an expressionless, paid-by-the-hour pollster asking a scant handful of scattered voters twenty questions in ten minutes.

In the current system, communications flow directly from the candidates and their staffs; they have replaced the kitchen table talks and ward captains. "Personally signed" letters from candidates refer to specific voter characteristics and pander to individual voter concerns. Phone banks deliver computer-tuned messages that easily could be mistaken for genuine, personal calls. Other media messages, although more generalized, still are targeted toward the voter's concerns, and mass media are restricted to negative ads and smears. The net effect of these contacts is the cultivation of a perceived relationship with the candidate. "They called me. They know I work for Chrysler. They know I'm married to Louise, have two kids and have lived here fifteen years. They talked about a possible layoff, my biggest, damned worry." People like to feel important, and they want to feel connected. Targeting feeds off these human desires, and by design, it encourages the perception of a growing relationship that is, in reality, false.

The switch from person-to-person communication to high-tech depersonalization that counterfeits the human element has led to the rise in selfish expectation. Candidates finger the voter's hot-button issues and vow to seek a fitting resolution. Politicians have always passed out promises by the buckets full, but the high-tech forum for these promises—personal letters and staff calls—makes them more tangible and convincing. It's one thing to hear a stump speech promising a chicken in every generic pot, quite another to read a signed letter from a candidate promising coq au vin in your pot. The latter has a higher order of credibility and merits a stronger sense of expectation. There is nothing wrong with an expectation as long as it can be fulfilled. The rub comes when the promises go unful-filled. Towering expectations cause more pain when they topple. Voters feel let down, and after a few disappointing episodes by several candidates, they know they've been played for suckers. The hurt then turns to the cynicism and anger we see among voters today.

There is a growing perception that politicians are in it for themselves and will do what it takes to get elected. A statement by President Bush during the 1992 campaign only reinforced the public outrage. Bush told David Frost on national television that he would "do anything to get elected." He meant, he said later, that he would quit Washington and take to the streets—using anything political the campaign called for.

Voters recalled promises uttered during the 1988 campaign and figured they were just in for more of the same. In a lunch counter interview on William Greider's "Frontline" program, a man described as an average voter said, "Politicians are like lovers, they chase you, then when they get what they want, they leave you." This statement expresses the feeling revealed in polls by a growing number of voters that candidates toss around promises like posies, then forget their pledges and their beloved constit-uents after the election.

Two points are worth repeating. First, broken personal promises hurt. This is why the increasing use of direct mail and other targeted techniques, with ever more specific reference to topics close to home, can have a sharper sting. By design, people become ego-involved in smaller forums—from limited seminars to small-group political communications, personal letters and phone calls. So, while people are elevated by the personal touch, they also fall harder when they discover they've been had. Polls reveal increasing public disgruntlement with the honesty of elected officials and with their ability to deliver on promises.

Second, politicians are growing more distant from their constituents in a very observable way, delivering fewer of the goods they promise during the heat of a campaign. Greider argues that the division between voters and politicians is widened by the legislative process. Most legislation today, he says, is general, laying out broad principles—often the grand principles expounded in a campaign. Congress expresses sweeping legislative goals for drug treatment, food-product labeling and cable television regulation, to mention three of many. But, the devil is in the details, and the details are determined at the federal agency level, not in legislation. Health and Human Services, the Food and Drug Administration and the Federal Communication Commission—the agencies—write the details of these broad principles, and here voters feel the sting.

Gary D. Bass, executive director of OMB Watch, was quoted as saying, "So much of the way government operates is controlled by these behind-the-scenes, boring agencies." While tax law debates engage the public, "the engine to carry them out is the regulations" (Lockhead 1992).

When sweeping legislative generalities appear as operational specifics, voters are surprised by things they did not expect. Drug treatment in practice looks different from drug treatment legislation. Product labels and cable television regulations don't conform to expectations built from the legislation.

The problem, Greider says, is that at the agency level, where corporations and monied interests prevail, voters rarely are represented. Details are chiseled by only a few hands. The disparity between the expectations and the reality of regulations arouses cynicism for the process and drives a wedge between the voters and their representatives. This may have been reflected in the landslide vote for term limitations during the 1992 elections.

Consider the automobile fuel standards laid out in general legislation in 1975. Congress expressed its desires for improved efficiency and left the dirty details to the agencies. Auto industry lobbyists intervened at the Environmental Protection Agency and other agencies, and the efficiency ratings of new cars actually worsened in the late eighties and early nineties. So, the laws become hollow. Voters see the philosophy of legislation, which they like, then face the reality of implementation and feel betrayed. It often looks like a double cross. Greider believes the people are becoming street smart about this shell game. As they recognize what is happening, they also understand how powerless they really are. That is the frustration and the source of growing public hostility.

Clearly, there has been legislative grid-lock made worse because Congress and the administration were of different parties. Individual interests came to the table unyielding and uncompromising, the power of the veto thundering through Washington as an effective force, frequently neutralizing Democratic majorities in both houses.[6] Legislation often was purged of detail in order to clear both houses and to squeak past a presidential veto. These are times when agency rule-making dominates and the process becomes a devil's playground.

Against this backdrop in Washington, voters at election time receive targeted messages—some direct and personal, some through narrow media—telling them how much will be accomplished in their name. The information is specific, and it is disembodied from the larger set of issues that relate to any significant national debate. Expectations are built and broken, promises unkept, legislation unmoved. After all the crest and fall, a population is bound to grow cynical, even one already conditioned to suspect sleight of hand from its government.

IMPLICATIONS FOR GOVERNING

The worrisome thing about targeting technologies in political campaigns is this: The fallout continues after the political campaign ends and incumbency begins. Berkman and Kitch (1985, p. 147) write, "Modern governing has become a permanent campaign. Once elected, politicians must continually seek public approval for support of their policies. Techniques used to get the vote are now necessary to maintain public approval."

Each voter understandably expects officeholders to fulfill expectations generated during the campaign. Officials now must address the seductive, key issues separately, not as part of a larger package. "No-new-taxes voters" want no new taxes as promised, no matter what happens with the economy. Proenvironment voters want no development, despite the impact on jobs and industry. Prodevelopment voters want economic growth; to hell with natural resources. It's everyone for his own special interest, with little regard for the larger context. Campaigns foster these selfish views.

In the process, public approval has become paramount, and it does not stop at the water's edge of a campaign. The Bush administration became known for its loyalty to the polls. In 1988, Bush's candidacy took full advantage of the targeting technologies, segmenting audiences and directing messages of particular appeal to ideological, demographic and geographic subgroups. It follows that his presidency was known for its Pavlovian responses to the polls and to public opinion.

The Middle East crisis of 1990 was a case in point. Iraq invaded Kuwait just as President Bush was about to embark on his summer vacation in Maine. Among the casualties of war would be a peaceful presidential holiday. Public perception became a problem for the president and his political advisers: Should he sit in Washington to direct the U.S. Middle East operation, or should he continue with his vacation to avoid being seen as a hostage to the crisis? Uppermost in the minds of his advisers was Jimmy Carter's absorption in the Iranian Embassy takeover in 1979. His preoccupations became overwhelming (magnified by the hostage countdown on nightly newscasts) and contributed to the loss of his second bid for the presidency. Public opinion assaults on Carter taught Bush a lesson. The presidential vacation set the stage for some interesting public relations posturing.

White House spokesman Marlin Fitzwater publicly explained Bush's careful balance. The *Washington Post* quoted Fitzwater as saying,

The president thinks it's good for Americans to "*see that he is able* to continue carrying on the business of government at the same time worrying about this situation in the Gulf. . . . He carries on the work of the White House wherever he goes, and it's important for the *American people to see* that he's not holed up in the White House, as has happened in the past. So we're comfortable with the

American people seeing that he's combining his work and his vacation" (italics mine) (Balz 1990, p. A15).

It is interesting that the president's pollster and political strategist, Robert Teeter, was prominent throughout this delicate public relations episode. The *Post* said: "Robert Teeter . . . argued today that it is only journalists who are upset with the idea of Bush vacationing while the gulf crisis deepens. . . . Teeter insisted that *the public supports the president's policy* and does not begrudge him some time for relaxation" (italics mine) (Balz 1990, p. A15).

Congress is no less immune to the grip of public reaction. It draws from the same well of technologies and is similarly affected. *New York Times* writer Michael Oreskes (1990, p. I22) laments: "In the past, when a President failed to seize the initiative, Congress often tried to. But now both ends of Pennsylvania Avenue seem immobilized by a politics of avoidance, where poll takers and advertising producers are more influential than economists or engineers."

Behind every political act lurks an ethical question. Granted that officeholders always have wanted to please their constituents, by custom they keep a steady eye on the next campaign. So what difference has high-tech communications made, and why do these practices raise the moral eyebrows of serious observers?

If ethics is about good and bad, right and wrong, it would be hard to characterize the process of polling as bad or wrong. Monitoring the public pulse has a valid place in a democracy as a tool of polity. The problem arises when the tool overpowers the polity, when the whims of public opinion dominate the formulation of public policy.

This republic does not submit every public issue for popular vote, because we expect elected officials to research the details of complex matters and to act on our behalf. We pay them to study the options and to use judgments, reasoned and moral, in making decisions that best advance the public interest. Public opinion receives its proper weight. But, the U.S. republican system of government was created to allow elected representatives to be the surrogates of the people on matters not best resolved through public vote. When officials substitute public opinion for their own judgment, they abrogate their responsibilities and dodge their constitutional obligations.

Senate Majority Leader George J. Mitchell has expressed his "frustration over what he calls the new breed of 'wet-finger politicians,' who spend more time sampling the political winds than reading policy papers" (Oreskes 1990, p. I22). When Hawkeye, in *The Last of the Mohicans*, raised a wet finger to the wind, he was using this as one of several skills in the larger venture of scouting. Wet-fingered politicians have no other purpose than to see which way the wind is blowing so they can conform to the public whim.

Besides displacing reasoned and ethical judgment, advice from the polls can be misleading. The public nearly always takes the easy way out. Survey respondents typically express personal preferences for utopian conditions without a sense of obligation to the system or accountability for the outcomes. People one-by-one answering a pollster's questions have no collective sense of responsibility. They also are unlikely to know much more about an issue than what they see in a few newscasts and, in a diminishing number of cases, read in a daily newspaper. Oreskes (1990, p. I22) says, "We have public opinion now, which is people's private reflexes. But we don't have public judgment." This is an understandable, although undesirable condition. It is a matter of political fraud when elected officials allow the substitution of such expressions for their own judgment. The matter becomes even more intolerable when the process is adopted for political expedience.

Not only that, but polls can distort reality. David W. Moore, writing an op ed column for the Sunday *New York Times* (1992), asked why Clinton had a double-digit lead before dropping to a five-point lead just before the election. His answer: The pollsters asked questions that led undecided, unsure respondents to say which way they were leaning. That encouraged them to commit themselves when their minds were not yet made up. Then, at the last minute, the 20 to 30 percent of uncommitted voters finally decided. Poll fluctuations prior to the election ranged so widely that they occasionally became news items alongside stories about the candidates. During the 1992 campaign, polls had front-page billing. The "MacNeil-Lehrer News Hour" on PBS even devoted most of an hour-long program to discussions about the frustrating, wild swings from day to day, from poll to poll.

Despite such pulsations in the polls, Lee AuCoin, former representative from Oregon, says his political consultants were not deterred. They paid too much attention to public opinion and coached him to do the same. He found little merit in the advice, noting that, for an officeholder, "the science of public opinion measuring is being misused to lock you in where you are today rather than to lead society to where you think you ought to be" (Oreskes 1990, p. I22). Even if accurately measured, public opinion offers a helpful statement of general impressions and values, but not much vision. It does not project. It may measure the present, but it offers little guidance for the future. Senator James A. McClure says the "polls are measuring emotional responses, not thought-out views" (Oreskes 1990, p. I22).

Put another way, polling data, which is bedrock to a campaign, may be quicksand for a government. Elected officials find themselves trapped by the technology that helped them achieve office. All those weak coalitions and strong special interests must be serviced. Voters become increasingly helpless to recognize the candidate's responsibility to sit in judgment on many issues and represent the public good, not just fractional passions and Johnny-one-note causes.

During the 1988 campaign, no single issue dominated more than taxes. Bush's unequivocal "read my lips, no new taxes" statement became the acid test for candidates of both parties. Political death would befall any candidate who uttered the "T" word. Since then, the classes of 1988, 1990 and now 1992 have been in office facing a frightening conundrum. The polls continue to register widespread public rejection of taxes, yet the national deficit climbs out of sight, and all the attending problems of a financially crippled nation come home to roost.

What's a politician to do? Fear of voters' wrath makes elected officials leery of any measure—notably higher taxes or lower entitlements—that could address the country's financial woes. In 1992, 63 percent of personal income taxes are needed to pay just the interest on the swelling debt. American families would have to hand over $45,000 each to clear the $4.4 trillion debt. Perot was the only one to speak the "T" word, and for that he deserves credit. Still, public opinion says "no," while all logic says "yes." The polls have paralyzed those who want to win before they can govern.

CONCLUSION

Like kicking a crack habit, it is not easy for a candidate to kick the habit of the new technologies. Candidates acquire a taste for the sense of control granted by voter information and targeted access. Politicians have cultivated tenacious constituency groups that demand promises of specific action on narrow issues be honored. Their indebtedness forces them to return to the surveys for guidance. They must raise that wet finger to the air again and again to see what the voters think about the issues today and about their performances yesterday. Thus, modern campaigning techniques resonate beyond the campaign.

We return to the time-honored concept for physics and politics that every action has an equal and opposite reaction. The new technologies have thundered into political campaigns with the promise of impacting large voter blocks through small, intimate communications. They have done that and more very well.

The opposite reaction has been the unplanned effects on voters, the press and the political system, all of which feel the consequences of a process that personifies numbers and brushes data in warm, fleshy tones. The process has benefits and drawbacks, blessings, and curses, and the balance will change as the technology evolves and the techniques mature. Already, there are warnings, but watch for the signs when voters become mere objects of a campaign, chess pieces analyzed then inched along, square by square, pawns in somebody else's game.

Voters are the owners of the process and of the government served by the process. When technology obscures that role, the balance tips sharply against its unbridled use. Marvin Kalb's instincts were right when he said, "I believe the use of technology can contribute to the growing irrelevance of the voter and, therefore, to the weakening of the democratic process." The voters must retain their power within the political process, no matter how wonderful and extraordinary these new technologies become.

NOTES

1. Stewart L. Udall, *The Quiet Crisis* (New York: Holt, Rinehart and Winston, 1963), p. 11.

2. The poor and middle class were lured into this policy that gave enormously disproportionate tax breaks to the wealthy.

3. One organization that contributed to the cynicism was the Competitiveness Council, whose sole stated purpose was to alleviate regulatory pressures on business. In 1992, the administration froze nearly all federal regulations to allow review by the Competitiveness Council, headed by the vice president. Quayle said a regulation would be suspect if it was "unnecessary" or came with "unnecessary costs." What constituted an unnecessary or unnecessarily costly regulation was the determination solely of the council. Moreover, adopting the most un-American bylaws, the council operated behind closed doors.

4. For instance, UAW membership has dropped from 1.5 million in 1979 to about 900,000 today.

5. See chapter 7 (note 4) for a quotation on the subject from the *Columbia Journalism Review*, reported in Molly Ivins, "The Media and the Election Press Asks Itself, 'How Did We Do?' Sins of Omission Count," *Atlanta Journal and Constitution*, November 28, 1992, A17.

6. President Bush vetoed thirty-six bills during his four years in office and was overridden only once—on his last veto of cable television legislation.

Appendix A

Elaboration on an Analysis Technique

This appendix supplements the information presented in chapter 6. It examines the components of a matrix formed by the intersection of Berlo's communication elements (source, message, channel and receiver) and knowledge, attitudes and behavior.

		Receiver	
	Source	Message	Channel
Knowledge	1	4	7
Attitudes	2	5	8
Behavior	3	6	9

1. KNOWLEDGE—SOURCE

The Basic Issue: What do voters know about the candidate (who is the recognized source of most information arising from a campaign)?

Anticipate two broad response categories: (1) Voters know nothing about the candidate (never heard of him or her), and (2) they know about the candidate. This ranges from having heard something (barely name recognition) to knowing everything possible.

Find out what these voters know along three dimensions: (1) What kinds of things do they know (characteristics, views and positions)? (2) How detailed is their knowledge (on a scale from knowing almost nothing to knowing the fine points)? (3) How accurate is their knowledge (is what they know correct)?

This information highlights the level of familiarity with a candidate's character and personality. A campaign should consider a strong public awareness program when voters are not aware of a candidate's character and background.

Such was the case for candidate Jimmy Carter, dubbed by the press at the beginning of the primary season as "Jimmy Who?" Clever PR work and success in the Iowa caucuses drew in a curious national press, which then filled in the Carter "blank."

Too little information, too late, can be a real problem. Consider the Perot candidacy in 1992. Early polls showed the public knew almost nothing about the man. It was an anonymity he appeared to enjoy. Perot quickly discovered, however, that the knowledge vacuum allowed other campaigns to define him, and it was not a definition he liked. Perot's campaign was slow to advance public knowledge about this unknown from Texas. At first, it seemed that the information void was a strength; later, they found that it came at a cost.

Don't let voters form impressions on incorrect information. Bring the candidate into sharper focus. It is difficult enough modifying negative impressions based on facts, but it is worse when impressions are based on incorrect information. Detect these knowledge gaps and misperceptions, and confront them early. How do you detect them?

The best way is through polls and surveys. Campaigns must dig for details, and usually open-ended questions work best. Once the campaign is underway, monitor voters' knowledge of a candidate with faster, more efficient, closed-ended questions.

Focus groups can examine the knowledge base, but don't substitute them for studies of representative voter samples. Even focus groups with a "cross-section of voters" do not provide representative data. Moreover, representativeness notwithstanding, vocal opinion leaders have a way of submerging the ideas of quiet participants and, in the processes, rob researchers of important perspectives.

Finally, examine the entire population, but also discover the many small clusters within that population. The prizes in targeted communications are the small groups. It is simple to discuss voters' views as though they were homogeneous, but people are not so uniform. Their differences become the defining elements for targeted communications.

2. ATTITUDES—SOURCE

The Basic Issue: What are the voters' attitudes about the candidate?

Because attitudes follow knowledge, you want to know how voters feel about the candidate. Easy enough, but along what dimensions: Do you care only if voters like your candidate? That may not be enough. Some-times, people like a candidate but don't vote for her. Maybe they like the other candidate more. Maybe they like a candidate, but only as a friend or public speaker, not as a congressman, senator or president. Will Rogers liked everyone, and everyone liked Will Rogers, but would they have voted for him?

If the like-dislike scale isn't enough of an attitude measure, what is? There are many answers, but here's a helpful, adaptable approach that draws from research that has investigated this question: "What is it that makes this person credible to an audience?" Three answers have surfaced: trustworthiness, expertise and charisma. These are meaningful, measurable and manipulatable attitudinal components that have found their way into applications as diverse as selling jam and promoting presidents. They offer a useful way to think about voters' perceptions, and they provide the basis for voter persuasion.

Voters must trust a candidate. George Bush understood this well when, in the 1992 presidential campaign, he hit Bill Clinton hard on the trust issue. Clinton's trust factor dominated Bush's strategy during the final weeks of that race. Bush obviously didn't make the case with most voters, and he also bore his own trust problems, which he failed to address.

If voters don't trust a candidate, they are not likely to vote for him. If they don't trust either candidate, they may sit out the election. Many people attribute low voter turnout to a lack of trust in the candidates: "They're all damned crooks, and I don't trust any one of 'em."

Trustworthiness is a generalizable trait, and this can work for or against a candidate. If people trust someone, they invest in her a sense of confidence that cuts across subjects: "Her word is as good as gold. She will be there for you. You can count on her." Such confidence is not often ac-companied by qualifiers—if you really trust someone, you trust her across the board.

But, this is a two-edged sword. Damaged trust on one issue damages trust on all the others. For instance, if a candidate is caught lying about his marital fidelity, he's through. Not that his personal affairs portend his professional actions, but trust is a thick, fuzzy line that does not partition well portions of a candidate's life. If he lied about this, he very well may lie about that. Thus, survey questions about voters' trust need not pinpoint specific items. When assessing voters' trust, there are different dimensions, but not different targets.

It may take one question or several to learn how much voters trust a candidate. Do they believe what she says? Do they think she is honest and forthright, a straight shooter? Trust questions should be asked several ways. As the most important attitudinal trait, it pays to dig deeply.

People expect their elected officials to have expertise, to know something about the job, or at least to be a fast study who can pick up the needed skills. Consequently, we observe candidates listing their credentials: education, experience, familiarity with a problem, insight into a solution. Besides college degrees and résumés (this society's measures of expertise), candidates propose programs and describe legislation, all of which validates their knowledge and skills.

While trustworthiness is a general trait, expertise is specific and does not convey from one subject to another. Doctors are experts—but in medicine, not French cooking. Itzhak Perlman, an expert violinist, probably knows nothing about repairing a transmission. It is important for a candidate to display a level of expertise in topics appropriate to the job. When the economy is sour, it helps a candidate to have knowledge of financial matters. It does a candidate well to have environmental expertise when CFCs (chlorofluorocarbons) are drilling holes in the atmosphere.

This means that survey questions about expertise must be specific. "Is she an expert?" is only half a question. Fix on the specific area of expertise. "Is she an expert on economic issues? On environmental matters?"

Charisma—or dynamism—is a multidimensional term encompassing traits that make a candidate appear active, interesting, personable and exciting. A candidate's charisma is important in forming his public image. These features say little about the candidate's abilities, but they reveal his enthusiasm and energy to do a job. Ross Perot projected charisma and a "go-getter" spirit. Supporters believed he was a doer, someone who could crack Iranian prisons, free MIAs, solve economic problems with the force of will. This society admires and respects action.

With the importance of television, charisma has assumed an even greater significance. The medium has set a new standard for all public figures. A trustworthy and knowledgeable candidate may suffer at the polls because he cannot generate the spark voters seek. It takes more than competence; it takes excitement and activity. That was one of Michael Dukakis's failings: He thought the 1988 presidential race was mostly about competence.

You can manipulate charisma. Coach candidates to have a more effective speaking style. Hot-wire their speeches with catchy phrases, clever references and humor. Suitable hairdos, ties, dresses and makeup can enliven a plain Jane or Joe. Balloons, Sousa bands and cheering crowds can create an exciting campaign environment, the way stage props and lights create a theatrical mood.

These props only can go so far, but they can add a touch of sparkle to a lackluster candidate. Let research isolate deficiencies in charisma. Do voters think the candidate is a boring speaker? Does she seem uncertain, exhausted or nervous? Does she blend in with the gray drapes? To some observers, these matters are trivial, but politics is awash in subjective judgments, and leadership is a composite of traits that goes beyond rationale measures.

These three elements—trustworthiness, expertise and charisma—provide structure for an inventory of attitudes toward the candidate. After they are measured, campaigns can address them in voter communications. Information programs can fortify perceived trustworthiness, improve voter perception of a candidate's expertise and pump the candidate with more charisma.

3. BEHAVIOR—SOURCE

The Basic Issue: How have voters' behaved toward the candidate; what do they think their behavior will be?

The big behavioral question is, "Will you vote for this candidate?" Nothing else really matters. Of course, if people would or could accurately foretell their voting behavior, most surveys would consist of a single question. But, people do not reveal such behavior. Many honestly do not know how they will vote. That is what campaigns are about: convincing people of the best candidate and sustaining that confidence through the election. Throughout a campaign, many voters shift with the ebb and flow of political currents, drifting first toward one candidate, then another. Decisions gel over time, but often for substantial numbers of voters, the decision is made only after the curtain closes on the polling booth.

The "big question," then, is not an accurate predictor, because, at best, it measures how a respondent feels at the moment, and this may not hold. Still, others know how they'll vote but won't tell. Some like to tweak a pollster's nose and report the opposite of how they plan to vote. The *Chicago Tribune*'s mischievous columnist Mike Royko has been known to encourage people to put pollsters through this hell.

"How will you vote?" questions have these things going against them: People think they know, but later change; they don't know; they won't tell; they lie. Still, everyone asks the question, because they don't know how to avoid it and because it gives campaigns something to go on. Answers help sort the audience into groups and offer a guide by which to interpret other items in a survey.

There was a time when the auto industry developed marketing strategies that presumed "once a Chevy owner, always a Chevy owner." Candidates thought "once a Democrat, always a Democrat." One of the strongest predictors of future voting behavior is past voting behavior. If you voted for a congressman before, you likely will vote for him again. Even though it is less certain today than it once was, if you voted for a Democrat last time, you likely will vote for a Democrat this time. Some people violate the pattern, but for most, the past is a reasonable predictor. Past voting behavior is an important card in the tarot deck.

Voting behavior questions, past and future, are the most important in this section of the analysis, but consider other behaviors. How else might voters behave? Would they attend a rally, write a letter to the editor, contribute money, talk with a friend, do volunteer work? These sorts of behavioral issues reveal the strengths of support for a candidate and for the opposition. In aggregate, they form a measure of commitment.

It isn't a bad idea, early in the campaign, to use open-ended voting behavior questions to understand why respondents lean toward one candidate or another. Don't just ask, "How do you think you'll vote?" Ask, "Why will you vote that way?"

4. KNOWLEDGE—MESSAGE

The Basic Issue: What do voters know about the message or the issues dominant in a campaign?

Issues in recent national elections have ranged from broad and philosophical (e.g., the U.S. role in the new world order, the role of government in the lives of citizens) to specific and immediate (e.g., mechanics of a health care plan, defense cuts, economic stimulation). Voters, candidates, the media and interest groups all add issues to a campaign agenda. Candidates can ignore some issues, while others, like timber wolves, howl at their camp and will not go away. Try as he might to shift the campaign agenda from the economy, George Bush had to be forced, heels dragging, back to the issue by voters, the media and Bill Clinton.

The purpose of this section is to examine voter awareness of the issues that are, or may become, a topic for political discussion. Approach the subject from two directions. First, find out which issues the voters feel are important. This is a task for open-ended questions and general discussions. Leave plenty of room to probe here and to find out specifically what aspects of an issue most concern respondents. If they say "the environment," for instance, what about the environment concerns them? Acid rain? Ozone depletion? Deforestation? Do they look at more specific aspects of these larger matters? Industrial coal burning policies, control of CFCs, timber industry practices? Voter attitudes (next section) will emerge along with the identification of issues, but for now, fix on issue awareness and framing.

The second direction forces respondents to address issues identified by the campaign. For instance, the candidate may wish to advance a program for government child-care subsidies. Have people thought about this? Have they read much about it? Which aspects of the program do they know best? Which are least understood? Test a list of issues.

The approach used to assess knowledge of a candidate is also used to assess knowledge of the issues: which issues interest voters, how much do voters know about the issues, how accurate is their information. These items depict the prominent public issues, and they reveal misconceptions. This information allows a campaign to assess the amount of effort necessary to push an issue onto the public agenda. Popular and correctly understood issues are the easiest to approach; unknown or poorly understood issues demand the greatest persistence.

5. ATTITUDES—MESSAGE

The Basic Issue: What are voters' attitudes toward the issues?

Most surveys gather knowledge and attitude information at the same time. Knowledge information identifies hot-button issues. Attitudinal information looks at the value loadings on the issues. Note the interplay.

Consider the energy conservation plank of the 1984 Walter Mondale campaign. People had been aware of conservation practices from the Carter years, and they didn't much like them. Who would? Conservation under Carter, and promised under Mondale, meant belt-tightening, driving smaller cars, doubling up in car pools, turning off lights, turning down thermostats. In was morning in Reagan's America, and the president had convinced voters that conservation was a thing of the past and that doomsayers like Mondale were crying wolf. Large majorities of the voting population did not want to hear about conservation, and nothing Mondale attempted could change that. People knew about the conservation problem, but their attitudes did not support Mondale's remedies.

Mondale also raised the national debt issue, but here, too, his words fell on a disinterested population. People knew about the debt; they just didn't give a damn about it, because most didn't sense its dangers. Too many were enjoying too much to be too concerned. Again, Mondale could not assert his issue onto the public agenda. He was bucking against knowledge and attitude problems of overwhelming proportions.

What do these examples reveal? People were comfortable with their attitudes about conservation and the national debt. The years proved them wrong, but at the time, their attitudes logically followed their knowledge. The questions were: Should Mondale change public attitudes based on incorrect assumptions, or first correct the assumptions, then encourage new attitudes. How could he correct the mistaken assumptions if people's attitudes innoculated them against new (and contradictory) information? What a conundrum for Mondale.

The example reveals a distinction between knowledge and attitudes. With issues less charged than these, Mondale may have been able to break the cycle. Perhaps he could have demonstrated that the debt was not about to vanish and that it really mattered to the nation's economic health. If he could have gotten this across, he might have budged public attitudes. Today, we know that many voters fear the debt, but it has taken a decade and a thousand horror stories to do it.

It is easier to deal with issues when the population seeks information and has not hardened its attitudes. Health care is a good example. During the past several years, the press has revealed how millions of Americans have lost health insurance. It is a complex issue that has captured public attention. Candidates educate people on their remedy (knowledge) and attempt to convince voters that their plan is the best (attitudes).

As they prepare their fixes for health care problems, candidates consult the polls to learn what solutions people want from the government, what they favor and what they oppose. What are their attitudes toward socialized medicine, voucher systems, tax write-offs, pay-or-play plans and the other options. This does not argue for policy by polls. It suggests that it isn't a bad idea in a democracy to get the public viewpoint on public issues. It is wise for candidates to chart voters' attitudes and to consider them along with other information.

What attitude questions do you ask? It is difficult to build a scheme flexible enough to accommodate the great variety of issues. Surveys typically ask respondents to assess issues along these measures: like-dislike, support-oppose, good-bad, strong-weak, wasteful-efficient. Any number of appropriate bipolar adjectives can be paired to gauge public thinking about issues. Likert scales and other semantic differential techniques give a reasonable fix on respondent views. These approaches trace an issue through a campaign and compare two or more programs side by side. Through factor analysis and other data reduction techniques, measures can be collapsed into useful issue assessments.

To understand the nuances of voter attitudes, though, particularly in the test stage of issue planning, there are no substitutes for open-ended questions. The best questions: "What do you feel about this issue?" "Why do you feel this way?" Follow-up probes refine the information and paint a three-dimensional picture of attitudes.

6. BEHAVIOR—MESSAGE

The Basic Issue: How are voters likely to behave toward an issue?

Think of behavior in three dimensions: past, present and future. Just as past voting behavior presages future voting behavior, past behavior toward issues foretells future behavior toward issues. Marketers, for instance, learn much about a consumer's future purchasing behaviors by learning about past and current product purchases. The trends are so strong that manufacturers offer coupons to break people from their customary purchasing habits. "Sure you always buy Tide; here's a dollar to try Dash." Companies make such offers to establish a new path in the purchasing behavior maze.

The concept holds for political issues as well. People who previously (or currently) supported prochoice positions are likely to continue to do so in the future. Attending rallies, contributing money or volunteer time, voting in public referenda, writing letters, participating in canvassing drives and other behavioral demonstrations of support in the past serve as expressions of activities in the future.

Expressions of past and present behaviors serve only as surrogates for what we really want to know, which is how this respondent is likely to act in the future. So, most surveys will attempt a direct question about anticipated future behavior. As with all projected behavior responses, we can look for two factors to temper the accuracy of a response.

First, projections weaken from the weight of time. We predict more accurately what we will do tomorrow than what we will do six months from now. New information arrives, conditions vary and decisions change.

Second, the personal salience of an issue effects predictions. People with strongly held beliefs are less vulnerable to persuasion and so are more likely to predict their behaviors accurately. Committed environmentalists are more likely to know that they will attend a national rally than someone less committed to the movement. Strong anti-environmentalists accurately predict they will not attend.

Predictions, then, are always tricky, but you can increase their accuracy with this information: Find out about past behaviors. Determine the strength of a respondent's commitment. Be careful of investing too much confidence in data too far from the target event.

CHANNEL

Details about communication channels are important for obvious reasons. In political communication, nearly all information comes to voters through the media—mass or targeted. While for many, information passes through secondary sources—friends, neighbors and other opinion leaders— just about everything voters learn evolves from media-borne information.

In developing plans for targeted information, it is important to know how best to reach individual groups. Which broadcast stations do they use, and which paper do they read? Which voters rely on the opinions of other people, and which make up their minds directly from media sources? Which sources do voters trust for information, and which do they trust for opinions? Apply the same sequence to channels that was used for candidates and the issues.

Existing records provide much of the information about channels. Arbitron and other sources offer media-specific information for demographic subgroups. Individual media often have detailed audience information they will share with potential advertisers.

In some cases, existing media information will be enough, particularly if campaigns plan to identify target groups by simple demographics. Media credibility and other attitudinal information will not be available on the street, and for these, campaigns must turn to public surveys.

7. KNOWLEDGE—CHANNEL

The Basic Issue: With what channels are voters familiar?

Test a general media plan. Are voters aware of certain shows on which the campaign wishes to advertise? Have they heard of named magazines, newspapers and newsletters?

While this effort may seek to confirm published media statistics, a more important data application will be to match voter targets with the media.

8. ATTITUDES—CHANNEL

The Basic Issue: How do voters feel about various channel categories and specific channels?

Which media do voters like and dislike, and why? Evaluate media on their perceived expertise, trustworthiness and charisma. Some people invest considerable credibility in the same media others discount. Supermarket tabloids are viewed as legitimate, believable sources by some readers. Papers of record such as the *New York Times* and *Washington Post*, paragons of American journalism for most people, are distrusted by others, who see them as champions of the establishment. There are sizable numbers of viewers who believe sensational infocasts such as "A Current Affair" over more conventional network newscasts. It is a good idea to learn more about how voters line up behind the media.

This is more than just an exercise in media popularity. The media are not just neutral conduits for information, but sources of influence on public perceptions. Consider the cheap image of mail-order products advertised on late-night television shows or those promoted in "junk" mail. This is true for all media. Even a billboard intruding on a bucolic, wooded roadside says something about the candidate who would choose to put it there.

There is more to media selection than just costs per thousand. Attitudinal information helps a campaign know something about the spin a medium puts on a message.

9. BEHAVIOR—CHANNEL

The Basic Issue: Which media do voters use?

In this section, the only time frame we really care about is the present. The past is less revealing of the future than is the present; questions about the future are meaningless. It is silly to ask respondents what radio station they think they will be listening to or what paper they will be reading at some future time. Most people will assume a continuation of their current patterns.

Information from this section is the best measure of how voters sort themselves among the media. Existing databases may be used; surveys will provide a more precise matchup between political attitudes and media patronage. The bottom line is, "Which media should you use to reach this group?" A secondary question, answered in the previous sections: "What impression will the medium contribute to your message?"

THE RECEIVER

Finally, obtain information about the receivers for two broad reasons. First, in support of the theme running strongly through this book, it will help campaigns improve the development of effective, receiver-specific messages. The more you know about the needs, interests and thinking of audiences, the better able you are to develop effective communication.

Second, receiver information is the basis for sorting a voter population into targeted communication blocks. Again, more information gives you more to go on when parceling an audience into clusters. Individual detail allows you to place people into groups. For instance, people below a given income level, with children, become a target group for a candidate's school breakfast program. Attitudinal information helps frame the most effective persuasive message. Self-employed and unemployed people are a natural target for mailings about a candidate's plan for group health rates. Of course, the process of group identification can involve more than two or three variables. There are practical limits, but each bit of data stands to refine a target group, and the analyst can decide on the best combination.

For the receiver, then, attempt to develop a detailed demographic profile with which to sort the remaining data and to form target groups.

Appendix B

A High-Tech Approach to Augment Voter Participation

This Appendix describes an innovative data collection approach that uses computer technology to reassert the role of the voter into American politics. We call the sample project The Voice of the Voter. It integrates computer technology and human interviewers in a process that catalogs the thinking of a substantial national sample of voters. It reveals what a representative group finds important and what these participants feel should be addressed by candidates running for public office.

The Voice of the Voter offers a significant contribution to the political dialogue taking place in the national press. It forms a basis for articles, suggests companion and follow-up stories, and augments the development of strategic press coverage for print and broadcast journalism.

Appendix B has two components: a general description of The Voice of the Voter, and an example of the data output.

GENERAL DESCRIPTION

Purpose and Background

The purpose of this project is to establish a public opinion data bank for print and broadcast media. This data bank will be developed from a series of in-depth interviews conducted with random U.S. population samples. Information will be used by reporters to assess a true national agenda and to understand the views of citizens toward national issues, politics and the role of government in American life.

Three times per year, the project will gather data using an innovative telephone data gathering technique. Data will be made available to major newspapers and broadcasters, wire services and other media through a computer bulletin board maintained at a specified university.

Three features make this project unique:

1. Interview structure. Most opinion surveys ask a series of questions that impose an agenda on respondents. Usually, these surveys also present a series of forced choices from which respondents must select. This limits respondent-initiated information and yields shallow and incomplete information about complex national topics. Many journalists have grumbled about the lack of detailed, representative information to guide their analyses and story development. Some media use focus groups in an effort to patch the gaps of conventional surveys, but focus groups, too, have serious methodological problems.

The Voice of the Voter will provide respondents with the opportunity to set their own agendas. It will allow them to ask questions and also to relate stories, personal experiences and individual concerns about sweeping national topics. This approach will introduce new insights into interpretations of public thinking about topics touched on only lightly by most polls.

2. Data quality. Data analysis will yield three levels of information: statistical summaries, information capsules and one-line statements, and complete transcripts of discussions that provide journalists with the important context of a discussion.

This layered data presentation will allow users to progress from summary to respondent-level data. The indexing scheme is intuitive and easy to use, allowing journalists to access data quickly as they prepare stories under short deadlines.

3. Data availability and delivery. Each survey will produce nearly one thousand pages of indexed information, all of it available immediately to news media through a computer modem. This electronic format eliminates the need for printed reports with all the attendant distribution and cost problems. It further allows convenient and fast movement through the data files and enables users quick access to specific details necessary for a story.

Over time, a library of data sets will be available for population comparisons. These data will provide the tenor of thinking at different times and offer a rich historical account not available through other survey forums.

Approach

This project will be an ongoing activity, with several surveys per year, more in election years. Outside funding is desirable in order to make the data accessible to all media, no matter their size and available financial resources. Several large media have expressed an interest in this project, but they have insisted on proprietary use of the data. The plan is to offer universal access without charge.

Data collection, transcription and preliminary computer analysis will take one week.

1. Summary Results

Numbers and Percentages of Respondents Selecting Each Item

	Total		Gender		Age			Income			Education		
			Male	Female	18-39	40-55	55+	<$19K	$20-45	45+	< HS	HS	Coll
	N %		N %	N %	N %	N %	N %	N %	N %	N %	N %	N %	N %

Abortion
Agricultural
Banking
Child care
Corp Ethics   *Numbers and percentages of respondents for*
Crime
Education   *the total and for each subgroup*
Economy
Energy
Foreign policy
Gov. ethics
Health care
Media
Military
Politics
Poverty
Religion
Soviets
Sports
Transportation
Unemployment

The Ten Most Important Issues

The statistics presented here are fictitious.
Percentages account for multiple responses, so totals exceed 100%

Total Sample

Economy	42%
Abortion	31
Education	28
Environment	21
Corp. ethics	15
Crime	13
Military	11
Agriculture	9
Child Care	7
Banking	5

Gender

Males		Females	
Economy	43%	Education	44%
Education	30	Crime	34
Banking	29	Abortion	25
Corp Ethics	22	Child care	20
Child care	14	Banking	15
Crime	12	Religion	12
Environment	11	Health	10
Abortion	9	Poverty	9
Military	7	Military	8
Energy	4	Energy	7

The Ten Most Important Issues
(Continued)

Age

18-39		40-55		55+	
Abortion	47%	Education	44%	Health care	45%
Agricultural	31	Crime	34	Poverty	40
Banking	28	Abortion	25	Banking	31
Child care	21	Child care	20	Crime	19
Corp ethics	15	Banking	15	Corp. ethics	18
Crime	13	Religion	12	Media	14
Military	11	Health	10	Education	12
Economy	9	Poverty	9	Transport	8
Environment	7	Military	8	Abortion	7
Energy	5	Energy	7	Military	5

Income

Under $19,000		$20,000-45,000		$45,000+	
Abortion	47%	Education	44%	Health care	45%
Agricultural	31	Crime	34	Poverty	40
Banking	28	Abortion	25	Banking	31
Child care	21	Child care	20	Crime	19
Corp. ethics	15	Banking	15	Corp. ethics	18
Crime	13	Religion	12	Media	14
Military	11	Health	10	Education	12
Economy	9	Poverty	9	Transport	8
Education	7	Military	8	Abortion	7
Energy	5	Energy	7	Military	5

2. Categorized One-Liners

(This sample is based on nine respondents)

This section provides a one-line digest for each question and advice item. The items are categorized by topic using the same typology employed throughout the report. Each item also is identified by a code number which corresponds to the text in Section 3 (Transcripts of Interviews). Because of multiple coding, one-liners may be included in more than a single category. While this results in some redundancy, it also provides a more complete summary for quick reference. This section also summarizes advice for news media.

(RC) and (DC) refer to questions and suggestions for the Republican and Democratic candidates respectively. The number next to each item is a code corresponding to the transcription identification in Section 3.

Abortion

Questions

(RC)   543   "I'd like to ask him about his stand on abortion. Why is he so opposed to allowing women to make their own choice?"

Advice

(RC)   431   "I think he's right standing his ground on the slaughter of human life. I mean abortion."

Agriculture

Questions

(RC)   258   "I'd have to ask him why he doesn't do something to help the American farmer."

(DC)   258   "I'd ask Mr. Harkin how he's going to help the farmer when there's no money left for the government to spend."

Child Care

Question

(DC)   543   (For Clinton) "What are you going to do about child care?"

Economy

Questions

(RC)   124   "Why couldn't he have some kind of arrangement to reallocate money into areas where it's needed?"

(RC)   311   "I'd ask him why he and Reagan have in ten years created a deficit bigger than all the debt incurred by the government since George Washington."

(DC) 258   "I'd ask Mr. Harkin how he's going to help the farmer when there's no money left for the government to spend."

Education

Question

(RC) 431   "I'd like to ask him why he doesn't make the schools get back to the basics."

Environment

Question

(RC) 245   "I'd ask him to clean up the water pollution."

Foreign Affairs

Advice

(RC) 431   "I'd tell him to finish off Saddam."

Gun Control

Question

(RC) 398   "I'd say, 'Mr. President, why are you so opposed to gun control?'"

Media

Question

(DC) 398   (For Cuomo) "Do you think you can do something about TV?"

Military

Question

(DC) 245   "I'd ask Mr. Kerrey about how he'd run the military if he got elected."

Advice

(RC) 431   "I'd tell him to finish off Saddam."

Political

Question

(RC) 135   "I'd like to know why he cares more about other countries than he cares about his own country?"

(DC)   124   "Does he consider himself a populist and does he believe in their values and standards?"

(DC)   135   "I'd ask Mr. Cuomo flat out, 'Have you ever been involved with the mob--the Mafia--or not?'"

(DC)   431   "I'd ask Clinton, a good Southern boy, why he's such a damned liberal."

Advice

(RC)   135   "I'd tell him to forget foreign countries for a while."

(RC)   245   "If I had some advice, I guess it would be that he not take so many vacations."

(RC)   258   "I don't know why he'd ask for my advice, but if he did, I'd say that I don't see much of the kinder, gentler America he talked about in the last election."

(RC)   311   "Fire Sununu."

(RC)   398   "I'd tell him to get his head out of the clouds."

(RC)   478   "I'd tell him to listen to his mother. She's 90 and probably knows a lot he doesn't."

(RC)   543   "I'd say, 'Quit acting like a wimp.'"

(DC)   124   "Be honest. That's a hell of a thing to have to advise somebody who's running for president of the United States, but we haven't had much honesty lately."

(DC)   135   "I'd say, 'Hell with the mob, go for it, Mario.'"

(DC)   245   "I'd say, 'Young man, I advise you to loosen up, relax. Laugh a little.'"

(DC)   258   "Keep up the plain talk and stay at the people's level."

(DC)   311   "Don't turn your back on Bush during this election. Look what they did to Dukakis."

(DC)   398   "I like Mario and I'd tell him not to pull any punches with Bush."

(DC)   431   (For Clinton) "I'd say 'Get back to your good Southern values, boy.'"

(DC)   478   (For any Democratic candidate) "Be like Roosevelt."

(DC)   543   "I'd suggest he start asking people if they think they're better off now than we were before Bush and Reagan got in office."

Race

Advice

(RC)   124   "I'm concerned about why young black men are killing themselves off."

Social Security

Questions

(RC)   478   "I'd ask him why Social Security or Medicare can't pay for eye-glasses."

(DC)   478   "I'd ask any of 'em what they'll do about Social Security."

Soviets

Question

(DC)   311   "How does he plan to use the resources we once threw at the Soviets?"

Advice for American Media
on Campaign Coverage

124   "Make the candidates answer your damned questions."

135   "Be more aggressive."

245   "Not much. I maybe would tell them they could ask questions about specific cases."

258   "Get the candidates to fix on specific things."

311   "Reporters should work together. If the candidate doesn't answer one reporter, the next reporter should say, 'Hey, why didn't you answer his question?'"

398   "They could do a lot better in comparing a candidate's answers with independent, objective information."

431   "Not much. Some people in TV make a big deal out of nothing."

478   "I'd say they should tell how these big plans the candidates talk about are going to affect the people, how they will affect our lives."

543   "Well, I guess it would be to keep pushing the candidates. Candidates are like kids, they'll never volunteer to do anything, you've got to push them."

3. Transcripts of Interviews

124   (Kansas, Female, Conference Coordinator, Some Coll., $31K, 53 years)

Republican Candidate Question

"Why couldn't he have some kind of arrangement to reallocate money into areas where it's needed?"

(What areas would you suggest?) "From defense to drug use research, for instance. These are real problems. This country spends so much money on things it doesn't need. I'd like to know why we spend so much for defense when the Soviet Union is dead. We see problems on TV. This society is deteriorating at a rapid rate. There's a big drug problem and poverty. We spend money to research why cows fart, but not much on so many other problems running throughout this country. Where are Bush's values? Where are the values of this country?"

Republican Candidate Advice

"I'm concerned about why young black men are killing themselves off.

"They're making themselves extinct! Why don't we have resources to do something about this? My advice is to pay more attention to and devote more resources to social problems. Look at the dynamics of poverty, because it's the basis for so many other problems."

Democratic Candidate Question

(For Harkin) "Does he consider himself a populist and does he believe in their values and standards?"

(Would you explain that question?) "I'd want to know exactly where he's coming from. I really like him and agree with him when I see him on TV. We've been fooled so many times by politicians. I mean, the 'Education President'--during the election only. The 'Environmental President'--who promotes timber cutting, oil drilling in nature preserves, cutting inspectors at toxic sites. They must think we're stupid. Maybe the American people are. Who is calling Bush on his lies and hype. Remember Reagan was going to balance the budget by 1984? I remember it. Why don't we hear people griping about these lies? I like Harkin, but I want him to tell the American people right out what he's for and against. What he's going to do. If he gets elected, he damned well better do it."

Democratic Candidate Advice

(For Harkin) "Be honest. That's a hell of a thing to have to advise somebody who's running for president of the United States, but we haven't had much honesty lately."

"We've had twelve years of deceit and lies. Promise the people, then rip them off in public view. Nobody complains, nobody gets mad, nobody probably even cares. Maybe we're so used to being lied to and ripped off. But I like honesty. I don't expect it from Republicans anymore. Maybe Harkin will be honest and be a pleasant change. That's all."

Campaign Coverage: Poor

(Why poor?) "They're nothing but a rubber stamp. They don't report, they just pass information through from the candidate's PR people to readers and viewers."

Advice to News Media

"Make the candidates answer your damned questions."

(Why this advice?) "I don't know how many times I've wanted to kick the TV when reporters ask the candidate a 'yes or no' question, then let him give a line of bull without answering the question. I wouldn't let my kids get away with that. Ask the question. Ask again. Ask again. I blame the press for being bullied."

135   (Pennsylvania, Male, Computer Operator, Some Coll., $27K, 32 years)

Republican Candidate Question

"I'd like to know why he cares more about other countries than he cares about his own country."

(Why would you ask that question?) "Why? He's spent more time walking around in front of the cameras in foreign countries than he has spent in his own country. I live in Philly. Do you think he ever saw the trash and vacant buildings around this place? People sleeping on the grates. I see them all the time. We have needs here, you know. He flies from Washington to his vacationland in Kennebunkport. That's all he knows."

Republican Candidate Advice

"If I had five minutes, I'd tell him to forget foreign countries for a while.

"Not forget them, just give them less attention. Drive through this country. Show Americans you care about us. I really think you did great with Russia and you showed Saddam Hussein, but that's over now. What have you done since, and what have you done here?"

(How would you advise him to do all this?) "I know I said show them you care, but I don't just mean do lots of show-and-tells in front of the cameras. We really have lots of problems around here. Make a list of things you will do to solve some of them."

(What three problems, for instance, would you advise him to address?) "Like I said, poverty. I've never seen so many people sleeping in public places. How about the environment, and how about hunger? I guess that's poverty, but it affects a lot of people, and we shouldn't have people hungry in this country."

Democratic Candidate Question

"I'd ask Mr. Cuomo flat out, 'Have you ever been involved with the mob--the Mafia--or not?"

(Why would you ask that?) "Let's face it. The guy has charm. On camera and in front of large audiences, he can move people. He's bright. I've seen him on Brinkley and he backhands even the toughest questions from guys like George Will. So with all this he'd have a hell of a shot at someone like Bush and Quayle. Why sit it out? Either he's crazy which he isn't, or he's got something big and ugly in the closet. I figure it's the mob. Under the spotlight of the national press everything might come out. Somebody would find out, and it's over, not only the presidency, but the governorship, Senate, dogcatcher."

Democratic Candidate Advice

"I'd say, 'Hell with the mob, go for it, Mario.'"

(What is your thinking on such advice?) "Personally, I don't care what he's done in the past, or even may be doing right now that's a bit shady. Tell me Bush is clean. Hell, he's been in all sorts of mud, he just uses his friends to clean him off and maybe hide the stains. Cuomo couldn't be worse than Bush. I think he really cares about this country and isn't so hot on making a big name for himself on the international scene. He has compassion for the poor and understands the average Joe a lot better than Bush, who was born into privilege and never bothered to look around at how the rest of us live."

Campaign Coverage: Fair

(Why fair?) "I think they could be more aggressive with the candidates."

Advice to News Media

"Well, be more aggressive. Make candidates get away from the script. They always say the same thing you see on their commercials. Everything is scripted. I'd tell reporters to throw them off balance. Ask different kinds of questions, then make them answer them."

(How can they do that?) "How about not taking the campaign line? How about saying, 'Mr. Bush, that's a prepackaged answer and it doesn't address my question. I'm going to ask you again?'"

245   (Arkansas, Male, Retired Mechanic, < High School, 67 years)

Republican Candidate Question

"I'd ask him to clean up the water pollution."

(Why would you ask this particular question?) "I've been a sport fisherman for fifty years, and I've never seen it so bad. Less fish, and half the time they look pretty sick and puny. He's a fisherman, too, you know, only he likes saltwater. We don't have much of that here in Arkansas. You hear on TV all the time about the poison in the fish. Maybe it's not the president's job, but he can get people in Washington started. Get them to find out why things have got so bad."

(What do you think pollutes water the most where you live?) "Well around here, it's factories, pure and simple. But I used to fish near Fort Smith, and it got too big, too many people. Probably a lot of sewage and whatnot."

Republican Candidate Advice

"I like Bush. I voted for him and Reagan. If I had some advice, I guess it would be that he not take so many vacations.

"It makes him look bad, with the recession and all. Lots of people laid off around here. They're selling off things to pay for food, and they see the president off on boats. Makes him look too rich. I think he should have rests and enjoy life. Just don't make such a point of it."

Democratic Candidate Question

"I'd ask Mr. Kerrey about how he'd run the military if he got elected."

(Would you tell me more about why you would ask this?) "Well, here's the thing. I know Kerrey's been in Vietnam and got the Medal of Honor, even got his leg blown off. That means a lot to me. I'm a World War II vet, and that sort of thing means something. Any guy who would go through that earns your respect. At least he does mine. But, you know, when he talks about the military, he sounds like he wants to cut it way back. I know the Russians may not be much of a threat anymore, but how about the Middle East and Cuba? There's always China and some other threat. You need a good military. He scares me on this one, though."

Democratic Candidate Advice

"I'd say, "Young man, I advise you to loosen up, relax. Laugh a little.""

(Why do you feel this is important advice?) "I don't know if it's all that important, but every time I see him on TV, he reminds me of a guy who keeps everything inside and can't have a good belly laugh. You need perspective if you're going to be a president, and I think it helps to open up a bit and don't be so worried about making a mistake. He's a war hero, and I respect that. Maybe the war made him tense, who knows what goes through a man's mind in war situations. I think he'd be a lot more likable if they could get him to look more at ease."

Campaign Coverage: Good

(Why good?) "I don't know, it's okay I suppose."

Advice to News Media

"Not much. I maybe would tell them they could ask questions about specific cases. Like the pollution thing I told you about. Sometimes the candidates drift when they're asked questions, and I think a specific instance would focus their responses. But I'm not an expert, I don't really know."

258   (Wisconsin, Female, Farmer, High School, $23K, 54 years)

Republican Candidate Question

"I'd have to ask him why he doesn't do something to help the American farmer."

(Tell me more about this issue you'd raise.) "Well, I'm a farmer, my family farms. And in the fifty-plus years I've lived on this place (or before I was married on my parents' farm), I've seen a lot of unhappy things take place. Farmers are real dependent on interest rates and the economy, and when someone sneezes in

Washington, we catch a cold. Lots of my friends had to sell out, and they sold to some absentee landlord who sent out managers to run the farms they were buying up. It's like selling your child to the Gypsies. My question asks why we can help the savings and loans and the big corporations like Chrysler and lots of foreign countries, but when an American family farm is hurting, we just let it go belly up. That bothers me personally."

Republican Candidate Advice

"I don't know why he'd ask for my advice, but if he did, I'd say 'I don't see much of the kinder, gentler America he talked about in the last election.'

"People have forgotten about that, haven't they? I would remind him that he said he was going to be more compassionate and caring. I still see on TV a lot of people in soup lines, and I hear about kids being shot in school and sick people dying because they have no insurance. Sometimes I'm ashamed when I see these things. Where is the kinder, gentler America? I'd tell him to read his old speeches and practice what he preached."

Democratic Candidate Question

"I'd ask Mr. Harkin how he's going to help the farmer when there's no money left for the government to spend."

(Why is this question on your mind?) "He was visiting Madison last week and said he thought it was time the government helped people in the heartland. I like that. I told you my feelings about the American farmer. But, I've seen a lot of politics and a lot of politicians and heard the speeches and everybody promises everything to everyone. I like the promises, but you can't eat a promise and you can't pay the mortgage or buy a tractor with it. Look at the deficit. I know Reagan ran it up, but we're stuck with it. How can Harkin pay for his promises. That's what I want to know. Not to be sassy, I really would like to know."

Democratic Candidate Advice

"Two things. Keep up the plain talk and stay at the people's level."

(Why these bits of advice?) "Maybe it's because I'm from a farming community, but I've gotten sick of all the slick talk from Washington. Harkin seems down-to-earth to me. He doesn't mind saying what's on his mind, even if it offends some people who think it's crude. I think it's refreshing, even if he uses more four-letter words than I'm used to. I also like the way he explains things to people. He doesn't think we're stupid, and he doesn't assume we know all about policies and programs in Washington. He discusses things and gives background information most people can understand. I'd just tell him to keep it up."

Campaign Coverage: Fair

(Why fair?) "I knew you'd ask me that. Because I think a lot of questions go unasked."

(What questions?) "How about questions about what's really happening to the American farmer. Do the candidates really understand? How about specifics? Bush and Harkin both like to talk in general terms."

Advice to News Media

"Get the candidates to fix on specific things. I mean, ask them flat out, 'What would you do. Don't give me a campaign slogan like build a better America, I mean exactly what would you do?' And something else. I'd check out all their facts. I've heard statistics that just can't be true. I think these guys come up with facts and figures on the fly. I'd tell reporters to check them out. Maybe they do, I don't know, but I'd remind them to do it."

311   (New York, Male, Bank Teller, High School, $30K, 46 years)

Republican Candidate Question

"I'd ask him why he and Reagan have in ten years created a deficit bigger than all the debt incurred by the government since George Washington.

"I can't understand why the press doesn't push this matter. They let Reagan off the hook, and now they're letting Bush off. How irresponsible--of the press for not pushing, of the White House for creating such policy. Bush now endorses what he once called Voodoo Economics. This guy has no conscience. Look what has happened to this country, in large part because of the deficit. Poor roads and bridges, poor education, filthy environment, unemployment, poverty, crime because we can't police the streets. Congress is to blame too, but the ship is guided from the White House helm. I pin this right on Bush. I'd make him sweat with some real questions about the economy and especially the deficit."

Republican Candidate Advice

"About what?"

(About anything you want.) "Well, apart from what I already said about the economy, I think first I'd tell him to fire John Sununu. That guy has an iron fist, and he insulates Bush from unpopular ideas, just the way Haldeman and Ehrlichman boxed in Nixon. That makes a president develop a one-dimensional view of things and keeps him from seeing the scope of concerns held by the people. I think Bush's getting bad advice. Fire Sununu."

(You said you had other advice.) "I'd tell him to keep Mrs. Bush around him. I like her. She's looks pretty solid, not like Nancy Reagan, who was a flake."

Democratic Candidate Question

"I'd ask Cuomo about his views toward the Russians."

(What about his views?) "How does he plan to use the resources we once threw at the Soviets?"

(Could you explain that a bit more?) "Well, look at all the money we spent chasing the communists--military, CIA, State Department. Look at the people, equipment and time we used up keeping an eye on them and keeping them in check. Now they're through. How would Cuomo redirect these resources? Beating the commies was an industry like building automobiles and running the phone system. If we should no longer need cars or phones, we would have a lot of surplus factories, people and money laying around. The anticommunist industry is lots bigger. What will Cuomo do with all this potential?"

Democratic Candidate Advice

"Don't turn your back on Bush during this election. Look what they did to Dukakis."

(Would you describe this advice more fully?) "Right after the convention, it looked like Dukakis was ahead. Then Bush's thugs took off the gloves. They dragged out Willie Horton and all that other flag stuff. Pure bullshit, but it worked like a charm. Dukakis fell fast and he never saw blue sky again. They'll try it to Cuomo or any other Democrat. They'll lie and cheat, they are the dirtiest. I'd say, 'Don't turn your back, Mario.'

"Can I say something else?" (Sure.) "I'd like to advise that Cuomo make education his theme. I only finished high school, but I see a lot of things. I believe half our problems are due to a failing education system. Hell, kids are graduating, and they can't read a newspaper or add a column of numbers. Bush talks about being the Education President. Mario should hit him for cheap talk and no action. Then HE should do something about it and make it a strong campaign theme."

Campaign Coverage: Poor

(Why poor?) "They just drop the ball. I think half of them are on the take from the candidates."

Advice to News Media

"Reporters should work together. If the candidate doesn't answer one reporter, the next reporter should say, 'Hey, why didn't you answer his question?' It seems to me that in the past few campaigns, the candidates have learned how to manipulate the press something awful. I blame the candidates, but mostly I blame the press for letting them get away with it. If one reporter's question is ignored, others should follow through. It's not ganging up on the candidate, it's just trying to get them to give answers that voters need to know."

398   (New Jersey, Female, Government Worker, Coll. Deg., $48K, 35 years)

Republican Candidate Question

"I'd say, 'Mr. President, why are you so opposed to gun control?'

"You say you're for law and order and yet, despite all the studies and all the testimony, you stand behind the NRA and let people buy machine guns. It's a shooting gallery out there, and you don't see it from behind your White House walls. But real people know what guns are doing. I read about a half-dozen murders every morning in the paper. They're so common the paper doesn't give them more than a tiny place in the back section. You want to stop crime, stop guns. That's what I'd tell him."

(Why would you ask him this question?) "Well, I think the guy's a hypocrite with a rubber spine. He's afraid of irritating the conservative fringe, and he hides behind the 'right to bear arms' defense like all the crazies. Mr. Law and Order. Just another example of being for the rich. Who gets shot? Mr. Bush's rich friends? The poor get shot. Kids get shot--in school. You can't pick up the paper without getting sickened by the descriptions of shootings."

Republican Candidate Advice

"I'd tell him to get out of the clouds. Get into the streets of America.

"He spent time on the streets of Moscow and Tokyo, why not visit his own country? Try to understand the little people. They have needs just like people overseas. See where they hurt, see how they have been neglected. I'd say 'Be our president instead of running for president of the world.' Enough's enough."

Democratic Candidate Question

(For Cuomo) "Do you think you can do something about TV?"

(Would you explain that for me?) "Well, you know he's been making speeches about television and the American family. He has talked about bringing the family back together. He also said TV can be a force to help kids, and that parents can use TV to help their kids. He never explains this. I have two kids, and it's a constant battle over the tube. I don't think it's something a president can deal with, but since he brought it up, I'd ask him to explain it."

Democratic Candidate Advice

"I like Mario, and I'd tell him not to pull any punches with Bush.

"Already Ailes or whoever has come up with some pretty foul commercials about a few Democrats. They'll get on Cuomo soon for being too liberal or too Italian or too something. Don't take it. Throw it back at them, or they'll kill you. It really gets me mad. I'd tell Mario to talk about Bush's wimpness. I still think he's fruity, and Mario's people should build that image. I'm Italian, too. I hate to see him get blasted."

Campaign Coverage: Fair

(Why fair?) "They could do a lot better in comparing a candidate's answers with independent objective information."

Advice to News Media

"If candidates didn't give me an answer, if I were a reporter, I would say, 'Mr. Bush, I'll get back to you. I'll call you next week and ask you for the detail you can't provide right now.' I don't see a lot of follow-through. We treat every day in a campaign as a separate event. I think we should see the campaign as a stream. Follow-through. Pick up this week on the things candidates missed last week. This just makes common sense to me. Maybe the public goes from day to day, but I think the press can't allow this to happen."

431 (Alabama, Male, Auto Mechanic, < High School, $26K, 55 years)

Republican Candidate Question

"I'd like to ask him why he doesn't make the schools get back to the basics."

(Would you explain that to me?) "When I was in school--I know it's been a long time, but some things are basic and shouldn't change. We'd start out with the Lord's Prayer and salute the flag. It taught us respect. We'd hand in homework. We worked on the three Rs and didn't involve in all this bull the kids do now. Watching movies and playing games. And if anybody sassed the teacher, he got it twice, first from the teacher, then at home. When we got out of school, at least we could read and write. Half of 'em now can't get through a newspaper. No wonder this country is going to hell."

Republican Candidate Advice

"About the school question?"

(That or anything else.) "Then I'd like to tell him first he's right in standing his ground on the slaughter of human life. By that I mean abortion. God said it is wrong to kill, and that means babies. God gave us so many blessings in this country because we follow His word, but if we let them murder babies, I fear for this country. God will turn His back on us."

(You suggested you may have other advice.) "Well, if he'd listen, I'd tell him to finish off Saddam. I mean we should have blown up his palace or whatever during the war, but since we didn't do it then, let's do it now. Iraq's probably got the bomb, let's finish him off before he uses it. That'd be my advice."

Democratic Candidate Question

"I'd ask Clinton, a good Southern boy, why he's such a damned liberal."

(Would you explain that one?) "It isn't really a question, just a poke. I'm pretty conservative, and I believe in the real American values--hard work, God, country. It's part of the South. I was in Korea with half my friends. We signed up. But Clinton sounds like he's from New York--I hope you're not from New York. (No, Texas.) Well, then, Clinton sounds like Cuomo. Big dollars for welfare, food stamps, paying people to have more babies so we can support them. I want to like him, being from Arkansas, but he sounds like a communist half the time."

Democratic Candidate Advice

"I'd say, 'Get back to your good Southern values, boy.'"

(Specifically, what would you suggest he do?) "Start talking about what this country is all about. List the values that made this country great. Talk about hard work and family. Tell people about responsibility and decency. Hell, he won't do it. He sounds more like a Russian than Gorbachev. Say abortion is wrong. Say welfare is wrong. Let people bear arms--it's in the Constitution."

Campaign Coverage: Good

(Why good?) "I know all I want to know about politics."

Advice to News Media

"Not much. Some people on TV make a big deal over nothing, but they're the liberals. I'd just say, 'Get out the facts.' That's all."

478   (Florida, Female, Retired Teacher, Coll. Grad., 78 years)

Republican Candidate Question

"I'd ask him why Social Security or Medicare can't pay for eyeglasses?"

(Why is this the question you would ask?) "Because I just got a pair and had to pay $90 out of my own pocket. An older person can't afford that kind of expense. It's all part of medical care, and I think the government in this country should provide it just like governments overseas. It's terrible to ask older people to pay for medical care when they don't have the money. Everyone should have free health care, I think."

Republican Candidate Advice

"I'd tell him to listen to his mother. She's 90 and probably knows a lot he doesn't.

"She's still alive and 90, you know. Of course, she's probably well off, but at that age, you've got to know something. Listen to the old people. They know a lot of things. Don't forget about us."

Democratic Candidate Question

"I'd ask any of 'em what they'll do about Social Security."

(Why that question?) "I haven't heard anyone talking about it, and it makes you wonder if they'll try to reduce it. You like to know what's going through their minds. This is an important matter. I'd ask them to say outright what they'd do."

Democratic Candidate Advice

"Be like Roosevelt."

(How do you mean?) "Roosevelt was for the people. He set up programs that helped people down on their luck. Since Reagan, things are going the other way. Take from the poor and give to the rich. Everyone seems to know about it, but nobody does anything about it. I think if someone's going to help the poor, it'll have to be a Democrat. Republicans never could see their way past corporations and the rich. I'd tell the Democrat to bring the government back to the people."

Campaign Coverage: Fair

(Why fair?) "They could tell more about how these candidates will affect the people, the ones who depend on government for their needs."

Advice to News Media

"I'd say they should tell how these big plans the candidates talk about are going to affect the people, how they will affect our lives. I know they think they have to get out the facts the way the candidates tell them, but lots of times it's more important to say what the programs will do for people, not just how much money is being spent. If the candidates don't talk about this, the newspapers should."

543   (Oregon, Female, Salesclerk, High School, $18K, 34 years)

Republican Candidate Question

"I'd like to ask him about his stand on abortion. Why is he so opposed to allowing women to make their own choice?"

(Tell me a little about why your question would concern abortion?) "It's an important thing with me. My mother told me about a friend who years ago, before abortion was legal, had one by some butcher and nearly died. It's hard for me to believe in 1991 that we could even think of going back to those dark ages. You'd expect that in Iran or someplace, but not in this country. I have two kids and I love them, but I don't want any more, I can't afford them. If I need an abortion, I want it without going to Canada or someplace."

Republican Candidate Advice

"I'd say, 'Quit acting like a wimp.

"They used to call him a wimp before he went through macho training, but I think he still doesn't know who he really is and floats along with what he thinks people want to hear. Like look at the environment. He says he wants to protect wilderness, but he goes along with big business who he can't stand up against. Same with the NRA. He's afraid of them, so he doesn't want gun control."

Democratic Candidate Question

(For Clinton) "'What are you going to do about child care.' That's what I'd ask him."

(Why that question?) "Because it's on my mind. My husband was laid off, then got a minimum-wage job in construction. I've got two kids but had to go to work. It's been lousy finding someone to watch them. I got a woman to do it, but she charges me a bundle. How the hell can the average person make it anymore? I don't know if Clinton can do anything, but he'll be the president if he gets elected. Let him find out some way to help out working Americans."

Democratic Candidate Advice

"I'd suggest he start asking people if they think they're better off now than we were before Bush and Reagan got in office.

"That was a big question in the past few elections, but nobody's asking it now. I think it's a good one. It'll help the Democrats, because people are a lot worse off, if you ask me. It takes both a wife and husband working to afford to live anymore. There's crime everywhere. Insurance costs are crazy. So how are we better off? We're still paying taxes and now have a lot less to show for it. I'd tell the Democrats to get people asking if they're better off or not."

Campaign Coverage: Good

(Why good?) "They do what they can with candidates that don't say much anymore."

Advice to News Media

"Well, I guess it would be to keep pushing the candidates. Candidates are like kids, they'll never volunteer to do anything, you've got to push them. I think the reporters have to make them explain what they'll do and how they'll do it. They'll never tell this on their own. They'll just say how great they are."

Selected Bibliography

Almond, Gabriel. *A Discipline Divided: Schools and Sects in Political Science*. Newbury Park, CA: Sage Publications, 1990.

Balz, Dan. "Turnout in Primaries Down Almost 12%, Study Finds." *Washington Post*, April 14, 1992, p. A1.

———. "President Mixing Business, Pleasure with a Vengeance." *Washington Post*, August 20, 1990, p. A15.

Bem, D. J. *Beliefs, Attitudes and Human Affairs*. Belmont, CA: Brooks/Cole, 1970.

Benveniste, Guy. *Mastering the Politics of Planning: Crafting Credible Plans and Policies That Make a Difference*. San Francisco: Jossey-Bass, 1989.

Berkman, R., and L. W. Kitch. *Politics in the Media Age*. New York: McGraw-Hill, 1985.

Boisseau, Charles. "Shakeout in the Newspaper Industry: No. 2 Papers a Tough Sell, Analysts Say." *Houston Chronicle*, October 7, 1992, p. 1.

Bradburn, Norman, and Seymour Sudman. *Polls and Surveys: Understanding What They Tell Us*. San Francisco: Jossey-Bass, 1988.

Broder, David S. "The Risk and Reward of Ross Perot." *Washington Post*, April 29, 1992, p. A23.

Brower, B. "The Pernicious Power of Polls." *Money*, March 1988, pp. 144–158.

Castro, Janice. "Are You Out There, Ross?" *Time*, October 12, 1992, p. 23.

"Census, CD–ROM, and You!" U.S. Bureau of the Census, 1992.

Coleman, Frank, M. *Politics, Policy, and the Constitution*. New York: St. Martin's Press, 1982.

Coulter, Edwin. *Principles of Politics and Government*. Boston: Allyn and Bacon, 1981.

Crenshaw, Albert B. "Credit Card Holder to Be Told of Surveys." *Washington Post*, May 14, 1992, p. D11.

"David Duke: A Racist Turns Populist." *Newsweek*, August 13, 1990, p. 37.

Edsall, T. B. "GOP Leaders Tap Frustration over Local Election Support." *Washington Post*, August 11, 1990, p. A2.

Fisher, Christy. "Hemorrhaging Halted, So Status Quo a Relief." *Advertising Age*, October 12, 1992, p. S14.

Fitz-Hugh, Susan H. "Registered Voter Lists Information." Prepared by the Secretary of the State Board of Elections, Commonwealth of Virginia, 1983.

Frank M. Magid Associates, Inc. "New TV Viewing: Summary and Conclusions." Study prepared for ACT III Communications, June 1988.

Freeman, Joseph. *Government Is Good: Citizenship Participation and Power*. Columbia: University of Missouri Press, 1992.

Frenkel, K. "Computing as a Political Force." *Personal Computing*, October 1989, pp. 99–106.

Goel, Vindu P. "CompuServe Still King." *San Francisco Examiner*, July 12, 1992, p. E14.

Greenfield, Meg. "Thinking Small." *Washington Post*, April 19, 1978, p. A13.

Greider, William. *Who Will Tell the People: The Betrayal of American Democracy*. New York: Simon & Schuster, 1992. Also on "Frontline"(aired on the Public Broadcasting Service), 1992.

Johnson, Haynes. *Sleepwalking through History*. New York: W. W. Norton, 1991.

Jones, Alex. "The Media Business: Press amid Dark Clouds of Gloom, Newspapers See Some Hope." *New York Times*, December 30, 1991, p. D6.

Joslyn, Richard. *Mass Media and Elections*. Reading, MA: Addison-Wesley, 1984.

Knickerbocker, Brad. " 'Project Vote Smart' Sticks to Facts." *Christian Science Monitor*, August 3, 1992, p. 8.

Kurtz, Howard. "Clinton Camp Beat Bush Ads to Punch." *Houston Chronicle*, November 6, 1992, p. A7.

———. "Network TV Anchors Sharply Criticize Campaign Reporting." *Washington Post*, July 13, 1992, p. A11.

Lawler, Peter, and Robert Schaefer, eds. *American Political Rhetoric*. 2d ed. Savage, MD: Rowman and Littlefield, 1990.

Leo, John. "All the News That's Fit to Script." *U.S. News & World Report*, May 4, 1992, p. 26.

Lockhead, Carolyn. "Clinton Might Rev Up Regulatory Agencies." *San Francisco Chronicle*, November 30, 1992, p. A5.

Lumley, F. H. "Synopsis of Methods." In *Measurement of Radio*. Columbus: The Ohio State University, 1934, pp. 227–32. Reprinted in L. W. Lichty and M. C. Topping, eds., *American Broadcasting*. New York: Hastings House, 1975, pp. 479–83.

McGrory, Mary. "Tracking the Font of Voter Rage." *Washington Post*, April 14, 1992, p. A2.

McLeod, Roman. "People in Small Towns Spend Most Time with Television, Newspapers."*San Francisco Chronicle*, April 9, 1992, p. E8.

Moore, David W. "The Sure Thing That Got Away." *New York Times*, October 25, 1992, p. D15.

Nielsen, A. C. "Report on Television." Pamphlet. 1993.

Oreskes, M. "American Politics Loses Way as Polls Displace Leadership." *New York Times*, March 18, 1990, pp. I1, I22.

Piekarski, Linda. "Answering Machine Households Not So Elusive." Survey Sampling, Inc. Reprint from *The Frame*, Spring 1990.

Rand, Ayn. *The Fountainhead*. Philadelphia: Blackstone, 1943.

Regardies, November 1986, p. 130.

Robinson, John. "Thanks for Reading This: Television Hurts Newspapers More Than It Hurts Books or Magazines." *American Demographics*, May 1990, p. 6.

Rogers, Everett. *Diffusion of Innovations*. New York: Free Press, Collier-Macmillan, 1983.

Rogers, Everett M., and F. Floyd Shoemaker. *The Communication of Innovations*. New York: Collier-Macmillan, 1971.

Sandman, Peter M., David Rubin and David Sachsman. *Media: An Introductory Analysis of American Mass Communications*. 3d ed. Englewood Cliffs, NJ: Prentice-Hall, 1982.

Scott, Andrew M. *Political Thought in America*. New York: Rinehart, 1959.

Sevareid, Eric. *Not So Wild a Dream*. New York: Alfred A. Knopf, 1946.

———. *Small Sounds in the Night*. New York: Alfred A. Knopf, 1956.

Shaw, David. "Inventing the 'Paper' of the Future." *Los Angeles Times*, June 2, 1991, p. A1.

Shields, Mark. "Played Out in Peoria." *Washington Post*, April 21, 1992, p. A19.

Simons, Paul. "All the President's Programmers." *The Independent*, October 26, 1992, p. 15.

Smith, Alfred. *Communication and Culture*. New York: Holt, Rinehart and Winston, 1966.

Stone, Bob. *Successful Direct Marketing Methods*. 4th ed. Lincolnwood, IL: NTC Business Books, 1988.

Toner, R. " 'Wars' Wound Candidates and the Process." *New York Times*, March 19, 1990, pp. A1, B6.

Trent, Judith S., and Robert V. Friedenberg. *Political Campaign Communication: Principles and Practices*. 2d ed. New York: Praeger, 1991.

Tustin, Arnold. "Feedback." *Scientific American* 187, November 1952, pp. 48–54.

Will, George. "Cooper's Character Hawkeye Still Sleeps Lightly in Most Americans." *Atlanta Journal and Constitution*, October 8, 1992, p. A12.

Willette, Anne. "Taxpayer-Financed Mail Helps Keep House Members in Office." Gannett News Service, September 27, 1992.

Woodward, Bob. "Origin of the Tax Pledge; In '88, Bush Camp Was Split on 'Read My Lips' Vow." *Washington Post*, October 4, 1992, p. A1.

Index

About the Author

GARY W. SELNOW is a communication research methodologist and analyst specializing in the social psychological aspects of human communication. He is an Associate Professor at San Francisco State University whose writings have focused on communications policy research, mass audience research, and research components of strategic planning. He is the author or editor of five books, including *Society's Impact on Television: How the Viewing Public Shapes Television Programming* (Praeger, 1993), which he co-wrote with Richard Gilbert.